About the Author

Dorothy Mitchell was a nurse by profession, and forced by adversity into business. Retiring, she'd eighty-four hours to fill each week. Without sporting or athletic ambition, not keen on coffee mornings and retired lunches, she's worked full-time voluntarily in the community.

Now physically decrepit, she doesn't see well, can't drive, and is unable to be an active social entrepreneur. Large print on Kindle and Sudoku being insufficient, she decided while she can still drive a desk, she would write about 'Old Nursing Times.'

Now complete and isolated from her children, grandchildren and friends due to Coronavirus, she is writing about living in a village 'Not on a bus route'.

Old Nursing Times

Dorothy Mitchell

Old Nursing Times

Olympia Publishers
London

www.olympiapublishers.com
OLYMPIA PAPERBACK EDITION

A CIP catalogue record for this title is
available from the British Library.

ISBN: 978-1-78830-814-4

First Published in 2020

Olympia Publishers
Tallis House
2 Tallis Street
London
EC4Y 0AB

Printed in Great Britain

Dedication

For my favourite only daughter Kathryn and my sons.

Acknowledgements

My first thanks are due to Christopher Aspin and John Simpson who suggested that writing this book was something useful I could do and for their assistance with regularising my random punctuation. I am very fortunate in having close and loving children who ensure everything I need is at hand and all my equipment is maintained, fitted and working. I appreciate my friends who chauffeur me to places I can go to and enjoy with them. I am lucky to have a wider family, friends and colleagues who combine to ensure I will never be lonely nor isolated. I appreciate their great contribution to my health and happiness. New additions to my thanks are the editors, cover designer and Kristina the Production Coordinator at Olympia for their patient and professional input and support in making this happen. Finally, thank you Barry for being a critical reader and to Ruth who not only read but corrected my punctuation and dealt kindly with my tortuous sentences.

Thank you all.

01 Permission to Apply

Were I ever to return to nursing, I'd be found to be theoretically sound, but practically useless. I can't understand how Registrars are classed as Junior Doctors when in any hospital, nurses wear scrubs and stethoscopes. I understood life when Registrars sat on the right hand of their Consultant, Residents clustered round the collective legs writing up the chart of the patient being blessed with the wisdom of the great man. Hordes of lesser beings scuttled under the bottoms of the patients; these were nurses carrying out the orders emanating from on high via the voice of sister. Important, august and superior as they were, they all deflated when Matron silently materialised in full sail and beribboned cap.

First a probationer then a student nurse I began at the beginning with babies. That's the origin of the theory. Assuming the unwell child does not have the language and the arrogance of the consultant who considers 'mother' as an unnecessary intrusion, it is incumbent on the nurse to know the signs, symptoms, treatment, complications, side-effects and prognosis of all known disease. I was entering my final year when I first used a stethoscope outside the classroom and even managed a postgraduate registration before I ever took blood. I'd been injecting oranges since PTS – (Preliminary Training School) to ensure I could stab, pull back and discharge content of syringe before the unsuspecting child felt anything other than the draught when the bedclothes were swept aside.

My parents hadn't considered nursing as a potential career for me and I don't think I had any idea about anything other than the way forward decided on my behalf between my parents and teachers. I don't remember anyone with ambition in my form at all. I'd won a bursary to James Gillespie's High School for Girls in Edinburgh for my secondary education. The attainment was the place, the money means tested. My dad earning £7 a week as a Company Secretary in 1945 meant not only did he have to find my fees but also books and uniform. My mother made sure I was conscious of the sacrifice at all times. I understand now. Then it just seemed to be another manifestation of the inconvenience, lack of consideration, unreasonable expectations and the unlikelihood of my ever amounting to much. Her constant refrain was that I was bone idle with my head forever in a book. I did have ambition. I longed to be 'common.' Had I been allowed to do all things I wanted to do; I might not have been bone idle. Everything I really wanted to do was 'common.' Ice skating, roller skating, Saturday pictures, joining a local young people's drama, sport and dancing group. Perhaps had she explained our financial situation I would have understood there was no cash for dancing, skating and the accoutrements. On the other hand, I would not have been considerate of the cost of maintaining my father's position. On a wage level with that of my school friends' dads who were painters and decorators or delivery drivers wearing free overalls, mothers headscarves and curlers and part-time jobs, we were the origin of 'fur coat and no knickers.' My mother believed she was born to be a lady but when she grew up there were no vacancies. Ladies do not discuss money. Parents decided on where you went next.

There were discussions at the time of the Lower Leaving Certificate which directed us to our Higher curriculum. The scene was set. I would do the mandatory subjects plus, shorthand, typing, bookkeeping, economics and economic history. At the end of the year, I'd sit the Civil Service Entrance Examination and that would be me sorted. Because numbers were my thing, my parents were assured by my teachers that I'd work at St Andrew's House, the prestigious building in Edinburgh where Civil Servants worked, become a statistician and if I never married, retire with a fabulous pension. The seeds of rebellion were sown when my appendix had to be removed at what was clearly an impressionable age. A gap may have previously opened up when I worked Saturday mornings at the Children's Shelter just off the High Street to get the experience needed for one of my armful of Girl Guide proficiency badges. A short stay RSSPCC (Royal Scottish Society for the Prevention of Cruelty to Children) home for children removed from their families by police, welfare or the 'cruelty man' as a place of safety. It wasn't in an area where you could take the children to a park. We would walk up and down the Royal Mile pushing prams with an infant at either end and toddlers hanging onto the handle till they got tired and had to be dumped back to back in the middle of the pram where the baby's feet met.

Appendix removal in 1948 wasn't in and out in 24 hours in case you got a hospital acquired infection. The hospital stay was ten days, the convalescent period six weeks. Prowling round looking for something to do, my dad suggested I might like to come to the office with him and I could practice my typing. That put the tin lid on the Civil Service and I broke the news I was going to train as a nurse. I applied, sat a test and was accepted to train as a Registered Sick Children's Nurse at the Royal Hospital for Sick Children in Edinburgh. I was delivered by both parents to the PTS (Preliminary Training School) on Thursday 3rd January 1952. That may sound easily done, assured and decisive; it wasn't. It took three months and the summer holidays to achieve the decision allowing me to choose.

My family dynamic may illustrate just what had to happen before I got to where I am today. My dad, Jim, being the second son was not apprenticed, but from school became a bookkeeper administrator. It was probably self-defence on the part of my grandpa who must, by the time Jim was 14 have realised he was 'not good with his hands.' Being not good with his hands didn't mean he didn't aspire to being good with his hands. When a potential 'fixer' came to our house he would produce a fully equipped and well-maintained tool kit for them to show off their prowess. So, words like chamfering or dowelling jig could roll off his tongue, he couldn't actually do any of the things you do with them. However, he was a master at 'preparation.' Whether decoration or repair, preparation was mandatory and took longer, was more labour intensive and involved materials such as sugar soap, sand paper, filler and a spirit level. This preparation overflowed into spring cleaning. When it was time, my mother was never left alone to grapple with it. Dad was there, work trousers, elderly shirt, sleeves rolled up to scour walls and paintwork.

My mum was the eldest child of her family, also a family of five. Only three reached maturity and my grandfather was killed in WW1. Of the two families hers was the most upwardly mobile and had her father lived she would surely have reached the heady heights of an 'Edinburgh Middle Class Snob.' This is something highlighted in the lifelong sorrow my mother carried. Pre-war, she was indulged and believed she was born to high standing. Post-war she was a war orphan and she never got over it. Dad was a disappointment as well. A kind, generous, gentle man, his main beneficiary was my mum. She wanted for nothing. Clothes, holidays, help in the house and his help around the house and taking far more of the parenting workload than was usual, were all hers. His love and care of her was his number one but never enough. Had she been in charge of finance they could have been well off. She really believed this would have been so. We used to eat out at weekends, and sometimes we went away to a hotel for a weekend, to give my mum a rest. Holidays were 100% given over to giving my mum a rest. She finished work the week before she married, was presented with a china tea set and was never gainfully employed again. My dad's wage, additional to maintaining his senior management position, a wife with delusions of grandeur and two daughters, had to cover his other family obligations. He paid for electricity to be installed at my maternal grandmother's, he paid her rent, and had to leave 15/- on the sideboard at my other grandparents' each week as his contribution to their living costs. In later years my mother claimed he was far too generous. We must not argue with our mother, 'if your mother says black is white, it's white'! That is why it took so long to reach agreement on my career trajectory.

I swiftly dispensed with the need to be eighteen when I learned that you could start to become a State Registered Children's Nurse at seventeen. I knew I would love working

15

with children such was my happiness at my Saturday volunteering at the Children's Shelter. Where was the point in increasing my typing and shorthand speeds which were already greater than those required for Civil Service entry and not much use to a nurse? Think of the savings on school fees and books. If I was going back, I definitely needed a new blazer and was it worth three summer dresses and a new Panama for just one term? No, I had no intention of hanging around getting under Mother's feet until New Year because I could go and work full-time at the Children's Shelter. And, I wouldn't be a volunteer anymore; it was a proper job and I would be earning. I would live in so they would not even have to feed me.

02 Work Experience

My stint at the Children's Shelter was the most valuable experience I could possibly have gained pre-entry to nursing. When I started training, I was experienced in dealing with distressed little children. Impetigo, ringworm, scabies, lice, fleas, red raw bottoms and nasty smells were commonplace to me. I liked living in, was used to night duty and accustomed to aching feet. I had become a competent cleaner, incompetent launderess and was no longer a faddy eater. The drop outs from PTS came about once we started on the wards and the s*** hit the fan so to speak. For me the culture shock was strict rules and regulations, the hierarchy that defined it and the contempt in which we were held by every man and his dog. One visit from the CQC and the Children's Shelter would have been closed down before they had the introductory cup of tea with whoever happened to be around. Little we did then would be acceptable today. We were almost casual in our approach; our accommodation was of a low standard but what could you expect when we were entirely funded by charity. Additionally, nobody stated staff employed had to be trained to a standard either. When I left, they were preparing to move to new premises with a garden and with accommodation and facilities suited for staff and children. Cheerful, casual and lacking in qualifications we were but we provided an exceptional service and the children in our care were loved, settled and happy with us. An invaluable skill I acquired was the ability to engage with a clinging, frightened, screaming child and persuade it to let go and come with me to explore untold wonders on offer.

The Children's Shelter was situated in Edinburgh's High Street/Royal Mile. Not on the front street but up a dank small corridor, below rooms above the shops. A heavy portcullis type gate guarded the entrance. A dark, spooky walk took you into a small yard where three steps led up to the front door. No vehicular access. Double fronted, it led into a hallway. It could well have been a school in a previous manifestation. The ground floor consisted of offices, a meeting room, boy's dormitory, toilets and staff accommodation. Upstairs was the girl's dorm/nursery, playroom, kitchen, bathroom and toilets. Upstairs we had loads of cupboards stuffed with second-hand clothes donated for our children. Under the age of ten, we had varying numbers but usually between 12 and 20 children were with us for varying lengths of time. Even the nappies we had were someone's cast offs and nothing in furnishing or toys were anything other than 'new to us'. I'd enjoyed my time as a volunteer and went on to enjoy being employed even more. My parents and sister having gone on holiday, I was dropped off by an uncle who came no further than the first gate. Just as well as I may never have been allowed to remain had he seen my living accommodation. My mother, calling unannounced shortly before I was due to leave threatened to remove me immediately from the squalor in which I was living.

Staff quarters were a room off the boys' dormitory. There was one window overlooking a wall so no chance of anyone looking in or seeing our knickers hanging on the line we had strung across it. Our accommodation was furnished with three iron bedsteads, three cane stand chairs, an old-fashioned chest of drawers, a wooden airing rack and an ashtray. As number three, I got the two small drawers in the chest and anything that needed hanging could go in a cupboard with a rail in the dormitory. We shared a toilet with the boys at the far end of the dorm. In addition to a large and small toilet, it boasted two wash basins and a changing shelf. No locks. The little boys had a bed and a 'one between two' second-hand hospital wooden locker. Our children tended not to have 'things' but acquired some when with us which made them protective to the extent of constant readiness to inflict 'grievous bodily' on anyone with the temerity to even 'look.' Having the little boys next door wasn't a problem, they were only there at night and if they felt lonely or sad, they would find their way into bed with one of us. I was very fortunate none of mine were enuretic. Not really a problem though because when the worst happened the mattress would be sent for 'stoving' and a spare took its place. We lived with the children and our modesty was maintained much as in motherhood by stentorian voice or strategically placed door stop when we were having our daily all over wash. We were permitted a bath each week in the one and only bath. The more refined among readers might shudder at the thought of who and what had been in that bath before. We had no such reservations; the water was always boiling hot and soap flakes freely available. Our after use ritual bath cleaning standards were so high that when it was your turn you absolutely knew that bath was free from grime, pestilence and body waste and yours for a lengthy soak, top ups and a good read.

There was more to the building. In the roof were attic rooms where the upper tier of staff had their accommodation. Matron was short, plump and ex-army so ideally suited to

19

dealing with uniformed officials, police and welfare. Her two cohorts were nursery nurses. Rumour had it they had a proper bathroom but the gate at the foot of the staircase to prevent trespass by inmates was equally prohibitive to lesser staff. We did not mix out of work but we were not despised as I would later experience in proper nurse training. Nothing fazed our seniors and they shared their skills and taught us without patronising us. When nursing, we did **not** routinely inspect baby girls to check they were 'hymen intact.' We did at the Children's Shelter. Such was my naiveté down to my sheltered upbringing; the explanations were sometimes beyond my comprehension. We also did full body examination for abrasions, scars, bruises and flexibility of joints. The cursory check for nits was about as far as a nurse was required to do on admission at Sick Kids. Had I ever been checked over in a similar way, I'd be found to be hymen intact but scars, bruises and abrasions to be present in significant numbers on all sorts of bits of me. Health and Safety has surely gone over the top and while weakly disguised within rules at Sick Kids, unheard of at the Children's Shelter.

I was no more accident prone than anyone else there once I got the hang of things. Once able to manage the risks arising from every day duties inflicted by dangerous appliances, I just limped from time to time, sported the occasional shiner but nobody ever broke my glasses. That was because not only were they NHS they had plastic lenses and twisted, yes but broken never.

I was 43 years old before I ever broke a pair of glasses and on that day, then, not only but also my spare pair. Nothing to do with the matter in hand but worth a mention being such a momentous event. It was 5p.m. Friday, I was in the ladies and removed and set down my specs exactly as always to do my face. As I drew them off, one arm stayed put, the other supported the lenses on the basin ledge. I was 90 miles from home. I did not panic. When you've been a nurse, then sole provider for five children, you don't. I completed the beautifying – disguising the bags; once in the car got my spares out of the glove compartment. Drawing them out of the case one lens and one arm came forth! I panicked. Driving with one hand I reached a chemist/dispensing optician which was about to close. There was nothing she could do. They didn't actually 'do' anything with spectacles. We were joined by another 'ready for off' experienced spectacle wearer whose helpful suggestions of sticking plaster were tried and failed. By now I was in full emergency mode, no way could I safely tackle Friday going home time on the M6 without my glasses. How to get the childminder to stay? Where could I find a bed for the night? Then there was light. The Pharmacist switched off his light but unable to leave without finding out what this female huddle was about, he completely saved the day. He had a small son with, but not very careful with spectacles so he had extensive experience. He picked up my glasses, made a decision, disappeared back into his cubby hole and a few minutes later emerged with the pair with the broken bridge drilled and stitched up with fuse wire. Safe to go and with a bit of more than usual foot down made it before the child minder was martyred and into overtime.

There was no accident book, we were just clumsy! I'll briefly mention the injuries I recall sustaining but suspect others had different hazards which rendered them clumsy too, but you can only really discuss what you know and experience is as always invaluable.

The greatest source of injury for me was the Laundry. The 'copper' burnt me regularly. The splashes were nothing, just a few wee blisters but the sides which seemed to jump into my arms when I was emptying it prior to the deep clean when it was still boiling hot inflicted long deep gashes which scabbed and scarred. The length and breadth of lesions were worth sharing and though I did well, I was never the winner. The actual sink injuries were my piece de resistance. Twice in my effort to get to an elusive piece of something lurking in the depths, I overbalanced and smashed my head on the taps. These taps for me were a safety device. If they had not brought me to a sudden stop, I'd have been head first in very hot water with legs flailing. I was super wary of the mangle though and only sustained a very minor, not quite a miss, with a pinkie.

The kitchen should have been OK but it was not just a place to cook. As far as cooking went, I learned to peel potatoes fast and could shred a cabbage in a flash of a sabre-like knife. We had a lot of cabbage and loads of carrots and swede. We had very little meat because it was still rationed. We only ever baked scones with an occasional sponge for a birthday cake. My only salutary culinary lesson was that if you are testing the texture of porridge which has been simmering all night and a drip lands on you, it eats right down to the bone. Even the iron left me alone. The stove was something else. It was enormous. It was not an AGA although it did have AGA features like the covers that come down on the hot plates. It had loads of these hotplates, manholes really with heavy iron manhole covers, different sizes and each with a different function below. Each manhole had a different sized tool to lift it and they could be hot but we knew that and had a lint square or the end of our pinny to keep the heat off. Two of the covers revealed nothing when lifted and we would clean them out with a chimney sweep vacuum. The big one opened to the fires of Hell and this is where we disposed of verminous clothing. Another was the vital fuel store and we had to keep it topped up with egg shaped anthracite kept in a hod. The hod was two floors down to re-fill and two floors up once you'd filled it properly – no half measures – use your head to save your legs. Another was something to do with draught but it was on its top that sat the bottom of the porridge pot. The oatmeal soaked there all day, getting a little warm. By the time the night staff came it was at the testing for texture stage. It could at that time be eaten by anyone needing feeding.

Our children were an ongoing cause of accidental injury. Night or day the most likely place for this to happen was in the bathroom. A quiet admission was unusual. Most arrived screaming and in great distress gripped in the arms of a strange man in a black shiny mac and peaked cap. The Cruelty Man. I found all the officers I met to be scary and not the kind of men that are paramedics today. Mr Mackay on Porridge with Ronnie Barker, but taller, fits my best recollection. I know cruelty and neglect have not disappeared, but it seems unlikely that today some of the awful physical states of these children can be reached; so closely are children monitored and parents generally unafraid of taking up anything on offer for them. Being let in through the massive iron gate by a woman in a mattress ticking frock, carried through a dark tunnel into a strange building didn't help. Tempted with milk in a chipped enamel mug and a Nice biscuit would result in a temporary lull. The man would leave with Nurse, and Nanny would do anything within her repertoire to instil calm. Mostly this was achieved quite quickly. The means varied. Singing to myself and remaining at a short distance worked most often and a two-way shuffle happened and the child ended up foul-smelling, wet and verminous on my lap. Sometimes inane chatter and a Dinky toy were the means of connection.

Worse was yet to come. Whereas there was me in my grey striped wardress-style frock and a supply of biscuits, Nurse would return from her take-over from the Cruelty Man in full battle dress. Her blue uniform dress was protected by a full length, heavy duty, rubber apron, hair scraped back and tucked into a head square and the outfit complete with red Marigolds. Desperately trying to sell the pleasures to come, Nanny and child followed Nurse into the bathroom. The floor was covered with newspaper and a lovely warm, soapy bubbly bath was ready and waiting. I don't recall our having newspapers delivered but we always had piles of Scotsman and Edinburgh Evening News in the bathroom. Maybe people donated their old papers as well as children's cast offs. The bathroom was steamy, not over brightly lit and contained a sluice, two long sinks with shelf between toilet and the bath. For most of our children the bath itself was a scary monster. Notwithstanding the kind words and gentle persuasion, the only things the child came with were stripped off and dropped on a waiting newspaper. If once the state of the body was ascertained, the child immediately thrilled to the bubbles or the wee boat or the fun of filling a cup and emptying it again, I moved on. Bundling up the newspaper I'd take it downstairs and dump it at the top of the cellar steps. With fresh newspaper I would go to our room, spread it and undress on to it – frock, stockings, pinny. Re-dressed, my bundle and that of the child went down to the cellar. My clothes went into the laundry and into a tin bath already filled with strong brown disinfectant where they would soak until they progressed to the copper. The verminous clothing was fed into the furnace. No forensic evidence bags, then. I could now return to the bathroom where a decision would have been made on whether the child's head could be treated in-house or whether we were bound for the barber shop. Bound for the barber was a nanny job and another shock for the poor child. I cringe writing this, but it was all surprisingly simple and apart from the biting, kicking and cursing on admission by some with spirit, it was a new experience for me to share with my charge and make it an adventure.

03 Children's Shelter

The building had many floors and went down as well as upstairs. If I am ever diagnosed with Asbestosis, that is where I got it from. I spent a lot of time down there doing the laundry. It wasn't a comfortable place. The corridors were dimly lit – think Ian Rankin's John Rebus and dead bodies deep below Edinburgh. A furnace space with piles of anthracite and coal which whooshed down a chute, which could be directed to whichever pile was being fed; three locked rooms, and two which were my empire. The laundry and the drying room. Twelve months on I'd be doing the same thing at Forteviot but with a Bendix! My co-probationers who felt washing was beneath them didn't have a clue. Hot water was never a problem, it came from any tap in the building as hot as delivered by today's Breville Instant Boiler. Not hot enough for whites, nappies and all things cotton which had to be boiled for long periods. For that we had a copper.

Our copper was a tank raised off the flag floor on blocks with a gas ring below. My mother had a copper. Her copper was fed from a hosepipe from her sink and had a tap at the bottom to drain it afterwards. Not so at the Children's Shelter. It was a tank and yes, we could run a hosepipe from one of the cold-water taps to fill it. What we could not do was run the water off – the mucky water had to be ladled out with first a bucket and eventually a soup ladle until empty. We hosed it down to clean the sides, ladled out again and eventually by dint of standing on a stool, lean in, balancing on the rim to dry out and polish. Overbalancing was a risk you had to take. You could not start with hot water to speed things up. Every time we had to attach the portable gas ring to begin and disconnect and wind up to put away.

We didn't have to carry all the washing downstairs. A small gap at the turn of the stairs allowed us to throw anything down from top to bottom. Care was taken with regard to who was in the building. It would have been unpleasant for any potential donors or committee people to see our goods in transit. My turn and I'd make my way down to the bottom and climb over or shift piles to reach the room. I fill the copper with cold and immediately light the gas. Next, I 'sort the washing,' then check it for any residual solids or potential hazards and one by one feed them into the copper. The one by one is imperative because there is no rotating drum. I had a wooden Posser a kind of cudgel to stir them frequently to simulate the rotation which would cause the dirt to escape. Now I began on my washing. The hand washing. I had two deep sinks – very deep and again there is a risk of overbalancing and drowning. With hot water, a washing board and elbow grease I started scrubbing while sink two was filling with clean water. The knuckles of my right hand were permanently grazed and scabby due to friction from the washing board. As I finished each garment it was wrung out and thrown into the clean water. Choice load complete, sink one was refilled with more clear water and after agitating the first rinse over they go for the second. I wrung out by hand then twist articles round taps and wring again before moving to the mangle. The article was fed through the rollers and dropped into a waiting basket. I was now ready to enter the drying room.

The heat assails you as you enter a room with hot pipes criss-crossing the roof and festooned with washing lines. The heat is so intense you never linger but quickly unpeg the dry washing and peg up the new. Dumping the ready for ironing at the foot of the stairs you return to deal with the copper. Unfortunately, there is only one way to get the laundry to the kitchen two floors up and that is by going up and down the stairs, one basket at a time. Our woollies were a disgrace due entirely to the drying process. We were told about warm water and soap flakes but could do nothing about the burning heat in that drying room – some things were even singed.

I had prior knowledge of how to care for woollens. I knew if the water was more than lukewarm, they could shrink. I knew if dried in direct heat they could mat. I knew they could not be pegged out because pegs damaged the article. It was permissible for school jumpers and cardigans to be dried outside if pegged on either the rib or cuff. Good woollens were only ever dried under the carpet. I exaggerate a little here, the carpet was only a rug. In the bedrooms at home we had linoleum and a bedside rug. In the sitting room a carpet square and a good place for the job. Even better was under the hall runner. The process for woolly wash was almost a doctrine. Only Lux soapflakes and lukewarm water; they were individually dipped one at a time just to ensure no colour leak spoiled anything. Each article was gently squeezed then lightly wrung and placed in a basin. Once all were washed the soapy water could be let out and the sink refilled with cool clear water. Sometimes though the soapy water wasn't wasted and transferred to the copper to start a 'brith' for whites or at others tipped over the flowerbed outside the back door. Rinsed twice before being squeezed dry in a waiting towel, we were ready for the next stage. Carpet rolled back; a newspaper was laid on the linoleum underneath. Now the garment was laid flat, shaped, then covered by newspaper and carpet returned to position. The position under the carpet varied so as not to cause uneven wear and tear as we used to make it normal practice to walk where the bumps were to hasten the process. Woollies were not ironed.

Nobody at the Children's Shelter knew how to deal with woollies beyond the cursory gesture of warm water and cheap soap flakes. They were dried and ironed within an inch of their lives. A toddler cardigan became a small birth to three months mat in no time. Ironing was a night duty job. We had loads of clothes. Cupboards full of the things we'd wrecked or were about to. Then there were the locked cupboards which contained the new and posh clothes donated to us and which were ceremonially brought forth when we were on show.

In general use, the children had Bakelite or enamel mugs and tin plates. We of the working class had thick white plates, cups and saucers. The office staff had a little tray with a brown teapot, three china cups and saucers and a wee milk jug for which they self-cared. I mean, they brought the teapot in twice a day and warmed it prior to returning to their office to infuse along with a just enough milk in their jug. After the event, office junior with a tray, used cups and a linen tea towel came to the kitchen and washed everything up ready for next time. Their own personal tea towel covered the tray for her return journey. They thought they were quite somebody but compared to the Committee, we could see they were not. The Committee room for which we were responsible for upkeep had a gleaming wooden floor, polished oak table with robust high-backed chairs with shiny leather seats and a sideboard. Two windows with a portrait of a man with a beard on the wall between. The sideboard sported a vase with a silver tray on either side. Within, was the best china with matching side plates, milk jugs, slop bowl, tea strainer, teapots, water jug and a two-tier cake stand. These elite personages were not served by us but by the office staff. The whole place stood to attention. We only ever glimpsed inside the room and never did any of the posh biscuits or fondant fancies reach us. We had to be prepared for inspection.

It would have been good had we been able to have the children's noses wiped, tidily clad, odourless and any bald Gentian Violet heads respectfully covered for their arrival. No, they met, had tea, then inspected. Our anxiety was twofold. We didn't want people turning up their noses at our children because of the way they looked or behaved. We were also aware that Matron would be furious with us if we allowed any of the 'don't let them see' or the children exhibited some of their primitive/feral behaviour.

Another very fussy time was when potential benefactors came. For these the show was a bit different and the poverty, disadvantage and neglected state of our children could be showcased. There was the opportunity for them to be shown 'one we made earlier' and understand what a difference we were making to the lives of these poor little children. Children learn fast and if eating with a spoon rather than your hands merits the reward of a chocolate drop then a spoon it is.

Unexpected visitors made no demands of us because mostly they never got beyond the front hall. These people would be people donating food or clothes or sometimes money from a Jumble Sale. Food was usually from Harvest Festivals or other church giving days. With wartime still a recent memory and many foods still not available or not even heard of then, the pickings were never really very interesting. Nobody for instance donated sweets. Some pre-war sweets were not back in production and when they did, advanced publicity sold them out immediately. My mother's favourite Duncan's Hazelnut Milk Chocolate was to be on sale at selected Confectioners and I was despatched to queue. I was permitted when I reached the front, hours later because they were not to sell them until lunchtime, to buy one two-ounce bar. There was no crowd control as there would be today because we were all resigned and queued quietly. For me queueing was a privilege, a pleasure and something my mother acknowledged I was good at. My book would go in the shopping bag and I'd queue for hours. She never overcame her need to ensure I wasn't wasting time sitting down with a book. When in her eighties, registered blind, she lived with me but were I to bend my knees to sit down the call would come. 'While you are on your feet would you just...'

The clothes the donors brought, we dived into like rats in a bin, before they could be seized and locked up. I remember a lovely little tailored coat I liberated for Andrew. Sometimes, only sometimes though, donors were asked if they would like to see the children. Granted this privilege they were ushered into the doorway of the playroom where anything could be happening. We could be cleaning. We did a lot of that. We might be playing which meant the floor was littered with Dinky cars and building blocks, a tattered doll's pram and we had a rocking horse. We had an antique musical box which I was told if in working order could play a selection of classical music as well as Brahms Lullaby. Unfortunately, it had lost the wind-up handle and the tune switch but if you turned the drum by hand it struggled through the Brahms. There was an untuned, upright piano which got quite a lot of action especially from me with my music badge which required me to have the ability to play God Save the King without music. Just another hazard, protestors could slam the lid down to take the fingers off me.

I don't remember the man who lived in the furnace room and swept the yard ever appearing in the main building. Somebody must have done bits of maintenance and bled radiators but maybe not in front of the children as many of them were wary to an extreme. I don't think the Cruelty Man was blameless; he'd have terrified me. We did our own cleaning. The floors were well polished, with heavy wooden boards in the Big Room and passages. Everything else was linoleum or oil cloth as it was known. I never swept or swilled the yard but I did do the front step and the brasses. The brasses were on the front door and doorbell. Our front steps were done with Cardinal Red. We had no gadgets, a variety of cleaning products, and a different process for each. The Big Room wasn't a room but a hall. It wasn't square, it wasn't L shaped but the disposition of the contents made it hard to define. It was a day nursery for napping babies or toddlers who could be popped into a variety of painted, donated cots either alone or with company. Our night nursery cots were white metal but lead sucked by those teething during the day was freely available. A couple or three playpens confined early years who may disturb games and we must have had a job lot of buffers. A buffer was a ground level little chair on wheels with a tray attached. All needing feeding got a buffer at mealtimes. Then there were the cupboards at ceiling height which were locked and held stocks of donated clothing not yet in circulation. Other cupboards we restocked from laundry. The dining area had two long tables and four long, low benches with the rest of the space given over to play and boxes to put the toys in when not in use. It would be good to record the walls had lovely nursery rhyme murals but they didn't. The walls were typical shiny brown scrubbable up to waist height then washable paint to the long ladder ceiling in pale green. Nowhere else was any different. In the toy department it was well-supplied but repetitive, dinky cars, manky dolls, wooden building blocks and a lot of cardboard stacking boxes. In terms of big toys, we'd a large once posh rocking horse, a couple of trikes and doll's prams, none no way nearly new. Yes, it was cluttered but we had a system and before every occasion involving food or bath or going out everybody joined in and we tidied it all away.

That more or less covers the building. The offices I never entered nor did I ever get to the fourth floor. There were high walls enclosing the yard and our only way out was through the close. The street gate was open during the day. I don't know what was either side of the walls nor if we had neighbours.

The Children's Shelter did what it set out to do and more. Established in 1889, their main focus was the Cruelty Man removing neglected and abused children from their parents, usually on the information provided by neighbours. Until 1875, the law treated children as the property of their parents who could do with them anything they chose. In 1875 the first child cruelty case was treated in New York by invoking the prevention of animal cruelty to a human. In 1968 Social Services became responsible for child abuse and neglect and the organisation continued to work in other areas where there was a need for safeguarding. The organisation became Children First and they still operate out of the premises they moved to in 1952. Their website says that Child Protection is as relevant now as it was then.

The building may have been spartan, but it was clean. It was as clean as Sick Kids but just a bit more worn. We didn't have the fancy cleaning materials or a Hoover or electric polisher but our floors shone. We didn't know about 'damp dusting' and all our surfaces were washed with soap and water and scrubbing brush as necessary. We were often handicapped in our approach due to most often working with a child on your hip and another clinging to your leg wanting 'up,' but nobody told me not to get attached to the children. I never saw a mouse there and my first experience of cockroaches was at Sick Kids. I will never forget that night. I put on the kitchen light and there was a carpet of black crisp scuttling cockroaches.

04 Our Children

Not all our children were physically or sexually abused, neglected, starved or infested; but they were all in need of protection. Protection could be needed for children who were evicted along with their parents for rent arrears. Some mothers and fathers would end up arrested on Friday night so their children would be delivered to us by the police. It was never a reason for Ma not to be locked up that the children were home alone. People were arrested, locked up, in front of the bench in the morning and in jail by dinner time. Nothing like today when you read of someone arrested, bailed for a long period, tried and bailed again until sentencing at which time all agencies would have made provision for dependants. Our drunk and disorderly children were never with us long enough to be potty trained or drink from a cup. The police today use an expression 'known to us' which indicates a person of interest or past misdemeanours. Some children became known to us.

These children behaved in much the same way as patients with chronic disease who on recurrent admission would come in and take over where they left off. King of the day room with the pick of the toys and exclusive ownership of the rocking horse. There were children who became a growing family with us. Every nine months when Mum spent 10 days in the Elsie Ingles Maternity Unit, they moved in with us for the event and moved up their family tree. I remember shortly after I began, a father coming to visit to announce the birth of his third child. Seldom did our children have visitors and a chap with a bag of dolly mixtures and a bottle of pop was a notable event. We did not, as at Sick Kids plaster the name of the child on the bag and the bottle to ensure exclusivity. Oh no, if Daddy hadn't stuffed the lot into his children before management was alerted, they were seized and were shared properly.

Hospital admission was another reason why children came to us. These stays could be short, maybe just until Granny could get there or the stay was something simple. One family was an army family, mum had TB and was incarcerated in the City Hospital. They had to be with us until he was demobbed on compassionate grounds. There would not be the benefits and after care to which he would be entitled to now. Now is not the time to be worrying because we've all moved on, the poor are still with us yet benefits abound.

The slum clearances were at fault for children being neglected. People had moved out of vermin infested, room and kitchens in tenements where there could be one lavatory per landing. Otherwise there was a privy for everyone in the 'back green.' The back green was never green and though it hosted washing lines it wasn't big enough to allow children to play and it was not just a dog toilet but often the place where people 'went' rather than hang about for the privy to become vacant. Children played out on the street. A bath was something you went to – the public baths.

My mother and her siblings never had to do this as even as a war widow, their room and kitchen boasted a bath, a toilet and an indoor coal cellar. It wasn't the same at my other granny's. Naturally I don't remember my dad rolling up a towel with red Lifebuoy soap inside, tucking it under his arm and going to the baths for a bath. I believe they all did and not one of them could swim. He was married and had me so my actual memory is what happened when 'the aunts' had their weekly bath. I could be staying there while my parents had a night out at the pictures. This was the early way of my dad, 'giving your mother a rest.' They had a toilet, (where they lived is now an Edinburgh 'des res'), only a toilet, no wash basin, the only water was from the kitchen sink and a tin bath had to be fetched in. I've no idea where it lived, maybe in their coal bunker in the back green but Grandpa used to fetch it. Huffing and puffing he'd leave for the pub out of the way of the women and not being comfortable in the front room. He was a bit downtrodden as he wasn't allowed to smoke his pipe there and if he was required to be there on occasion, it was a starched collar, tie and a jacket. The front room was at the front. With dark green silk curtains, three-piece suite, a draught screen, embroidered foot stools and a china cabinet, it never felt right. Once the aunts had filled the bath, they were ready to take turns. Granny and I were sent off to the front room till they were done. Between the front room and kitchen was a bed closet where the uncles still at home slept and 'the girls' had the only bedroom. Granny and Grandpa slept in the box bed in the kitchen. This is unrelated information but I don't think the aunts would ever undress in front of each other during the time they had to share a tin bath. When I was grown up, I saw this extreme modesty as comical.

Back to the slum tenements, the lighting was gas. All the hassle of cleaning the soot off and having to buy new mantles if the soot had been allowed to get away with itself. Washing was done in the 'steamie,' a wash house, a very 'common' place because unlike the later launderettes they were not always ladylike. People were admitted to casualty following disputes over criticism of their whites.

The tenements were self-contained communities with standards maintained by a matriarch. Clean pinny after dinner, arms akimbo, she reigned supreme. She set the stairs rota and heaven help anyone who missed her turn. Well managed, not only were the stairs scrubbed and toilets bleached but mothers were supported, and everyone knew what was right. Any issues within the close were settled by a 'stair heid row' headed up by the matriarch and at the conclusion all knew, understood and complied with what was right. Within prescribed but invisible parameters, the children in the close were regarded as common property and skelped, bawled at and kissed better as necessary.

The hype surrounding the new estates was such that there was overwhelming demand on the housing. They came with not just a toilet but a bathroom. The kitchen was for cooking and washing, you didn't sit there and there was no box bed. Families got two- or three-bedroom flats in low level blocks. Older people and couples were housed in one-bedroom units somewhere else. Re-housed, former neighbours may not even end up on the same estate. Their support system was scuppered. New neighbours were an unknown quantity and unlikely to criticise even obliquely if they thought parenting wasn't up to scratch. New neighbour was unlikely to say things like 'they bairns o' yours want their heads seeing to' or drop hints like 'your lot were making a racket last night, wis ye baith oot?' On the new estates, hearing children crying or underfed and they'd be straight down to the phone box, cash in hand, alerting the Cruelty.

At the Children's Shelter, not all children were stripped naked onto newspaper, soaked, scrubbed and de-loused then clad in brand new second-hand clothes and despatched to the barber for a head shave. Some were just undressed, head and body check, bath, shampoo and introduced to institutional clothing. If the clothes we removed were neither dirty or verminous, they were carefully folded and wrapped in good quality brown paper, tied up with string and a prepared label tied to it with name number and date. We did not wantonly destroy or otherwise deprive any toy or comfort item though sometimes we persuaded a 'swop' so the item could be fumigated prior to return.

It was a noisy place, but I don't recall any long-term distress. Distress was much more likely to arise over ownership of toys or people having too long 'turns'. During the day there were, at any time children playing, squabbling, sleeping or sitting on potties. During the morning and afternoon, if fine we were out walking the streets making sure they all got fresh air. We were really into fresh air. On wet days, prams were parked in front of the wide-open barred windows just to make sure. We went out in pairs. Each with a battered high pram, it meant eight at a time got fresh air. Under two years old were top and tail and the older ones walked for longer or shorter distances hanging onto the handles. We were quite well-known and when we walked along George IV Bridge we would 'wave to the trams' and many of the drivers clanged their bell. That never happened to me when I ran with the Olympic Flame in 1948. Think the London Olympics. Recall the constant all day, all channel availability of people lining streets to watch the progress of the Flame.

When I ran from Greyfriars' Bobby to Edinburgh City Chambers bearing the Olympic Flame aloft – not even my Mum and Dad were there. My Guide Captain turned up to make sure my badge was gleaming, my uniform ironed and shoes shiny but departed immediately after the pimply Scout handed over the torch. It was pouring with rain so she agreed I should wear my school Burberry but my tie had to be on view and the ghastly beret at an angle that made my cap badge prominent. I raced off all by myself. Would it have made a halfpenny worth of difference if I'd just walked? Had that been today – perhaps the tramcar that passed while I paused before crossing George IV Bridge having looked both ways, might have rung its bell. No policeman holding up the traffic, no bystanders, no TV. It was a weekday, a school day and awfully wet but you'd have thought my granny could have made the effort. It could be none of my family thought it was anything more than a Guide thing for another badge to sew on my sleeve. I didn't meet a single person till I handed over to a Fettes schoolboy with long shorts and a running vest. (Fettes boys were always right posers e.g. such as the likes of Tony Blair.) He was allowed to enter the City Chambers. All I had left to do was trudge down the Mound to Frederick Street to get the tram home. I could have waited in the rain at the top of the Mound for a tram to Princess Street but that would have cost 1d. I don't remember what the conversation was at teatime but it was more than likely about the wetness of my coat and how it could be got dry for the morning. I have watched the progress of the Olympic Flame on television and felt cheated all over again.

When we went out with the children, every effort was made to ensure we could be proud of our little family. Second-hand clothes, yes, but if they needed shoes, new ones were purchased. We knew the brand; it was the size and the X-ray of the feet that was important. Everyone, ourselves included, got to look at our toes wiggling inside our shoes. No television then.

Some of the children were unforgettable. Andrew was three years old, slightly built, blond and delicate looking. His mummy had died of TB, as was common at the time, and his dad needed time to deal with organising the funeral, getting a job and somewhere to live outside Edinburgh where he could get help with looking after Andrew. He came quiet and sad and beautifully dressed. He had navy shorts, knee socks, a check Vyella shirt and a little bow tie under a smart little tweed coat with velvet collar. Naturally these were wrapped and labelled. I couldn't bear to see him in less than smart second-hand outfits. To ensure this I'd spend a lot of time rummaging for good stuff and even hiding some so he always looked like one of the models in Patrick Thomson' shop windows. A lovely coat came in once, very like his own and I grabbed it before it got put into lock up. I wasn't alone in this dressing up fad because we all did it. We liked our children to look cared for and admired. The children themselves quite quickly found themselves a surrogate mum and that was more or less what happened. Andrew was one of my regular hipsters during his short stay.

Mary and Euphemia were from a family I've never forgotten. Mary was the eldest and was about five or six, Euffie as she was known would be about four and there was a baby. Euffie, Mary and the baby were admitted at night which may be why they are so indelibly printed in my head. They were the dirtiest, smelliest, infested and infected I'd experienced. The baby's bottom wasn't just red raw, it was bleeding and the nappy rash spread all the way up his back and down his little legs. I had the little girls steeping in the bath together and we played boats and shops for ages once I actually got them persuaded to try it. After a while we marvelled at the scum on the water and started again with a clean fresh lather. Mary asked a lot of questions and I dearly hope she made something of herself as she was so interested and needing explanations of why and what we were doing. Eventually hair hacked off to skull, liberally painted with Gentian Violet and with more hot milk, they settled easily, and the next day they had the full head shave.

Often, we had no idea where these children came from or why they were with us but Mary and Euffie were 'in the papers'. They were known as 'the children who burned the bibles. With an older brother they had taken shelter in a church and because they were cold, the brother had made a fire with some hymn books. It was amazing how quickly they recreated a family for themselves. Mary was really mature and looked out for Euffie and the baby. She absolutely loved it when we went out and usually in the hearing of passers-by would address me as Mammy. The first time she did it I was mortified but you can get used to anything. They were with me in the shoe shop, with nice outfits and head coverings. Euffie had a pixie hat with a string tied under her chin but Mary had a really classy red beret with a small stalk in the crown; how she loved it. Neither of them was being shod, just along for the ride and another go on the X-ray. I had never said – 'on pain of death you do not remove your hat' but she did. All of a sudden, she said 'Mammy can I have a go' and whipped it off and there she was bald with purple patches. The salespeople knew who we were because we came with vouchers and didn't pay but the other customers with clean well-brought-up children were backing off.

When some weeks after they came in, they were joined by their arsonist brother, Terry. In what sort of custody, he'd been I don't know but his hair was beginning to grow. He was cheerful, cheeky, charming, and helpful. He'd go about stealing things to give us presents and when we made him give the gifts back to the owner he did so with charm and no shame. He had, prior to the church incident been a lookout for the unofficial bookies who operated around the estate. I next read about Terry years later when he was up before the bench and was sent down. Later, in 1962, there he was again in the newspaper – larceny again. It would be lovely to think maybe Mary and Euffie and the baby turned out well after their experiences with us but we never knew where they went afterwards.

I never was a doll and pram child, but I settled in to playing happy one parent families at the Children's Shelter. The other nannies were a bit older than me but they were hooked and I just followed suit. We had so much to instil into these children; to bring our idea of what was right and proper. Sitting at a table to eat was an achievement for some used to having a jelly piece on the go. Once seated, cutlery was a big thing but we didn't rush. We settled first for a spoon then by example introduced knives and forks. Grace had to be said before any food appeared. Saying Grace after the meal was another non-starter as attempts to keep them at the table till everyone was finished was seldom achievable.

If an activity was in any way geared to gracious living, we'd give it a go. We fought a constant battle against green snot. Nice little boys don't wipe their nose on their sleeves or on my frock; they have a hanky. Nice children don't sniff, they blow their noses in their hankies. In the days before tissues we had hundreds of hankies. Not of the lace edge variety but proper ones which unless lost when out getting fresh air, were committed nightly to the laundry pile. Ready to take the fresh air – have you got your hanky? Mary took to hankies in a big way and would wipe any nose she came across with hers. Another opportunity to show her how it was done in the best circles. On reflection she likely ended up as a matriarch somewhere.

We were confined in the building for security reasons but only later did I realise we were only ensuring the children didn't escape. When you came in having bumped your pram up the front steps, rung the bell and been admitted, you had to double check the door was locked – top and bottom. Torn from the loving arms of their parents you'd think two 16-year olds issuing forth with eight vulnerable children to get fresh air the organisation was taking a massive risk. Regular as clockwork, anyone could be lurking to snatch back their child. Of course, the children looked a lot different but a mother knows her young. They could have been photographed or interviewed. Nothing went wrong when I worked there and shortly, the Shelter moved to a place with a garden so walking the streets for fresh air would no longer be necessary.

05 Below Stairs

At the Children's Shelter our working and living conditions were not unusual nor much different than those at the Royal Hospital for Sick Children. The squalor of our room was entirely down to our not having shelves, drawers or somewhere to hang things. The day my mother made her unannounced inspection, throwing open the door to see me sat on my bed. On my bed – a place meant for sleeping with counterpanes unwrinkled – reading a book. It was untidy. It was not dirty. The same standard of cleanliness that covered the entire premises was maintained in our bedroom. I was quietly reading in the only place available and in the room where another of us being on nights, was asleep. We had nowhere else to go when off-duty. Nowhere else to sit. I backed her out and quickly and quietly closed the door while she ranted. The shame; how it had come to this? Not leaving me here and of course what would people think? I grabbed my coat and we left the building and by the time we got down to the West End and McVities' Snack Bar, my explanations had calmed things down and I got a cup of coffee and a cake. In order to learn the value of money and refund some of the expenses still incurred on my behalf I had to give her 10/- every week and was allowed to keep the two half-crowns that made up my wage. Once I was at Sick Kids and earning more, I got a raise to 10/-.

We nannies took our turn on night duty. Our senior night cover was provided by two interesting, capable, older married women. They were paired with us skivvies, providing us with useful skills and entertainment. Most of the night was spent between the kitchen and the big room where serious cleaning was undertaken. The day staff could manage the nursery and dorms because the children were either out getting fresh air or in the Big Room. I am not saying we did no cleaning in the Big Room during the day because we did. It just wasn't deep and meaningful. At varying times and after specific activities the room was returned to order. Before meals, toys were put away. Afterwards, tables were wiped clean, chairs washed free of stickiness, children ditto and floor swept/mopped. Toys were always tidied away with the assistance of the children before we went out, all part of the need for order, discipline and continuity which we were encouraging. Friday night was big floor night.

The last task of the day staff was to prepare the room for action. So, picture the scene. The tables having been cleaned were doubled up with the chairs on top, the buffers were accumulated in a bunch, cots shoved up against each other, toy boxes stacked and trikes and dolly prams clustered. We had piles of toys. Our proper perambulators were kept downstairs. On every day except Friday, we would move a pile, lugging a heavy metal bucket of hot water and stuff that smelled like creosote we mopped with a stringy mop, using a knife where necessary to scrape off lumps. Move another pile and carry on till all every bit was mopped. By now your starting point was dry so it was time to polish. Polish was in a large paint tin and dollops were wound onto bits of stick and splattered on the floor. On hands and knees, using a cloth we caressed the polish into the dry sort of matt brown floor. Once deemed to have soaked, in we leaned hard and rubbed vigorously with a new dry cloth to bring back the shine.

Fridays were a whole new ball game. Scene set the same as any other evening and Friday the day chosen due to the potential for our having visitors over the weekend. When you shifted a pile on Friday it wasn't to mop but to scrub. The entire week's build-up of polish had to be scoured off right down to bare patchy board. For this task we wore rubber gloves so as not to take the skin off or burn our hands in the very hot water liberally sprinkled with washing soda. Our brushes were about ten inches long with extra-long wiry bits at one end to ensure we got into the crevices between the boards. Making up for the very hard scrub, on Friday night polishing was a doddle. Once all dry, our buckets were filled with fresh clean water to which a measured amount of a proprietary product made by Johnson's was added. We wet mopped and waited. Once dry, all that remained was a quick buff with a dry mop to take any smears off the shine. Thereafter, night after night we built up on Johnson's instant shine. Till Friday when we started all over again.

Another night was radiator night as a job not suited to day time. The bottom half of the walls were shiny brown and scrubbed during the day but the radiators were guarded by wire cages almost as sturdy as the bars on the windows. A wrench and gripper were used to remove the guards and once we were in, we had short mops on sticks to clean between the gullies and our thick red Marigolds to prevent the removal of the skin on our hands for the rest.

Every night we bottomed the bathroom. Sinks, sluice, benches, potties and taps got thorough attention with scouring powder. The nappy bucket was carried two flights down to the bowels of the earth and contents transferred to the dolly tub which was the copper pre-soak. Another tub was pre-charged with foul-smelling disinfectant ready for foul wash. It is the middle of the night and going down one flight of stairs gets me to where the boys' dorm is, I'm fine. Next set of steps is to the cellars and that is spooky. The lighting is poor, once down it is a long walk to the next light switch. There are locked doors and not only possibly burglars or ghosts of the long dead, but rodents. I'm terrified.

The rest of my night was spent in the kitchen. Not sitting down or anything like that unless there was a baby to feed. The stove required filling up at least twice and a trip down for fuel another job. If it was having one of its turns, I might have to drag out the chimney sweep vacuum which was sat to one side and suck up soot via two of the smaller plates. If the stove played up the irons didn't heat. The ironing was all down to me. Everything was ironed. We ironed on the kitchen table on a blanket covered by a sheet. When you picked up the iron using a pot holder, you spat on it and it would hiss back at you, the sign for all systems go. Back at the table, I tested the iron on the sheet and if there was no scorch smell and the sheet didn't have a footprint, you were good to go. I had such a lot to learn. At home once the main ironing was complete and the iron cooling down my mother would instruct me to 'do the hankies.' I'd been taught about the importance of my Dad's hankies having to be totally crease-free. But I was clueless about anything that wasn't square.

Ironing sleeves, smocking, pleats, trousers and shirts were lessons to learn and I had a good teacher. Betty had worked in a laundry. She could do a man's shirt in two minutes. I never quite made the two minutes and ready to fold, but I got quite fast and to a good standard. Every night Betty would produce a large shopping bag full of damp, rolled up shirts for me to practice on. Under supervision I ironed and hung them to air. Once they were adequately aired, I'd take them back to the table and fold in the manner shirts were returned from a laundry. Betty was a right laugh and we had good times and she always had good tales to tell. It was not for me to ask why there were so many men's shirts; I just had to make sure all the full baskets were empty and the children's clothes packed back into the cupboards. Did I ever truly believe that out of the kindness of her heart she was fetching in her man's shirts for me to practice on? Was I really so unquestioning that I never suggested that for a brewery worker he had a lot of shirts?

It wasn't just cellar trips that were scary. On night duty we had to answer the door. During the day, visitors could walk up the close, into the yard and ring the front doorbell which was equally as strident as that of the gate to the close. Somehow it hadn't the heart-sink clang of the bell at the gate. We might be expecting an admission or we may know staff members are out but it is dark outside and dim inside and the bell rings and the fear strikes. You don't waste time because it could be one of us coming home and at risk from loitering drunks. It could be just one of the said drunks or happy chaps having a laugh and ringing the bell. Two things could happen. You'd get there and there would be nobody but you'd open the gate to make sure and hear them singing their way down the Pleasance. Or as you psyched yourself up to enter the ginnel, the gate would rattle and you'd be invited to 'come on hen, come fer a wee dram wi me' or less attractive offers. If you were the person waiting at the gate, it was a nerve wracking wait and the usual greeting; 'what kept you?'

We didn't go out often after dark. We hadn't much money and when we did, we'd go out with another unless returning from a day off when, like it or lump it, you were on your own. It was so scary at night; I took to coming back before dark just in case there was anyone around. If I'd dared tell my parents, my Dad would have driven me back but I was on very thin ice with my choice of career. When I was at Sick Kids and later the Western it was common practice for Dad to keep the car out of the garage till it was time for me to go back at night. Occasionally we'd go out to get chips. Just chips, we couldn't afford the fish.

The hours were long. We started at 7 a.m. and finished at 8 p.m. once all the children were in bed and supposedly asleep. We had time off during the morning or afternoon with one day off and one evening. The evening was usually the one before your day off so you finished at 5.30. We could go out during our day breaks, but more often would retire to bed and sleep till it was time to go back on. I only realised about fifty years later when I discovered work experience youngsters having a kip in a towel bay in the afternoon, that it wasn't just nurses that got tired in the day.

The uniform was no worse than many being a black grey mattress ticking stripe worn with a white apron. No cap. We laundered in-house so our aprons were not the stand-alone style of hospital, but they were starched. It wasn't spray starch as such, just a basin full of cloudy water which we sprinkled on and rolled up after drying and before ironing. If they wilted a bit you could always throw on another handful of the brew. Ownership of the frock and aprons was joint and there was no set changing day. What with nose wiping, baby sick and other spills we'd never have lasted. Honestly, we must have been much more hands off at Sick Kids because we had three dresses personally owned and identifiable by Cash's name tapes, one on, one off and one at the laundry. Laundry was weekly, bagged up in your embroidered soiled linen bag with six aprons and a cap, thrown into a truck for that purpose on your way to the wards, but returned beautifully laundered to our rooms. I just wore my school shoes and we had black stockings and either roll on or suspender belts to keep them up.

In our room we had a centre light; just the one. One of my roommates had a portable radio and we always had piles of magazines. I learned to smoke. I wasn't very good at it to begin with but got the hang of it and not quite shoving a pin through it to get to the fag end, but certainly no tabs of any consequence. People not wanting to waste a smidgeon of tobacco but at risk of burning their fingers would stick a pin through the 'tab end' to gain the maximum nicotine hit. I smoked Craven A filter tip because my Auntie Peggy did, she being the only female on either side of the family to smoke. When money dried up about Wednesday, we'd copper up and buy five Woodbines between us. I moved on to Embassy when I started nursing because there were tokens you could save up and cash them in for stuff. There was a greater value token in a packet of 20 than in a 10.

It wasn't a big room and we'd nowhere for shoes and definitely nowhere we could fold and reverently place the bedspread. A mortal sin in our house was to sit on a bed. We washed our knickers and stockings each night and they hung across the window on a line. You could not have sat on our personal chairs because they were always dressed with the clothes you'd wear when you got out of bed and of course your dressing gown. Slippers and your going out shoes, added to the mix. Underneath everything it was clean. Our sheets were changed, blankets flapped and pillows plumped. Just like the Big Room upstairs, we put stuff away and stacked everything on the beds. We took our little bedside mats outside to beat against the yard wall. The bed frames, chairs and the chest got washed and the floor properly and thoroughly mopped.

The High Street was not a salubrious place to live. The Royal Mile today is brightly lit and full of boutique shops, coffee shops, restaurants, genteel public houses, tartan galore, and even a five-star hotel all ready and waiting to bleed the tourists dry. The street-lights were still few and far between and a common expression was – 'as bright as a Toc H lamp in wartime'. People still lived in the closes and the shops were just ordinary. Pubs there were many and the unemployed and inebriated more in evidence than tourists. They were even hanging about at dinner time. They wore a greasy squashed flat cap, always grey. I don't remember seeing a full set of teeth, they were either 'gummy' or missing at the front. The shirt was collarless and the top coat a tweed jacket with a solitary middle button fastened. A kind of uniform really. An alternative was a khaki ex-Army blouson with row of medals, looking for the price of a pint of 'heavy' or a 'wee dram.' I think I was more embarrassed than scared. The long-term effect of coming into contact with these chaps is with me still. I still come over all unnecessary when confronted with drunken behaviour. I'm not against drink, from the time my uncles took me in hand and taught me what to drink and how, I've taken to it, enjoy in moderation but can't cope with the way it affects people. My parents were tee-total. Well they were then, but learned in middle age.

It's taken me a long time of life experience of highs and very lows to realise that my resilience has its origin in the Children's Shelter. Much of the experience there was absorbed without analysis and realisation only emerging at odd times. I was working in another hospital where a nurse was feeding her family out of patient meals. A penny dropped and I realised Betty had been 'taking in washing.' Had I not been at the Children's Shelter, I may easily have been one of those who dropped out after Preliminary Training School on discovering what it was really like. I left the Children's Shelter on Friday 21st December 1951 so I'd be home for my Dad's birthday on the 23rd, Christmas and my own birthday before I was delivered to 9, Rillbank Terrace on 3rd January 1952.

06 Preliminary Training School

I applied, sat a test and was accepted to train to become a Registered Sick Children's Nurse at the Royal Hospital for Sick Children in Edinburgh. I was delivered by both parents to the PTS (Preliminary Training School) on Thursday 3rd January 1952. There was a list of items which were obligatory and a list of those suggested. Suggested was about the number of vests, knickers and pyjamas and the navy cardigan.

If only we could ever wear the navy cardigan. This was not as was wont to happen at home when new things were kept for best and outgrown before they wore out then passed down to the next in line. The cardigan could not be worn on-duty. On-duty meant full uniform and regardless of temperature night or day cardigans were not permitted to be worn. Even in the middle of the night when cold and tired and despite the heating going off on April Fool's Day regardless of snow or frosty nights, the cardigan was forbidden because cardigans carry infection.

Obligatory items were scissors, watch with a second hand, a trunk, loose leaf folders, contents of a school pencil case but requiring a 12-inch ruler, black stockings, white Kirby grips (to anchor cap on head) black shoes, rubber soled, large safety pins and a gross of Cash's name tapes. The salary of £5/2/6 a month included board and lodging. The tooth fairy offers a better return now. Gross pay about £11 a month. When I was a staff nurse after three years, I got £16 a month. Nobody ever explained to me why, when I ate no more, got any better accommodation and had to provide my own belt and frilly cuffs for rolled up sleeve time which was all the time, that the board and lodging deduction increased. We were to work a ninety-six-hour fortnight which was a gross underestimate. There was no overtime. We would be twelve weeks in PTS before we were let loose on any unsuspecting patient.

The twelve-inch ruler became a souvenir which should be in my memory box but went missing possibly purloined by a child. I've never kept a diary except for places to be and reminder of birthdays. My ruler was a record of my life between 1952 and 1958. Each time it came out for classroom time I carved events since last time on it. With one of the spare safety pins attached to my person I very neatly scratched course and date and black inked it. It was very neat and nobody else had one like it. It may have been graffiti but it would have been handy now when I could be doing with knowing when, where and what.

The address was not the hospital but 9, Rillbank Terrace. Rillbank was a street directly behind the hospital and wholly owned and converted inside to a Nurses' Home on one side. Across the road, the conversion was accommodation for the matron and assistant matron who had flats, bedsits for, ward sisters and the doctors' residence. On our side of the street there was only the one front door at No 9, the only way in or out during permitted hours for the use of residents only.

Trunks were carried in and set down with others in the hallway. Parents were dismissed and probationary students with hand luggage directed into a sitting room where shortly twelve of us sat round and said little. A large teapot with a supply of thick white china cups and saucers was wheeled in by a uniformed person; no cap so clearly a minion and we were told to 'help yerselves.' A bit of shuffling and we helped ourselves and returned, still in outer garments and even a few with hats, to perch on the edge of the chairs. These chairs we'd later slump in, sleep in, smoke in and study in as this was our common room. Now it was an alien, hostile place but not for long as the door opened and two uniformed women entered.

Home Sister who wore state blue with a frilly Sister Dora cap was plump and apparently pleasant and Sister Tutor. Home Sister was occasionally pleasant, but mostly a prison warder come highly starched Madam guarding our morals, criticising our underwear, behaviour and state of our rooms. Sister Tutor was in a navy tailored dress with a veil and attitude. Generally, she did not approve of us, considered us stupid and not the calibre of people who should have been allowed to enter her hallowed halls. We'd never make nurses. This was definite. She did get enthusiastic about things though. When a bus was hired to take us to the Sewage Works, (intake and output and waste disposal were key subjects in PTS) she was really animated and jumped up on a mound that covered a pumping station with such enthusiasm we saw she wore white knickers with long legs, elasticated below the knee. Size wise, she was less than five feet and may have weighed six stone. The power of her oratory and the sharpness of her tone was unique and her opinions absolute.

Very meekly we answered to our names once Home Sister and Sister Tutor had introduced themselves and terrorised us with rules, regulations, policies and procedures for behaviour within the PTS and the Nurses Home. If you felt this was not for you, now was the time to leave before they wasted any of their valuable time trying to train us. Things moved quickly now.

While we'd been incarcerated, porters had taken our trunks to our rooms and we were now directed there. Mostly the trunks were in the passage outside the room because the single rooms were not big enough to accommodate a standard trunk on the available floor space. Single rooms were ideal for lazy people. You could do everything from the bed. There were double and occasionally treble rooms. My room was different. The houses on the streets behind the hospital had gradually been subsumed to be nurses' homes, classrooms and across the road the upper echelons. The elite had their own dining room, everyone else ate in the hospital dining room. In order to eat at all, you had to make your way to the hospital in full uniform or do without.

My room must have once been a back-entrance porch and scullery. Not only was it an odd shape but it had a sort of lobby then into the room which had a large walk in cupboard. Even more different, there was a trap door in the floor of the cupboard which led down to a cellar. As with all other ground floor rooms, the sash window was fixed so as to only open enough for a draught. All to stop us escaping and coming back after lights out. Nobody in my PTS was good at joinery so the window remained fixed. The wee lobby and the cupboard were a community benefit. Gathering in rooms was not encouraged but we managed fine in mine. Any time after 10.30 the night staff patrolled to ensure we were in darkness and where we should be. Eating, drinking, talking, laughing, complaining; room 17 was the place to be. Because of the tiny lobby we had an early warning system giving time for my guests to get into the cupboard taking their cups with them and for me to be quietly reading and ever so surprised when it was suggested she'd heard a noise.

In double rooms the wardrobe was the place to hide, but that failed me when the visitors couldn't take cup and toast with them and night sister checking up on me, needed to know a) where the toast had come from, b) why three cups? The toast could have got me sacked. As I was junior night nurse on the ward next to the internal entrance to Rillbank I was responsible for checking the lights were out and front door locked. I'd made toast for my starving friends transporting it in the bib of my apron. This was theft. I became a seasoned thief.

Having been allocated rooms we were to unpack and get into uniform, ready to be marched to the dining room for supper. Measured in advance our uniforms were in the rooms. We got three bright pink dresses, eight aprons, three caps, a belt and a pile of buttons and studs. A little more up-market here, the buttons were not rubber as at the Children's Shelter. We were not responsible for the laundering so no risk of our mangling buttons. Just another job though as every time you changed your uniform the buttons had to be removed and transferred to the clean garment. Never leave sorting your uniform till morning, it takes time you never have.

As you grew more senior, the pink faded. Neither the system of coloured belts nor the stripes on your sleeve were necessary to indicate your seniority. Towards the end, your frock was almost white with pink patches.

A terrible thing happened to me. Very shortly before I qualified, the assistant matron called me in and gave me a chit for new uniforms. I had fourteen patches on the one I was wearing and though they were of varying shades of pink, the stitches were small, no lumps and a living testament to the rule about 'economy in the use of hospital property.' Nothing I said made any difference and I had to go to the sewing room and get three bright pink frocks which I swear were pinker than they used to be and miles of tapes to sew on the eighteen stripes round the sleeves. The shame. I hadn't quite finished when I graduated to staff blue.

Having done as we were told first night in PTS, we were led in single file for supper, a spectacle of poor specimens who may or may not be able after three months, to casually enter the dining room and sit where fancy took. After supper it was back to our rooms to sew on the name tapes, make up our beds and be in them by 10p.m with the lights out.

Our training began with Anatomy and Physiology and practical nursing. Sister Tutor did most of the lectures with an assistant who sometimes took half of us for practical. When I was working at the Children's Shelter, we none of us undressed in front of the other. When going to bed you took pyjamas and dressing gown and went to the boy's bathroom to undress. We made progress in practical nursing because although sometimes the dummy was a dummy, sometimes it was one of us. Nobody can do a bed bath with a patient fully clothed. Neither of course, should you ever shove a Ryle's tube down anyone's throat unless you know what it feels like. Everything we did was scrutinised, examined and tested and we were ridiculed daily and made out to be fools. Everybody in the whole place was more important, smarter and more worthwhile than we were. Yes Sister, no Sister and keep out of Matron's way. The ward sisters were all harridans and merciless in their condemnation of probationers. After being battered in this way for three months there was little self-esteem or confidence left in any of us.

Wendy, one of us who lasted less than a year and left to be an actress, had a bit more about her. She did not put up with the freezing conditions where we were not allowed to wear a cardigan and brought a hot water bottle into lectures with her. Naturally we all wore vests and very soon we were all wearing camisoles as well. If we could get away with it, we added a jumper under the uniform. but only if the neckline was low enough. Though we began to look chubby, it was clothes, not fat. We didn't get enough to eat to get fat and once on the wards it got worse. Food was forbidden in the nurses' home and meals you didn't always manage to get to. In general nursing there were gifts of food from patients; in Sick Kids there was none. All the food on the ward was locked up. The doctors were persuasive and there were those among us who perhaps working towards 'going out with a doctor' could be blackmailed, incentivised or cajoled into making them toasted egg sandwiches. A rare delicacy often much sought after when they had a middle of the night theatre case and their boss was disparaging of the 'nice' biscuits the hospital provided for such occasions. I could make scrambled egg with one egg and a pint of milk! I had to because some greedy sod had used the eggs, I was supposed to make it with.

I was the only local in our intake. Children's teaching hospitals were few in number. Edinburgh, Glasgow, Sheffield and London were the big four. General hospitals had children's wards and State Registered Nurse (SRN) students would spend some time there 'doing kids' as it was referred to. Six weeks to us elite RSCNs was derisory and we absolutely knew, what they knew after six weeks, was inadequate. Sick Kids opened its doors to Edinburgh Royal Infirmary and we had a constant feed of their students on six-week placements. Compared to us home bred, they were pampered, cosseted, and not expected in sluice or bathroom.

The January '52 intake had girls from Wick, Skye, Tain, Stornoway, Inverness, Jedburgh and more local from the Calders, and even two English from Sheffield. Being the only local, placed a heavy burden on my mother because none of my peers could go home for off-duty. Towards the end of the month when nobody had any money and were off in the afternoon, I'd take along an off-duty person or two and my mother would feed us. It came to pass that even after I had moved on, nurses would descend on her when they had an afternoon off and were hungry. Strangely enough, she relished this; they kept in touch and she was a mine of information on their offspring and career moves. There were fringe benefits though because their mothers would reciprocate and send back butter, eggs and home-grown all sorts to her.

We had off-duty, but the studying was intense and weekly exams meant there was no time to let up. I learned to knit properly when I was in PTS. Wendy, who came from landed gentry, additional to her hot water bottle also brought her knitting to class. She claimed it to be boring and kept her mind on the lecture. It's true, it does. Once I got going, I realised that if my mind strayed from my notes it landed on the knitting and the boredom of moss stitch so knitting turned out to be good for me too. You can't knit and sleep either.

When we went out, we had to sign out and say where we were going and the door to No 9 was locked at 10p.m. sharp. Nobody had any reason to be anywhere near that door after 10p.m. so no chance of being let in at 10.05 p.m. It was the walk of shame to the back door of the hospital where you had to sign a late book and wait till someone could escort you back to No 9.

Going out in PTS could be a trip to the cinema but it had to be the early showing so you were out by 9.15 latest to get back in time. Our finishing work time meant we were too late for the start. But all was not lost, it was the time of continuous showings so we'd get in say half an hour into the big film and watch through and catch the beginning of the late showing. The origin of 'this is where we came in.'

If it was an afternoon and not raining, we'd walk through the Meadows and end up in a café where we could get coffee and divine home-made chocolate sponge with buttercream for 9d (3.5p). Another drop in out of the rain was a Milk Bar at the West End and if it was the beginning of the month then it was afternoon tea in McVities and we'd splash out a shilling (5p).

We didn't, as in later times, take to our beds of an afternoon because, though brain weary, physically we were fine. Sometimes though we just couldn't be bothered getting changed and would end up in the common room smoking or eating things which had come our way via food parcels. It was all about dressing and undressing really. We were in the classroom, but we were in full uniform all the time, caps starched and no safety pins on show but we couldn't go out like that. To go out you had to strip to underskirt and wear your own clothes and since black lisle stockings did not do a lot for anyone, they had to be changed as well.

Though our education was intense, there were gaps. During our entire twelve weeks in PTS our only hospital experience was a one-off whistle-stop tour. Sister Tutor had no umbrella, but as we caught up with her at each stop, we were given a quick resume of what we were about to see, urged to keep quiet and not touch anything. Everything in the classroom was adult size and children were never mentioned. We knew about milk teeth and second dentition, vaccination and immunisation, but milestones and feeding and signs and symptoms were for later.

Cleaning, apart from care of equipment was not on the curriculum. Our rooms were cleaned for us and other than leaving classrooms as found, they were nothing to do with us either. Was this deliberate? Once sufficiently indoctrinated and aware of the role we could aspire to, perhaps they thought we would accept with a religious fervour that for the next year, ninety per cent of our time would be taken up with foul wash and deep cleaning. Care and economy in the use of hospital property, was in-depth and involved practical and book learning.

Equipment didn't come in sealed sterile packs for single use and we learned how to use and care for hundreds of pieces of apparatus becoming guinea pigs for each other under supervision. The personal outcome, regardless of which role you had been allocated, meant you were either a lousy nurse or a difficult patient. There was a procedure for absolutely everything. You could do nothing when given a task until you had carried out the preparation and afterwards reversed the preparation. The before and after of a bed bath was more time consuming than the bath itself. Preparing for a bed bath required a trolley and twenty-three separate items. In PTS it did and on the wards, there was a bit of kit involved, but in moderation.

There was a bit of a ceremony when we passed out of PTS. No parents or guardians or dignitaries though. Matron delivered a sermon on our future and the sanctity of the profession and we were summarily dismissed to the notice board where we would find our postings. We were given a week's leave before we presented ourselves for duty. As far back as then I can safely say I was theoretically sound, but practically useless. There is nothing lower than a student nurse. On the wards top dog was sometimes a power struggle between sister and the most senior ward orderly. Even the Resident, (that was junior doctor then) despised by sister and bullied by registrars and consultants could look down on us with contempt and make us do things. Things for them that could cause us serious trouble like making them a cup of coffee. They too, were hungry and would lead us into temptation and have us steal for them, but they never shared. We were usually moved every three months and spent at least three months a year on nights.

07 On the Wards

Straight from PTS you spent most of your time in the sluice. The sluice being the place where you did what you did with dirty nappies and sheets splattered with sick and other bodily fluids. It was also the place where you started the process of washing feeders – note started. Cleaning feeders were a two-step process due to the fact that dribbles had to be soaked off first. Clean rinsed, they were placed in a basin for transfer to the bathroom where the process was completed.

Sick Kids was a good starting place because although we thought poo smelled bad it isn't as bad as grown up poo. Once you'd sluiced and cleaned bed pans there was the laundry to prepare. Nothing stained went to the laundry. Shut in the sluice with a high pile of dirty linen, each item was inspected for stains. We then tackled the stain in fast flowing cold water first to sluice it off then a hard bristle brush till it was a shadow of itself. A ward sister comment on poor sluicing – 'you can't expect the laundry staff to deal with this.' Once swilled, and scrubbed it was folded and laid out to be counted by a senior person into a bag, a source and content label was attached. We wore a gown with tape ties at the back to protect our aprons, just like embarrassed outpatients, but we tended to be damp most of the time anyway.

Thirty or so children create a lot of washing and not only did we count it out to the laundry, we counted it when it came back. Part of this checking beyond ensuring we had not been short changed, was also to check for any holes or rips or missing tapes. Tapes were always coming off feeders and nighties. Sewing them back on, was a night duty privilege. Was the height of the mending pile due to aggressive laundering or poor-quality night nurse sewers? Apart from being hauled out to assist with big cleaning, clean up spills, make beds or help with meals, the day was spent in the sluice.

When the next PTS came on stream you got immediate promotion to the bathroom. The bathroom wasn't a great deal more appealing but to me preferable to 'the flowers' which was the next step up. Children were bathed in the bathroom and used the toilets, but a lot more went on there. There were storage cupboards to be tidied daily and scrubbed out weekly. Everything within was also cleaned so all our vases, building bricks, push along cars, board books and assorted stuff got taken out and dealt with. Masks and feeders were hand washed here except when sister came over all derogatory about the shade being grey rather than Persil white. If so, prior to the wash and hang up in the bathroom they went to be boiled up in a pan in the ward kitchen with a bit of bleach. There were large well-scrubbed and bleached boards placed across the end of the baths. Their primary use was as a place for the child to be undressed and then dried afterwards. The secondary use was for flower arranging. A task for PTS + 3 and I'd swap this for the bathroom any day.

There were no floral arrangements in 1952. The flowers came in bunches waiting for a probationer to arrange artistically in what were really big jam jars. We were supposedly a well-endowed hospital, but our vases were rubbish and my flower arranging, worse. Sister was very keen to tell me day after day after I'd spent ages changing water and arranging, to 'take them back and do them properly.' Somebody paid good money for these flowers. Wreaths were complex arrangements which often came our way. It was seen as a good thing – a lovely thought – for people to bring them to us after a funeral. A wreath is a floral tribute and unless it is stripped out there is nothing you can do so it looks anything other than a wreath. A wreath in a ward in any hospital is not acceptable. Stripped out it was amazing just how few blooms were involved in a wreath. The left-over greenery, ribbon and wire had to be sorted and re-cycled. We wasted nowt. Ribbons, ironed and rolled up and wire were valuable stuff for use when we began preparing for Christmas in September.

Our duty hours were at the mercy of the ward sister, who planned off-duty each week. No point mentioning an event you may like to attend. Probationers and student nurses don't have life away from the ward. Thursday was the day we knew where we were from Sunday. Everybody started at 7.15 a.m. You could have either a morning or afternoon off so be off 10 till 1 or 2 till 5 and if you were lucky had two evenings when you finished supposedly at 5.30 p.m. The night staff came on at 8 p.m. We had one day off each week but times improved and shortly before I qualified, we got a half day as well. The half day was seldom attached to the whole day so no chance of a trip home overnight if you lived away.

Meal times were fixed. If you couldn't get there, you didn't eat. You had to be in uniform in the dining room. Lots of times I missed supper because I fell asleep. We had three meals and two short breaks. There was no menu. No vegetarian option. On night duty you had supper for breakfast and breakfast for your evening meal in the morning when you came off. One supper in the morning when I was coming off after 12 hours on night duty, kippers and rhubarb. We moved rooms usually every time we changed wards. Night duty meant walking about half a mile to a house provided for that purpose. We were only policed there by a caretaker making sure there were no men but there was an official visit each day to check we were in bed. The guardian of our morals was a good sort and had so many odd sorts of jobs we were always sure of entertainment. He had been an undertaker once. Washing a corpse with a new apprentice when trapped gases made it groan, he said 'water too hot for you?' and the apprentice fled.

We got very skilled at packing our trunks, which would appear outside our room on the morning we were to move. When we came off-duty at the end of the day, our trunk would be outside our new quarters. The porterage was very efficient and I never knew of any lost luggage. Our laundry was just as efficient – put it out and take it in on the day. We made our own beds, but our rooms were cleaned. Cleaners never put your stuff back where it had been. Probably just so we knew we'd been done or maybe they just knew better where things should go. I never gave into this irregular way of things. When I'd 'been done' my first action on entering my room was to put things back to where they'd been since the first day I unpacked my trunk, in PTS. Day duty, night duty, new room anywhere, my dressing table was laid out in exactly the same way.

We got clean linen every week. You stripped your bed, put the top sheet on the bottom and took the former bottom sheet, one pillow case and your bath and hand towel to the linen room from 6.15 – 6.45 a.m. Our assistant matron, Sister Fisher, always referred to as 'Fish' supervised and made sure we gave back what we took out. She unlocked the store and stayed until everyone had been. We exchanged a 'Good Morning' and she was then free to comment on any aspect of us she had reason to be suspicious of. The length of your hair or you may have been seen with brown Kirby grips rather than white anchoring your cap, charges there were many, but it meant each of us was physically 'seen' on a weekly basis. I liked to be early because there was a gradual move from boring white towels to coloured, and it was first come first served.

There were seven wards at Sick Kids and three outhouses. Two of the outhouses were in Edinburgh and one in Gullane near North Berwick. Forteviot in Edinburgh was much like a children's hospice today and the children were under two years old with life limiting or chronic illnesses. It was at Forteviot that I first became emotionally involved and, in fact, encouraged to engage with and bond with the children. I did my second posting and first night duty there. After my experiences on the ward, it was a holiday for me. A bit like the Children's Shelter, but a lot less physical activity. I fed babies, washed feeders and masks, did the mending and I could sit down. There were two of us on-duty and I had to make supper for both of us, ensure the kitchen was tidy and the children ready to 'get down from the table' after breakfast for the day staff.

Whilst I revelled in the doddle of a job, my senior, a final year student was in panic mode. I was too inexperienced to realise this was abnormal behaviour. She was fearful of everything and in particular that any child might cry and wake Sister who slept on the premises. It would not have mattered; Sister was as mother to each of these children and any sign of distress and she'd have known which child and choose whether or not to intervene. A few nights in and a baby snuffled and she lost it and herself roused Sister to help. She was promptly sent off and I finished the night with Sister. Next night as I came on-duty, I was called into Sister's sitting room. It was explained to me that not all nurses were strong enough to cope with very sick babies and nurse whatever she was called would not be on-duty and I'd have a new senior. She went on to tell me very kindly that I had a natural aptitude which was fortunate and that my feelings were transmitted to the babies so it was easy for me. She went on to explain that babies were very smart and able to manipulate grown-ups. That wee scrap would hear me walk in, think to himself – 'that's the night nurse, if I cry, she'll rock my cot.' She had no idea where I had been before and my 'aptitude' was a learned ability.

The new senior was two feet taller than me and extremely competent and I thought we'd settled down well till she accused me of eating more than my fair share. At 11p.m I had to go down to the kitchen and carry out instructions to finish preparing our meal. I would eat mine and leave hers in the warming oven. Next night I left three quarters of the shepherd's pie and she accused me again and decided I could not be trusted and thereafter, she would eat first. Forteviot was a lovely old house in beautiful grounds and as she drew what were formerly the drawing room curtains next morning, she saw a man leaving the summerhouse – we had been sheltering the homeless.

My Grandpa died the first time I worked at Forteviot. Just after PTS his was the first dead body I had ever seen. It was good experience for me in that I realised that once dead, the person no longer occupies the body. I don't think he'd ailed anything apart from old age; he was eighty. He'd gone into the scullery to shave and dropped. Granny heard the clatter and realised he was dead so she just got down on her knees, leaned over and closed his eyes!

There were no iPads or CBBs when I was small, and his shaving was one of the things that kept me occupied. There is no performance quite like it. First there was the shrugging off his braces and removal of his shirt which was cast aside in the kitchen prior to entry to the scullery. The braces remained dangling and he unbuttoned the buttons on his 'semmit.' Face and neck were washed which involved a bit of splashing and a dip into the basin with his head and a shake of his still considerable head of hair. The splashing was not just to entertain me as the mess in the scullery was a constant refrain from the aunts. I never knew any others who cleaned with such venomous thoroughness than the aunts. Always at speed before they went to work. Once the 'rough' had been rubbed off head and face, the preparation for shaving began. It involved a stick or bowl of shaving soap and a badger bristle brush to work up the lather. Once lathered the cut throat razor was swiped back and fore on his 'strop' which hung behind the door. Now he was ready and silence was called for as he peered into a small mirror on the window frame and began screwing up his face and scraping up and down. Once done to his satisfaction, there was a splashy rinse, a dabbing with the towel and any wee nicks were zapped with a styptic pencil.

His funeral was typical of the time. We all gathered in the front room after the undertaker had asked if there were any more viewers. While they did what they had to do, the minister said a prayer and the men left. A blind was raised and Granny was helped over to the window to wave goodbye. That done, my mother and the aunts went about preparing the 'boiled ham.' The men meanwhile, black ties and bowler hats, walked behind the hearse to Slateford Cemetery where they would be met by the other men who would attend at the graveside. Women did not go to funerals. When I was working in Inverness a keeper for the Laird in Tain died and as he was vaguely related, the funeral took place from the 'big hoose.' The gathering there was in a very big hall and all the men were fortified with a 'nip' before they set off carrying the coffin with every other male for miles around following on foot several miles to the graveyard. On their return to the 'big hoose,' the women were waiting to serve a hearty stand up carvery buffet meal but only after they had been offered another dram. A bit like before the hunt sets off there is a stirrup cup.

Douglas House, another former stately home was mainly for orthopaedics. Children in plaster or complicated pulley contraptions went there for the time between plaster changes or operations. Local, so there was no expense for their consultant and his team to visit. I only did a very short stint there, but experience there wasn't with the Douglas House children, but the ones next door. A little residential unit for children with behavioural problems had been set up in the grounds. The staff who were 'mental nurses' were not allowed to modify the behaviour of their children by raising the voice or using any method other than reward. These children were feral escape artists with amazing command of unsuitable language. Being neighbours, we were first on call before the police if they got beyond the walls, or fire brigade if they were on the roof. I was fluent in gutter language and could hector as a 'stair heid matriarch' without a script. When there was a mass breakout to make a snowman and attempts by staff were beaten off with snowballs, we got a telephone call to see if as neighbours we could 'do something.' Oh yes, I could – I did my best arms akimbo outraged woman whose poor sick children were being tormented and terrified by their outlandish behaviour and seeing as how there was nothing, I was not about to do them, they returned indoors.

Gullane, near North Berwick was long stay. Twenty-three miles from Edinburgh, children with long-term conditions not requiring frequent appointments were transferred from the wards there by ambulance. Some children went there between operations if their home conditions were poor. This often happened with children with extensive burns who were waiting for pedicles to 'take' or grafts to heal before the next batch. Night nurses were delegated to accompany them. It was a random selection and you would be informed by night sister when as junior night nurse you took her on the 2 a.m. ward round. Having worked from 7.15 p.m. to 8 a.m. and had breakfast, 8.45 you presented yourself still in full uniform at the front of the hospital to meet the ambulance. It was over an hour each way, but we got a brew at handover but it was midday before we got back to Edinburgh where we had to sign in then walk to the night nurses' home. Being out on the street after 12 noon was not a sin punishable by a visit to matron on ambulance duty days. Going to Gullane, was a little holiday for the children and we'd sing along to the ten green bottles and such like. If we had no return passengers, we'd lie down and have a cigarette.

It was hard work and there was little leeway any time and not much to choose between wards and departments. We did a stint everywhere. It took us three years to learn all we needed to know about sick children. Nurses doing general training were also required to learn about sick children. The Royal Infirmary had no children's wards, so during their three years' training they were seconded to Sick Kids for six weeks. We so looked down on these pampered student nurses. They never came in at sluice or bathroom level and so much of what we had to do they were excused. When I did general, I realised that their lives were different and drudgery was not required of them. Cleaning, big cleaning and special cleaning were not nursing tasks. We had ward maids, but we probationers were a lower caste. Ward maids did general cleaning and dish washing, but everything else we were responsible for. We were always responsible for lockers and trays, bathroom and sluice. When it was big cleaning every week, we had to drag out the beds and do the high dusting and the bed wheels, trolley wheels and often got a turn with the 'bumper,' a heavy slab on a stick with a cloth underneath which polished the floors.

The junior night nurse was required every night to clean the doctors' side room. Coming off night duty in the morning you went for breakfast but may not leave the building till after 9 a.m. If you had gone to the night nurses' home, you'd have to walk the half mile back again if you had to be called back for something you had not done. Once I got called back to do the doctors' side room again. I did it in the night, but we had admissions and the doctors and surgeons were in, and had used the ash trays, had biscuits and coffee and scuffed the floor!

After we had been there a year and passed our Preliminary Examination, we were quite useful and with three PTS below us we got to look after the children. This was the same examination required for any state registration in Scotland and England. That'd be why among the 23 items needed for a bed bath in a children's hospital a denture cup was listed. There were no excuses for not completing what was supposed to be completed. No matter what happened during the night, when the day staff took over all the beds had been stripped, mattress turned, babies fed, mending done, feeders washed, masks boiled and children having their breakfast.

Sitting or leaning were forbidden, the only time you could be off your feet was when feeding an infant and it was a mortal sin not to pick up a baby to feed. Had you several to feed and you fed one on your knee and propped another holding the bottle with your spare hand to try and lower the volume, that was wrong. The slightest hesitation and sister would want to know what you were doing, where you were going and why you weren't already there. Eating on the wards was forbidden. There were no breaks, just meal times. If you ate quickly you had time for a quick wee and a cigarette in the nurses' home. Once you finished eating, and we all ate quickly, you had to catch the eye of the senior person in the dining room to ask to be excused. No, you could not interrupt their meal, you had to wait till they looked up and the clock would be ticking and you'd be wondering if you had enough time. Toilets on the wards were for patients only. The burning feet and aching legs and bone tiredness were chronic. One thing common to both Children's Shelter and Sick Kids was the piece of wood used to splodge the polish from gallon tin to floor. After the 'Prelims' we were gifted white tape but no cotton to sew a single stripe round each of the six sleeves of our now not quite so bright pink dresses.

08 Coping Strategies

We may have been overworked and underpaid, but off-duty we enjoyed ourselves and on-duty, found ways to circumvent the draconian rules.

As junior on night duty, I'd far too many small babies needing to be fed at two, three-and four-hourly intervals. Additionally, there were the other children between two and 12 years old. The rule was that no matter how busy the ward was, no child could be woken before 6 a.m. By 7.45 a.m. the night staff had to have medicines done, babies changed and fed; all the older children toileted and had a bit of a lick and a promise, beds stripped, mattress turned, feeders on and breakfast ready to serve. Think about it – we could strip and turn in two minutes, but babies take as long as it takes. There's the need to caress, till the wind's up and deal with post-feed nappy filling. The jury never came back on whether you washed the little bottom and made it comfy then fed. Once sated and wind up, you hope it will settle, but ever aware of their inability not to seize the opportunity to fill the lovely clean nappy with warm wet poo. The alternative was feed, wash and change which kind of reduces the post prandial somnambulance so they have no intention of lying down quietly. As soon as all that was complete, the bread had to be buttered, empty feed bottles returned to the milk kitchen and breakfasts collected.

I just knew I'd never have time in the morning, so I'd butter the bread – with margarine, when things were quiet, and cover the plate and place it in the bread bin. Caught in the act, I listened to the lecture from night sister about giving these poor children dried up bread and butter. She was impervious to my difficulties and dismissive of my wrapping them in greaseproof paper. Next night I did what I always did, instead of the bread bin though, I put it on a shelf in the oven. Sister comes along and whizzes open the bread bin, sees no greaseproof wrapped bread and commends me on having seen the error of my ways. I collected the breakfasts first because I knew I had no last-minute rush. I whipped my parcel out of the oven and to my absolute horror; the corner of the bread had been eaten away by mice. OK, start again, but what to do with the chewed-up parcel? I could not put it in the pig bin because it would be found. I went to breakfast with a great wodge of bread and butter in the bib of my apron. I rustled a bit. On the way to the night home I put it in a public pig bin. Waste food was collected for a long time after the war to be fed to pigs. I'd learned a lesson and next night I put my parcel in the crockery steriliser. No entry from the bottom and a sealed lid.

Breakfasts were collected from the kitchen on the top floor. There was a lift, but we were not allowed to use it. The only exception for the likes of us was when we had the breakfasts on a tray. We couldn't use the front stairs either; they were strictly for sisters, doctors and visitors; and there were never hordes of them. Visiting was very limited and, in some wards, not allowed at all because of infection. We had to go everywhere by the back stairs. Unlike the wide gracious grand front staircase, there was always considerable two-way traffic. Steep, narrow, spiral and very worn was our route to everywhere.

Preparing to collect the breakfasts, we had a narrow metal tray which accommodated three crates of eight used feeding bottles, scrubbed and ready for autoclaving to the milk kitchen. Any more than three crates and the extras were clutched in your hands along with the handle of the tray and 'nurse please try not to rattle.' Up and up and round and round, not brave enough to dare to use the lift because it made a noise and we'd be caught. On presenting yourself at the kitchen with your now empty tray and a freshly laundered linen tea towel, you were given a deep conical shaped metal container of porridge and a serving dish of whatever was children's breakfast. With these side by side on your tray you made for the lift. On reaching the gates, you raised a knee to support the tray and pressed the button and threw open the lift gates. Hands back on tray, into lift, knees up, close the gates and press button. On landing, do it all over again.

Once when my counterpart on-duty on the same floor couldn't possibly spare the time to do the trip, I offered to fetch her breakfasts along with mine. This was a sin even greater than the bread and butter but so far, we had got away with. The lift had issues and didn't always stop level with the floor. On this day with two buckets of porridge, the breakfasts which were sausages were balanced, one on each bucket. The lift didn't stop level, I tripped. I saved the porridge but the sausages shot over the corridor and under the show piece hall table.

Food again. It had been decided that night staff should have breakfast in the evening and a proper meal in the morning. On day duty there were fresh rolls and toast. On night duty we never got rolls, just cold leathery toast. Scottish rolls are a delicacy and it wasn't fair. One morning on my way from the kitchen to the lift I noticed a tray of baker fresh rolls. I did my knee up routine and a couple jumped under the cloth covering my tray. My senior was delighted and we had one each before the day staff came on-duty. She couldn't help herself and next night her mates had instructed their juniors to supply them. So that night, the kitchen was fourteen rolls short. Then I thought why stop at one each, so we had two. Then everyone had two. The bakery was contacted re short delivery and rolls were locked up on arrival.

It was a student duty to clean the mortuary and inspect the residents. Nobody could be spared to accompany you, but we had a system. If you were the chosen one, you arranged for one of your off-duty mates to meet you on the back stairs and go with you. Such was our commitment to each other that we'd get dressed in full kit and loiter while the mortuary key was collected. Please understand that off-duty you were usually sprawled on your bed in your dressing gown either studying or asleep. To help a friend, meant black stockings, shiny shoes, pink frock, clean apron and cap and starched belt and cape. When the designated cleaner issued forth with her covered tray; looking as if she was about to carry out a minor procedure, we'd scuttle round the back to the mortuary. The tray looked very professional. When you whipped off the cover there was a covered silver bowl and a clean sheet. Remove the lid of the silver bowl and there you have dusters and metal polish.

There were no refrigerated drawers. Instead there were four white sheeted trestles with little occupants awaiting collection by an undertaker. It was a very cold but beautiful little chapel with murals on the walls in classical Italianate style of, 'suffer the little children.' Each little body was covered with a sheet up to the chin and a fine pure white linen cloth covered the face. The altar had a convent embroidered cloth, crucifix and fresh flowers. The metal polish was for the cross. You unlocked the double doors into a small unlit porch. Opening the chapel door there was some daylight. However, the key was very large, the doors heavy and creaky and I was always spooked by the time I actually got into the chapel. You could immediately see how many bodies there were, more or less than the day before and your first task was to check them to ensure there was no seepage. Once I'd lifted the face covering, I was fine, I could see the little person was really dead and not about to say boo. I never liked to just manhandle, to see if all was well and would lift them up, so my companion could check the under sheet was clean. Dead weight is very heavy and the smallest child is icy cold and rigid. That little person had been the entire world to parents who were bereft and there it was all alone in the cold and the dark. If there was any actual body work needed doing, that was not our business. We reported it to the ward whose child it was, to remedy. Only once did I have to do a daily re-dress and each day, I was gutted all over again because I had known and loved that little girl as she'd been with us a while. Today she wouldn't have died. When the undertaker had been, the clean sheet would be needed and if we were extremely fortunate, he'd have left a shroud. We had to make our own. We had a few we'd made earlier on each ward and stock replenished by the junior night nurse. Sometimes there was nothing the right size and you had to make one on the spot. There was a pride in being the creator of a pretty shroud. Just another of my talents, along with trifle, stuffing and fish pie.

The pathology lab itself was nothing like Silent Witness. A metal table in a room with shelves all around the walls and decorated with things in jars. We got anything abnormal from all over Scotland, hence the jars. Once when I was there a parcel was delivered by the postman with a little body! Once, a stillborn baby was found in the toilets in outpatients. Despite there being a virtual lockdown and inquisition, the mother was not found to be a member of staff. On-duty in outpatients, a woman arrived without a child, but with a paper carrier bag. She came straight to me, handed over the bag and said, 'That's Terry Jones for post mortem' and left.

More things happen on night duty than any other time. Once when I was more senior, I was on the isolation ward by myself. It was really a hut with a baby room and a small ward and the capacity would only be about 14 so no need for two. There were low floor lights and a desk lamp covered with a cloth where I could sit to mend or write the report. There was an entrance porch and fire doors both ends. In the porch was a 'break the glass' fire alarm. Night sister came to see me unexpectedly, not wanting me to worry, but just to let me know there was a prowler. Off she went. I couldn't lock the door – no key. So, I picked up the container full of disinfectant with long forceps and placed it at my right hand on the desk. I appropriated a 'snowstorm' from a locker and placed it to my left. Armed I sat down listening. The steriliser came to the boil and I couldn't cope with that very loud noise and listen out for the prowler. I got up and sidled to switch it off with eyes looking both ways and jug with forceps in hand ready to throw. Eventually sister came back to do her round and hoped I hadn't been worried. I told her about my plan – I had the forceps and the snowstorm to throw at him while I got to the fire alarm to set it off. 'Oh dear,' she said, 'you shouldn't have done that; you might have wakened Matron because it rings in her flat.' Know your place.

I'd heard about 'night nurse's paralysis' but only experienced it once. On night duty, all children asleep, all ready for night sister's round, I was sitting at the desk. I was not asleep. I heard her come through the swing doors. Normal procedure, would have closed the left-hand drawer where my cup was, stood up and walked to meet her at the ward entrance. I could not move. I heard her walk along the corridor past the ENT theatre and side wards and I could not move. In my head I am desperately trying to move, but I can't. Just as she stepped into the ward, I was able to stand up. We did eat and drink on the ward, but you kept your cup in the drawer then slid the drawer to, so if you were interrupted there were no visible signs.

Christmas was competition time in Sick Kids. Wholly and entirely and only between the ward sisters, it wasn't bitter, but it was secretive, intense and hard work, beginning in September and going on until the display went up in December. The ward and children got little beyond a few streamers, paper bells and whitewash with cochineal and green food colouring on the cubicle glass. Supposedly wash on wash off. Were this today and spending far too long taking the glass back to shining clarity, somebody would have been on to Trade Description. There was a tree protected by a waist high fireguard between sluice and bathroom which caused traffic chaos.

For whose benefit? The party piece was a display set out on top of the twelve-foot run of almost eye-level cupboards running from the swing doors into the corridor and opposite three glassed cubicles up to the ward entrance. Going back about two feet, it was a fair stretch to furnish with a storyline. Over the period you could be involved in more than one display. Only when all the bits came together and the scene built was the theme announced. I spent a long stint on a village scene, it wasn't a fairy tale, just an awful lot of little village people doing Christmas. This is where the green bits and wire from wreaths came in handy and other peoples' rubbish became gold to those prospecting for stuff to create with. Every little pipe-cleaner figure was hand-made and individually dressed. Structured from light card, (The spec was only available from a 'modern' till receipt to be collected by all staff family and friends) buildings were created and decorated. These people ate Christmas dinner, sang carols, walked their dogs, went to church and rang the bells, shopped and pushed their children in prams to see the Christmas tree. There were rows of houses with vehicles outside, a pond with skaters, a school with children at playtime and old people sitting in the park and the entire panoply sat on virgin white cotton wool. Sister truly ensured we gave every flying moment something to keep in store. Alongside the mending and list of swabs to be made there was equipment and instructions on how to make whatever was next on her list. We did as instructed, but it was never clear what the end result would be. Children could only see if allowed out of the ward and lifted up. Unless over five foot four and three quarters which was me, grown-ups struggled to see what was at the back.

One of the defining moments of my life occurred just over a year into my training. I failed an exam. We may have been out of PTS, but the lectures didn't stop and we had to attend regularly for different subjects then sit an exam. At the end of our first year, we sat Prelims (Preliminary State Examination) and were then proper student nurses. Lectures were in our own time. Sometimes it was inconvenient to be allowed your off-duty to coincide with a special occasion. There never was any difficulty in ensuring you were off-duty for lectures. In order not to inconvenience the wards by messing up the off-duty and to accommodate night staff there was a choice of times. You could attend at 11a.m or 5.p.m. In theory 5p.m was good for night staff as it didn't entail having to stay up till after lunch thus only managing about five hours sleep. If you were not working in Edinburgh neither time was a good time.

I was at Gullane for the nursing course. It should have been easy-peasy, because it was all about bed baths and catheters and pressure points, no Latin words or dosages or dangers associated with. Bus times made it impossible to attend the morning lecture. If I could have got there in time for the 11 am I could have been back by three but I had to do the 5 p.m. arriving back late so forcing a day staff member to stay on till I could run all the way up from the bus and get changed. The bus times meant leaving at 1.15p.m so, off-duty at 9a.m, bath, bed and up again at 12.30 to get ready and walk to the main road. I slept through much of the course and only achieved 60% which meant a re-sit. Pass was 65% and the de-brief leading to having to re-sit was cutting. If I had managed to stay awake and pay attention, I might not have found myself in this sorry situation. I resat and achieved 98% on my new method of learning. I know to this day that there are twenty-three pieces of equipment needed for a bed bath, nine reasons for catheterisation and fourteen functions of the liver. When it came to finals, and there were two lots of exams; hospital finals and state finals. I won every prize there was going. Anyone failing hospital finals could still pass State Registration, but never be awarded the silver and enamel Sick Kids badge.

09 Sick Children

The Royal Edinburgh Hospital for Sick Children is a teaching hospital and in 1952 one of very few in the whole of the United Kingdom. Children came to us from birth and up to the age of twelve when they would be admitted to a general hospital. Children were admitted from the city and surrounding areas with any kind of illness or surgical emergency requiring hospital admission. Rather more children came from much further afield. They came because their need was for specialist care or seeking a diagnosis from a particular consultant recommended to their parents by the family doctor.

The regime in comparison to now was authoritarian and completely disregarded parental bonds. Visiting was three times a week for a short period in the afternoon. Your child may be in a ward with no visiting at any time, or in isolation. The child was handed over to a nurse for admission which meant TPR, (temperature, pulse and respiration) clothes off, bath, head check and hospital clothing. By the time Sister had completed the paperwork and had signed consent for treatment, the child's clothes would be returned and the mother, usually alone and tearful, left for home. No box of tissues or cups of tea. Admission was conducted in the corridor as was the way of things then. Siblings were not allowed access under any circumstances. There was never the queue or the unseemly rush seen in general hospitals because the numbers were few. For many parents the journey was too difficult and too expensive. For local children admitted with ailments aligning to poverty, visitors were few and far between either, because they couldn't be bothered or had to stay with their other children. Hence, the very few people using the grand front staircase.

There was by this time National Dried Milk, but it was not fortified with vitamins. Vitamins were provided separately to children, nursing mother and in pregnancy along with concentrated orange juice. Babies admitted to hospital were automatically put on National Dried with Abidec drops added. At a separate time from milk feeds the baby would be fed diluted orange juice. Attention was drawn to the problem of children with vitamin deficiencies and the fact that clearly, they were not getting their vitamin allocation. Babies weren't keen on Cod Liver Oil and it was easier not to bother. Orange juice however had other uses in post war times. Rationing was almost at an end, so rather than buy what the government had decided was a balanced diet, people were free to buy what they chose. It was no longer necessary to buy vegetables to fill up with and there was bread other than the fortified National Loaf.

New housing estates and prefabs moved people out of overcrowded homes, but they became immediately less well off as they were now paying more rent, had bigger places to heat and hot water was at a cost many had not previously paid for. The result was that places were colder and because they were no longer living in one room the other rooms were unheated. There was much more to spend wages on with no more clothing coupons and utility furniture available. Keeping up with the Joneses and top show was far more evident in places like Craigmillar and Longstone than it had been in the tenements and closes down the Pleasance or Gorgie or Leith.

Babies with congenital abnormalities were admitted straight from the city maternity units. The number of live births with gross abnormalities is low, but Sick Kids was the only place they could be cared for. For these babies, for whom there was no hope, and dependent on which consultant they were admitted under, a simple regime of warmth, love, fluids and gentle care was implemented, but no invasive procedures carried out. The heartbroken mother was kept in maternity for the usual ten-day post-partum before she could visit and hold her dying baby in her arms had it lived that long. Our lives were hectic and time for extra care unusual, but there was always time for these little mites. There was always someone who'd stay on to give comfort. It was at times like these the lesson I learned about 'smart babies' was confirmed. By remaining calm and sharing your peace with child in your arms, it becomes mutual and there is no longer any fretfulness just a gentle giving in to the warmth. Years later, I found it worked for adults too.

On the surgical wards, early arrivals presented with Pyloric Stenosis, projectile vomiting of great reach and ferocity in one so small which was surgically corrected. Common baby operations were to repair hernias, Intussusception, Hypospadias, Perthes Disease, and TEV (Talipes Equinovarus – club foot). Less common were Hermaphrodites, tumours and casualties from car accidents. Children fall off out of and into things giving us the complicated fractures that needed pulleys and splints or rods fitted. Appendicitis was common but too often too late for a simple appendicectomy because it had already burst, spread the infection and become 'dirty.' That means no operation could take place after this child until theatre had been completely scoured, cleaned and disinfected which took at least two hours to get back to ready to set up. Why it wasn't spotted in time could be due to the child not having the language to describe what was making it out of sorts and cranky. Younger children with appendicitis would present with a sore throat and while that was being treated the bit of trouble in the gut would heat up and explode. Many surgical beds were taken by children with burns.

From several months to age eleven we had a steady occupancy of children who had fallen into fires and sustained serious burns requiring months and even into adulthood of operations for skin grafting and release of scar tissue. These children were the reason no visitors were permitted to Ward 3. During my time at Sick Kids the treatment was exposure. Our consultant had worked with McIndoe during the war treating army personnel and civilian casualties and they led in their field. We had special McIndoe forceps and our chap Wallace's Rules of Nine is still in vogue today. Wallace's Rules told the admitting doctor the extent, depth, likelihood of survival and the immediate treatments regime of intravenous fluid replacement. Finding skin to graft could be challenging but initially it was about pain relief, fluid replacement and creating a structure for them to lie on which did no further damage. This was achieved by creating a frame above the mattress into which sponge rubber blocks were placed and on which the unburned sections rested. A cage fitted over this construction and a sheet thrown over so the complete nakedness was hidden from view. Other burns were caused by irons, kettles and hot food and affected lesser areas, but could still require long intensive care.

Parents of children on Ward 3 could visit the ward, but see their children only through glass. One lad burned by a bonfire to a marginal live or die extent had a face from chin upwards untouched. He eventually made an excellent recovery and we had him dressed and exercising. It was decided he could leave the ward and meet his mum and perhaps go out for a short walk. When dressed in grey shorts, shirt, round neck pullover and knee-high socks, he had scarred knees and a keloid scar just visible under his chin and we were proud to take him to his mum. He stood there and she stood there, but not even moving to hug him, she said, 'His neck's an awfy mess.'

Other reconstruction work covered hare lip and cleft palate, removal of birth marks and rodent activity. We never met up with the 'Cruelty Man' at Sick Kids, but it beggar's belief how any mother could sleep through her two-year-old being eaten by rats.

On the medical wards there was a constant throughput of children with poverty, living conditions and ignorance exacerbated poor health. Chest infections and pneumonia were common and we'd find underlying rickets or scurvy and a few lice making things worse. A lot of our babies came as Marasmus or 'failure to thrive.' Investigation could diagnose a physical cause such as 'tongue tie' cleft palate, establishing feeding for Down's babies is often difficult, Coeliac Disease, Cystic Fibrosis, learning incapacity and others, but rather more were due to maternal anxiety. Parenting wasn't supported by the leaflets and books there are today. A new parent with a windy baby who possets all the time may decide to change the formula, not just once, but several times. They don't know all the different ways to 'bring up wind.' They get overtired and their anxiety is transferred to the baby who gets fretful. Babies come with inbuilt guile with which to torment their parents and firm expectations as to how they wish to be fed and when. Lack of routine can often be a cause. When presented with babies of this ilk it was incumbent on us to discover what would break the habit. One time I had one who liked to be sung to while in the next cot a colleague found Shakespeare helpful. Babies need to be secure when feeding and how they are held is important. Wrapped or unwrapped. Later in life I would start the process with these babies by sitting with the mother and watching.

Many medical issues in children are not translated into adulthood so there are many syndromes and diseases inconsistent with longevity which general medicine never experiences. This is not so today as advances mean complexities in systems which could not be fixed and manageable means of supplying oxygen and nutrients are now available. Meningitis, Epilepsy, Nephritis, Quinsy, Diphtheria, ear infections, PUOs (Pyrexia of Unknown Origin), Tuberculosis, Gastro-enteritis and tonsillitis provides just a flavour of the menu. Tonsillitis provided a full house twice a week in ENT (Ear Nose & Throat) when they made the top of the waiting list to have their tonsils and adenoids removed.

Only rarely was the one parent bedroom in use. The parents of desperately ill children who lived at a distance could be accommodated. An exception could be made for a mother breast feeding if she lived too far from the hospital to express her milk and fetch it to the ward twice a day. We didn't have peel off labels in the 1950s. Labelling of any milk delivered was done by cutting off a piece of Elastoplast from a two-inch-wide reel and attaching it to the bottle with time and name of child. The Elastoplast had the same effect on bottles once heated as on skin and required an extra action in the cleaning to properly remove the black stuff.

Progress in the manufacture of Penicillin was made during the war, but it wasn't the treatment of choice it became, and Sulphonamides were widely used in hospitals. Sulphonamides were not given to children routinely because of the dangerous side effects. Patients were advised to drink copiously to prevent calcification of the kidneys. On the wards intake and output was recorded meticulously. With older children this is not difficult, but with babies it is tricky. It wasn't a case of looking at a nappy and gauging the shade of yellow through to amber indicating danger. The child was weighed daily at the same time. Input was set out and adjusted as necessary. Output meant we weighed the nappy when it was applied and as we took it off when changing. No, you can't agree a nappy weight because they varied between heavy fluffy and light from frequent washing. Feeders also are before and after so you know how much you shovelled in had been spat out.

Children imprint themselves for different reasons and Irene not least because she was the little girl, I had to return to the mortuary daily to care for. Irene had been treated with Sulphonamides for a urinary infection, but no instructions given regarding the need for fluid intake. The damage was done. She became a cause celebre as the Sunday Post told the story of 'The Minister who delivered the rolls.' Her Dad was the local baker and once he'd baked the rolls, he would come straight to the hospital to join his wife at Irene's bedside. It was hopeless and one sad day the Minister came with the little baker's van to take home the bereft parents. Today the lawyers would be rubbing their hands – somebody will have to pay. Some months later their other child, a little girl they had adopted when Irene was a toddler and they were unable to provide her with a sibling, was admitted with nephritis. A ripple ran through the whole hospital, but there was a happy ending.

Cynthia's in my head for a different kind of reason. Cynthia was a routine admission for Ts & As, (Tonsils and Adenoids). On night duty, she was one of a completely new batch and before I could settle to the mending and swab-making, every last one of them had to have cocoa and a biscuit after which it was nil by mouth. Once that was over, all would have a wee, maybe even a story and then sleep till morning. In the morning all were toileted, washed and dressed in theatre gowns and long pirate socks. By the time I went off-duty, the theatre staff would be all set up and just waiting for the ENT surgeon to start the list. Cynthia suffered from insomnia. She clearly came from Morningside, being quite imperious in her demands. Inability to sleep was nothing new and her mummy always brought her sleeping spirits so she had lovely dreams. I explained that we had no sleeping spirits, but because she was so special, I might just be able to get my hands on some fairy medicine. Into a minim medicine glass, I poured two teaspoons of orange squash and a splodge more into the unbreakable ward drinking beaker. I had to explain apologetically that unlike sleeping spirits, fairy medicine, though even more effective, didn't taste very nice. So instead of just a wee glass of spirits, it was one mouthful of fairy medicine and a very quick follow-on quick drink of orange to take the taste away. Effective.

Marianne came to us because of a mix up in her gender. This was normally addressed at birth and in discussion, suggest the parents choose an either-or name like Frances or Lesley. The Edinburgh regime saw the child in outpatients and if in doubt they were admitted to perform a Laparotomy and have a good look around and decide. They came from Glasgow and some preparatory work had been done without a laparotomy when for some reason, doubt arose, and they were referred to Edinburgh. The parents were on the elderly side, devoted, embarrassed and upset. Exploratory surgery and a debrief held and agreed name change to Martin made. A number of operations over eighteen months followed and I was there at the first and in theatre for the last. Each time Martin came in his mother travelled every visiting time all the way from Glasgow to Edinburgh by train then tram. At weekends his dad came as well. They were obviously very conscious of their duty to Martin, but the 'shame' of having such a child clearly made them keep themselves to themselves and could well have explained the change of hospital. Everything about Martin's mum was buttoned up, no dinky curlers and headscarf. Her coat, which she never removed when visiting, and the close-fitting hat combined with the tight grip on her shopping bag and the smile which never revealed any teeth prevented any unwarranted approach from anyone. With Martin always delighted to see what they'd brought him and keen to engage, it was clear the prison they made for themselves was to ensure a safe place for their child. My last contact with Martin was at the removal of some temporary metalwork from his new working willie.

The McKays were a large family admitted from the far north. Large not in numbers – there were only three of them – but in size. Each was grossly obese. The boy, the youngest, aged about six, was eight stone; his older sister weighed ten stone and the big girl, the eldest, had to have an adult bed brought from the Infirmary. Both parents were smaller and thinner than their children and the Scottish expression 'shilpit,' (kind of small wet through and a paler shade of pale) could fit either. Experience later suggested they might be this way due to frequent squashing by their exuberant children. When you are asked to prepare for the admission of three obese children, you don't quite envisage two fat women and a Billy Bunter. We had to keep their clothes because we had nothing to fit them and we had to protect the other children and ourselves from accidental injury. We had to import a dining table and chairs. They broke things. When it was meal times and the food trolley was wheeled in all the other children remained in cot and bed till the McKays sat down. The Assyrian coming down like a wolf from the fold could give you an idea, a squeak of the trolley wheels and they set off en masse from wherever they happened to be.

The dietician was in her element. She had never been faced with such a challenge and was keen to try anything that might work. The calorie-controlled meals vanished quickly and they were always keen to help out anyone they thought needed it. I think the only bulk she didn't add was straw, but she tried. Then she had an idea that if they were full before the meal that could make a difference. To this end each was given a full-size bottle of fizzy pop before meals. It didn't make any difference. They still roamed about scavenging and since all comestibles brought by visitors were subsumed by Sister there was never anything to scavenge. There was no television and no entertainment lady. A teacher came in if we had long-term patients and provided some tutoring. The physio devised exercises and we all steered clear of the flailing limbs while these were carried out. They didn't stay long. A weight loss was established and they went back to where they came from with diet sheets and tablets and an appointment to see an endocrinologist in Aberdeen who would continue their care.

10 RHSC Staff Nurse

Not everyone who started at Sick Kids finished and few were offered staff nurse placements. Most people went on to do General training then Midwifery. Few came from Edinburgh and most were a long way from home. The age seventeen start meant you didn't need to hang around for a year after leaving school. You could go as a cadet to some of the major teaching hospitals, but there was no reduction of the training period. As a State Registered Children's Nurse, (RSCN) you already had the Preliminary State Certificate and need only to do a further two years training to become a Registered General Nurse (RGN). Prelims were common to all Registration courses. However, you couldn't do midwifery unless you were a Registered General Nurse. Most, when qualified, went back to England or Aberdeen or Inverness to train. Two who trained with me were Gaelic-speaking from the Highlands and Islands. They both finished, but shot back up North to be nearer home. No flying in these days, so they only ever got home on annual leave. They had nowhere to go when they were off-duty. Well, nowhere to go that didn't cost money. Off-duty with me, they'd tag along so my mother could feed us. She was really good at this and once they knew the way, she had nurses dropping in regularly to raid her tins. Even after I was long gone, they kept up with her and newbies they fetched with them from time to time.

Maddie McLean was a friend we kept up with at a distance. Maddie was very tall, well-built, but not fat, and always hungry. She was embarrassed about her appetite so, would initiate eating competitions which she always won. Her dad was a Co-op manager so she always fetched back food. The time our supper/breakfast was kippers and rhubarb she won hands down scoffing the lot because none of us could face it. Once we had a panic situation on my ward and Maddie was sent to help out and given the Temperatures (TPRs) to do, but she hadn't a watch! I lent her mine while I got drafted away from TPRs and into the panic. She cleared off and so did my watch. She denied all knowledge and the ward was turned upside down, but no sign. No nurse could present for duty without a watch with a second hand. I had to spend five shillings buying an enormous man's pocket watch with chain to get a little sixty second sweep at the bottom of it. Everyone was interrogated and eventually Matron said the hospital would replace my watch and I must ask my father for the receipt. I took the receipt in and was subjected to Matron's deep sorrow that I had lost such a valuable watch and what a sacrifice my parents must have made to buy it for me. Just like my dad every time I lost a pen. It had cost £15 and now I do understand it was expensive. Before the claim could be submitted, out of the blue and all of a sudden Maddie found my watch! It was just lying somewhere and the matter was closed. I suspect she pawned it till the end of the month.

Maddie had a new boyfriend, well an old man friend really. Jack was a technician in the pathology department, which was attached to the mortuary, and of advanced middle age. Our contact with that department was as little as we could manage it to be. Maddie was besotted by Jack, but as soon as it came to the attention of Matron, words were spoken, strong words in both directions. Her parents were informed and it was generally accepted that this undesirable clandestine affair had been terminated.

One afternoon, when we were both off-duty, she invited me to her room to listen to a new record. Maddie being the only one of us with a record player, I accepted with pleasure. We all bought records, but had to wait till Maddie could play them for us. While we listened, I was required to 'get yer feet up' as she packed up some of her stuff to change over. She had loads of clothes and she did from time to time swap her wardrobe for different ones from home. This was not a trunk, just a suitcase from the top of the wardrobe. She did not have her trunk. I would have noticed that because she had one of the rooms where trunks had to be packed and unpacked in the corridor. Next thing, she was gone. She'd done a 'moonlight' with Jack. When it was my turn to be interrogated, Matron thought that I must be thick in not even considering she was packing to go. Matron never raised her voice; she just had the rhetoric to reduce any one of us to recognition of our failings. Disowned by her family and living in a poor flat in a poor district, Maddie gave birth to twins. They did marry, but continued to live in squalor. She quickly had more children and the twins were feral, completely out of control and wrecked everything they came in contact with. Mollie and I visited on the birth of the third child, when the twins were about three. They swarmed over the furniture like alpine climbers wearing what looked like crampons. She was as scatty as a mother as she had been as a nurse. Her parents never became reconciled to the situation. Jack would be retired by the time the twins went to school.

I'd never liked Jack. He was coarse, had an untidy moustache, wore a brown coat rather than a white and never looked clean. He took delight in showing us the jars on the shelves containing foetal abnormalities, which he had to assemble for medical student pathology lectures. Once when I was on mortuary duty and I had just lifted an icy cold, stiff child, the door behind me opened suddenly and I almost passed out. He said 'Boo' and thought it was funny. That was Jack. He wasn't good looking; he was old and even to seasoned nurses his humour was coarse.

My first staffing post was in theatre. There was only a staff post there for six months each year to cover the spring week and annual holidays of the two theatre sisters. When you did a stint during training, you never 'scrubbed'; you were 'dirty' all the time. You could watch the rituals, but never participate. I remember the day I was invited. The senior sister was very much royalty, tall, elegant and very hard to please. She came up behind me on my last day and whispered 'Would you like to staff for us'? Oh yes, I would. Not having had any 'scrubbed' experience, I had to learn fast when I joined them.

Jean the other sister introduced me to Tunnocks. She came from Haddington, where Tunnock's factory was and we'd go out for a coffee and to 'support home trade' we had either a Tunnocks's caramel wafer or a Tunnocks's chocolate teacake.

There are sets of instruments for different operations and there are specific instrument brand/types that surgeons swear by. Every morning we had a 'list' of operations, an order of play, name of the principal operator and first off got out the tools for the job ready to be sterilised. You knew whose list it was and their preferred forceps, scalpels, needles, sewing materials and other weapons. Now they come in a sterilised pack ready to break open at the table. I wonder now if at Sick Kids they have all the different packs required to meet the different and exacting operators. We had to know exactly what was needed and how many, then set out one's trolley in the right order. You had to be one step ahead of the surgeon all the time. You scrubbed first, so while he was scrubbing, you were essentially setting the table.

The nail brushes were scratchy and you scrubbed hands and arms up to your elbows for ten minutes. Having turned off the taps with your elbows, you advanced to the bench, where bundles were set out. Top of the pile was a sterile towel, which you used to dry your hands and arms and discard. Then you picked up your gown and climbed into it, then a 'dirty' nurse fastened the tapes. Now to get your gloves on without any skin touching the outside. Gowned and gloved, arms out like a sleep walker, you advanced on your trolley and proceeded to the next stage of preparation. Swabs were counted out loud. Bundles first, then bundles counted down to individual in a variety of sizes to a 'dirty' nurse, who chalked the numbers up. The instruments you have selected are collected off the main sterile trolley and transferred to your smaller active trolley. If all goes to plan, you do not disturb your main sterile supply till next on the list.

When the patient was transferred from trolley to table, a nod, hand signal or vocal prompt was given and you handed out the sterile dressing towels that would cover everything except the operation site. You are now ready for the word 'scalpel.' I never knew any surgeons as casual as those in Holby. Our surgeons tended to be tense and the slightest hesitation in passing forceps or finding what they wanted wasn't what they wanted after all could result in a tantrum. The tantrums were most common when they were allowing a lesser mortal do the operation while they assisted. Sometimes a registrar asked for a different kind of spanner, which led to a hot debate. Some brave mortals actually answered back.

Our Mr Wallace had been one of the leading plastic surgeons in the Army, and just as McIndoe had forceps named after him, Mr Wallace was the initiator of the Wallace Rules of Nine, which calculated treatment regime for burns patients. He was very much against using antibiotic powder while his registrars swore by it. When we'd get to the final stages of a burns dressing or graft, Wallace would leave the registrar to finish off. One of his mates, who was 'dirty,' would approach the table and whip a jar of antibiotic powder out of his pocket and sprinkle to order. There were always a lot of burned children. For some it seemed there was no skin to be found to graft and they would keep coming back time after time to have yet another little patch.

While we had a list starting every morning Monday to Friday and finishing when we got to the end of it, after and even during, we had emergencies. Every evening, every night and over the weekend, we had emergencies. Student nurses working in theatre had to be on call several nights a week and if they were out of bed after midnight, they were allowed to delay reporting for duty till 9 a.m. next day. Sisters and staff nurses didn't qualify for this kindness. If there was something happening, we were there, day and night. Our perk was alternate weekends off. A weekend began at 5.30 p.m. on Friday and you didn't return to duty until first thing Monday morning. On one of my marathon weekends, I came on at 3.30 p.m. for an emergency which would definitely over-run, to let the weekender go. I was in the same place doing the same thing at 5.30p.m. on the Monday. I remember during the Monday afternoon doing an appendix with a registrar I had another the same evening and one on the Friday. He said to me, 'You must be tired, Staff' and all of a sudden, I was. Something upset the system and I didn't get the next weekend off either. It wasn't really much better. I got a refill of my stomach mixture and a lecture from assistant matron, 'I'm not surprised you have an ulcer the hours you keep.' All my fault – working day and night, missing meals and short on sleep. However, on this occasion there was a concession and she organised for there to be a jug of milk in the serving kitchen fridge from which I could help myself at any time.

Every day we hosed theatre down, scrubbed and sterilised anything not fixed to the floor after the 'list.' We did a more limited clean after an emergency unless it was a 'dirty case' and if so, the whole thing had to be done, walls and all, before we could leave or do another. It took an hour and a half and you could not accommodate another case till it was done. Saturdays were different and we did extra cleaning and the dishes. There were hundreds of different-sized needles that were not in regular use as well as dozens of weird shaped drains, pipes and pieces of rubber. All these things were displayed in glass dishes with a silver cover on glass shelves above the slab where we got ourselves attired. It took five hours to do the dishes. The artefacts were in pure phenol, which could burn you down to the bone. They had to be removed and sterilised then the painstaking job to replace all exactly as it was by size and type in the proper dish using sterile forceps. When I was setting my table for a case, a dirty nurse would lift down a dish for me to choose needles and bits and pieces for the job in hand. It had to happen to me. I'd finished and gone out of theatre when there was an almighty crash. The shelf had collapsed. Glass everywhere and all that dangerous liquid and my designer displays to do all over again.

Autoclaving which is steam sterilisation of silver drums was another risky job. Autoclaves could blow up and if you allowed the pressure to exceed the legal limit it emitted such horrible bells and hooters that the entire hospital knew you'd cocked up. Once you refilled all the drums used for a list it was time to consider how many swabs, wool balls and masks you would need to make to keep the back stock. Ready to get the autoclave working you loaded it then set the dials. It looked menacing and when you pulled open the heavy front opening, a bit like a submarine door, you packed it with drums then reversed the process to close. Once closed, you manipulated the wheel till it was secure and chose a series of smaller wheels, which set dials to carry out the programme required. You were still not finished then because the programme was staged. The steam level was varied and at specified times you returned to read the dials and alter the switches. All about pressure. When you removed the drums, you closed the vents in the drum and the colour of a label indicated whether a drum was sterile or not. Human error was all that could go wrong! One cardinal, wasteful and shameful sin was to overcook gloves. Gloves had only five minutes at high pressure. Over cooking would not be noted till, when carefully inserting your fingers, the whole glove disintegrated.

If eight surgeons one after the other removed an appendix, no two would do it in the same way, use exactly the same instruments or suture material. There was no music or jocularity, it was a serious business. Cotton wool balls didn't come in packets, we made them. Swabs had to be cut out and folded to size. You don't get profligate with swabs if you know you will only have to find the time to make more. On the wards, the night staff did this job because they assumed, you'd nothing to do once the lights were out. Our swab and ball making in theatre was more specialist. We had reached modernity in that the gauze had a blue thread which would show up on X-ray were one to be left behind. How that ever happened or any instruments got left is hard to understand because we counted in and counted out. When we made swabs, they were counted into bundles and tied with packing gauze tape. When I set my trolley, a 'dirty' nurse counted how many bundles I was starting with. I only ever gave the surgeon another if he gave me one back. They were counted as discarded by 'dirty' then, after it was all over, the whole thing was 'audited' and the clean and dirty recorded in a book. We even weighed them for blood loss.

For a list you knew what was coming, but emergencies were a lucky dip. No mobile phones or pagers so, on call you had to be on site and reception had to know where you were. Sunbathing on a lovely sunny Sunday afternoon, I was called for a baby with an ovarian cyst. Cyst – not tumour, baby not grown up – I set myself up with an extra gallipot (a small stainless-steel dish – mini yoghurt pot). When the cyst was eventually levered out, I had to send for a bowl to put it in. Only a few days later, another surgeon called me out as he was operating on the seven-year-old son of two GP colleagues whom he suspected had a cyst on the mesentery. I learn by my mistakes. Another cyst, but a larger child. I provided range of receptacles, starting with pimple size and up to the biggest in our stock for sterilised stainless steel. Wrong again, this time it had to be a bucket. I wasn't the only person wrong footed. The child was slightly distended, but as the cyst was eased out and the incision extended, it was unbelievable that such an enormous mass could have been inside the abdomen of a small boy.

My room was the first in the nurses' home so, being called during the night nobody else in the building would be disturbed. The home could be reached directly from Ward 1, but this was forbidden except for the person locking up at 10 o'clock, night sister on the prowl or getting theatre on-call called. Two doors and a squeaky floor board. So accustomed did I become to being called in the night that I'd hear the first door, second door and squeak and when they came into my room I was out of bed and sufficiently dressed to walk back with the caller. There was only a 30-minute gap from decision to operate, and ready to start. That went for the anaesthetist as well, as they were called from home. After the operation, surgeon, registrar and anaesthetist swanned off to the ward for coffee and toasted sandwiches prepared by some already demented junior night nurse. She may have already cleaned and polished the doctors' side room, but they'd leave crumbs, dirty cups and fag ash and she'd have to do it all over again. We were only free to go off-duty when all the jobs were completed to the usual high standard required.

My room was the only one the ground floor in which the window was not nailed down. All windows on all floors could be raised just enough for a draught. Mine opened wide, made little noise and was the only way into the Nurses' home after 10 p.m. People out late were out without permission. Their names were not in 'the book' on the front hall table, so they would not be missed. The window was a fair way off the ground and required stepped assistance from a drainpipe joint. There was frequent traffic, but only once did it coincide with night sister calling me. I'd be asleep then be aware of a bit of bustle and a whispered 'it's only me – go to sleep.' On the occasion of the near miss, the breaker and enterer became aware of the knock on the door and backed out again, but sprained her ankle. She couldn't get any purchase on the leg on the ground so I had to climb up, hang out, drag her in then leave her to find her own way once I'd gone.

Some rituals were traditional, like after-the-operation routine. Patient entered stage left, but left by the main doors, which opened on to the main corridor. At a given signal, a dirty nurse would bring in a trolley from stage left and the patient transferred. A further nod and she threw open the double doors and leapt out into the corridor to stop traffic. Her exit left or right depended on the ward the patient was being returned to and immediately she was in position the trolley hurtled out and was raced to the ward. I don't know why; it was just how we did it then. After the almost holy silence of what went before it seemed really rowdy hooligan behaviour.

The crossword with the senior sister was a ritual and oh how I feared that. We sometimes got a coffee break in the plaster room, even the preparation was a performance. She may have been an early barista. The cups and saucers were fine bone china with a wee milk jug and sugar bowl. It could have been a pleasant interlude were it not for the Scotsman crossword. Wednesday and Saturday the compiler was a sod and when asked, I never seemed to be able to come up with an answer. Though much more regal, the senior sister was a female *Dad's Army*, Captain Mannering and I the 'stupid boy.' The other weekdays weren't so bad, Monday and Thursday and Tuesday and Friday had obviously very clever chaps making them up, but Wednesday and Saturday, no chance. When I moved to Forteviot we had the Times and Observer on Sundays, which were a picnic compared to the Scotsman Wednesday and Saturday.

Blood tests clearly told us little compared with today and there were no MRI scans. The way to find out was to open them up and have a good old rummage. No keyholes then. Our older surgeons were dismissive of small incisions. No little jeweller's eye glass, just get in there and rummage then demand retractors to open things up a bit more. No wonder they kept appendices in for ten days. A child of indeterminate sex would have an exploratory operation to see what was inside and based on what was there the decision would be made.

Having done this stint as a staff nurse in theatre, my next stop was Forteviot.

11 Forteviot

My second stint at staffing was different. Forteviot was a gracious mansion in Edinburgh not very far from the hospital. It was home to sixteen very young children with a long term, life limiting illness. Few would reach school age. I have a photograph taken by the Edinburgh Evening News of the Christmas party and by the time I completed my General, only McDuff was still alive. The main part of the house was a dining room and morning room downstairs with a drawing room, library and sewing room upstairs and a bedroom wing. The dining room and drawing room were wards, the morning room two cubicles, and library was sister's sitting room and the sewing room her bedroom. She was never far from the children night or day. Downstairs off the ward there was a large conservatory which was where the children played and ate and we generally spent our days.

Domestic and nursing staff were in the bedroom wing. I got a room to myself, everybody else shared and we had a common room. The grounds were magnificent having manicured lawns, flower beds and a summer house. All these children were loved and despite the severity of their ailments it was unusual to have squalling or niggly babies. We did not use Calpol, it hadn't been invented, but very occasionally we administered chloral hydrate if prescribed.

We were never overwhelmed with visitors. Some parents came regularly but few daily and some not at all. Alistair McDuff spent a lot of time there between operations. His parents never visited. He had Hirschsprung's disease and was deaf. His aunt was a friend of my dad's cousin and through her intervention in 1952 I was asked to visit the ward he was on and find out about him. That would never happen today because parents visit freely. We did get a lot of dirty children and dirty parents along with poverty and disadvantage. Today the poor are not unwashed as much and have designer trainers and in comparative terms they are not really poor but they still suffer from poor health. In the 1950s many had no inside toilet or running water, they cooked on a coal fire and benefits for the destitute was doled out by charities. Some parents didn't visit because they couldn't afford the fare and didn't ring because they had no telephone. Our only means of contact was to ring the police where they lived, and the local Bobby would go round with a message. It was normal practice then if somebody knew a nurse they'd be asked to visit and feedback. I took an interest in Alistair from the time he was a baby and now he's 68 years old and we are still in touch.

In the hospital everybody in every ward knew Alistair. He was admitted with an obstruction shortly after birth and despite a colostomy he was prone to recurring obstructions and he seldom left the hospital for long. At Forteviot, he was a bit like a trusty in jail. Despite his deafness he was bright and tuned in to everything. Towards mealtimes he would go around all the little lockers and fetch the correct feeder for each child. Having discovered he was deaf the ENT people had been involved and he was referred to Donaldson's Hospital which wasn't a hospital but a school for the deaf and wherein clinics were held. He began attending there once a week and the third week I took him.

A taxi collected us and returned to pick us up. We had a session with an audiologist who involved all three of us bbbbing into a balloon and picking up wooden animals and saying cow or sheep. When we'd had our turn, she asked us to wait. The 'high heid yin' came in and explained that Alistair had now had three sessions and was making no progress. We were completely getting it wrong because on each occasion a different person had brought him. He would never stand a chance unless he had a 'mummy.' I was told to go back and explain to the hospital. They didn't have case conferences in these days but his surgeon spoke to the ENT people and the ENT people spoke to the physician who was in charge of Forteviot who spoke to Sister. They decided I could do the 'mummy' role. From that day on, I would pick him out of his cot in the morning and he would accompany me round with the night nurse who was handing over and I'd keep him with me till I put him to bed.

It worked, he was my little shadow copying everything I did even to picking up laundry and checking for missing tapes on baby gowns and feeders. I'd take him with me if I had the afternoon off, so he'd go home with me and became part of our family. I had to buy him clothes because I didn't like being out with a child in what the hospital provided. Then my parents began to chip in and when we went to the Zoo for lunch on a Sunday, he was a proper little Lord Fauntleroy. He did really well and in no time, he understood every word I spoke. When I left Forteviot to do my General we kept in contact and I'd pick him up for my day off and try to have my off-duty so we went to lipreading together. When he went to Donaldson's as a boarder, he'd spend weekends with my parents.

He went home for a school holiday and I rang his mum to check when he'd be back to organise picking him up and she said 'he's no right well, why do you nae come doon?' I did and when she opened the door this little waif with sunken eyes held up his arms to me, I rang the hospital and took him in. It was touch and go. When he was ready for discharge his mother didn't want to risk having him and the hospital wondered if my mother would have him. He was discharged into her care. When she took him back for an appointment, she had one of the proudest moments of her life. Because Alistair was so special, she didn't have to go to outpatients but to the ward. As they came into the front entrance there was a porter up a ladder who called out 'it's McDuff' and Matron was passing and called out for assistant matron and they all greeted them like royalty. They went up the stairs, the grand front stairs and his surgeon was coming towards them and he said, 'Somebody knows how to look after McDuff.' The first few days after leaving Forteviot, I was completely bereft.

Much later, his mother told mine, that her having mumps during pregnancy was the cause of Alistair's problems. Her GP told her she had to be prepared to 'give up' her baby. She did exactly as the doctor said. They lived in the borders and his dad worked in one of the mills and I'm sure had she not taken the advice literally that they would have visited when he was small. His condition settled down after he went to school and he'd go back to Jedburgh for the holidays just spending leave outs and half term with my parents.

I don't understand nursing today. The situation with McDuff was very casual and would never be allowed today. It isn't possible to care for someone if you can't touch them. The baby you lift to feed needs to know and feel loved. You can't switch off and not care though you do need to be able not to come over all unnecessary when a long stay patient goes home or when patients die. It isn't easy.

One Christmas, I think 1954, I was 'floating,' and Anne was in charge of the Milk Kitchen when we had a flurry of baby deaths from what they called 'Silent Pneumonia.' In that period of ten days Anne and I did the Last Offices for nine babies. The baby would be fine on going to bed and either dead or close to dead in the morning. The next-door neighbours of one of our registrars were an elderly couple absolutely thrilled that their first grandchild was coming to stay and to be baptised where his parents had married. They'd borrowed a cot from him. He and his wife had been called in to admire the evening they arrived. A lovely chubby smiling infant. There was no Christening. One of our surgical registrars had twins; a boy and a girl. The little girl was on her feet chattering and shaking the bars of her cot and he reached in to the other cot and said 'wake up sleepyhead' and the little boy was dead. People were referring to Anne and me as 'the morticians.' We were going to a family party on Hogmanay but not finishing till nine so a taxi had been ordered to collect us and it never turned up. I rang home to say we'd not be coming and burst into tears. It was all too much. Six days, dead babies, grieving parents and the last straw – no taxi.

Charles was beautiful, he had very sparse, blond curly hair and a bluish, deathly white complexion. When undressing him you could see his little heart fluttering. He fed very slowly and seldom cried. Mostly, he was awake and alert. He had a very wide forehead and I'm sure he would have been clever. Charles never sat up or did anything except smile and wiggle very lightly, his very large for his size expressive hands, which would tinkle a mobile across his cot and smile some more. It was a very distinctive tinkle of the sort that made you smile when you heard it. His story is sad. His mother, the wife of a miner in Fife with a large family had a fling and the outcome was Charles. Her husband threw her out, so homeless and mother of a very sick baby in hospital she got a live-in job as a cleaner at an Edinburgh hospital. She came every day she could. His father clearly married and of managerial ilk visited too, but never at the same time. He would arrive, suited and booted, Scotsman newspaper under his arm, stand by the cot then leave again with a curt salute to whoever happened to be around. When Charles died, his mother and her oldest son came to Forteviot and Chris Edgar, the sister in charge carried the little white coffin on her knee to the crematorium where the father was waiting. It was a cold, wet foggy day. When the service was over, Chris suggested to the mother that she and her boy go to a café for a hot drink then go to the pictures so they would be out of the cold. The poor woman had no home to go to and she couldn't take her grown up son to her lonely room in the hospital. A few days later, crossing the hall, I heard the tinkle of the mobile. I felt so sad I had to find a replacement for the child who had been gifted with it and find a replacement with a more robust jingle.

William wasn't with us very long. He was nine months old when he was admitted. He had Hydrocephalus and his head was enormous. Not only was it bigger than a large beach ball, it was heavily tilted because of the way he had been lying all his life. Shunts for babies with Hydrocephalus were quite routine. There was criticism for his previous care in allowing his head to become so distorted but it was too late. When William was first seen it was too late. Born at home in a remote community he'd not been seen till a few days before he was admitted for observation to Sick Kids. Cerebral irritation causes a cry that has the same effect as a fork scraping the bottom of a pan. In Wembley Stadium you could pick out a lone cerebral cry they are so distinctive. William cried. Most of the time one of us was with him just to try and comfort him. If he'd lain on the other side, his neck would have snapped with the weight. The best way to nurse him was to lie down and let his massive head rest on your chest. If you sat with him or walked with him the pain in the arm supporting his head grew cramped and painful in a very short time. I did something for William I have never done before or since. I went out and bought a dummy. Dummies were forbidden and just not the thing. Chris Edgar and I had a discussion and the outcome was an undercover outing. I changed into mufti and walked to a Boots the Chemist out of the district. Even in disguise I found it difficult to play the part. It was worse than having to ask for sanitary towels or later in life Durex. Not only did I sneak it in, I disposed of the packaging in the street. I sterilised it and with hope in my heart picked him out of his cot and offered it to him. He spat it out.

Elaine, a baby with Cystic Fibrosis was with us because the authorities were trying to find somewhere for her to go home to. Her parents were both at university in Edinburgh and very immature they were. Mostly they were accompanied by their own parents when they came to visit and they were all regular visitors. I classed them all as remote. At Forteviot we not only welcomed visitors at any reasonable hour, we encouraged contact with their children. Neither of the birth parents had enough nous to leave a child with, never mind a sickly one. Their parents acknowledged that their offspring had fathered a child not expected to live beyond the age of two. That was as far as it went. Neither couple were up for taking on the poor wee thing.

Then there was Johnny. He was a blue baby and as McDuff was to me so Johnny was to Chris Edgar. Not only had he four different heart malfunctions, he was slow with everything else. Chris had high hopes that once he could be operated on, he'd pick up on his milestones. He was amiable, had fond parents and an older sister. He'd been at Forteviot all his life till he went for operation age four. He survived the operation and the day after he'd been bright and no cause for alarm. In fact, Chris was absolutely charmed when she came back because as she'd walked on to his ward, he'd heard her footsteps and called out 'here's Edgar.' He died that night. It was only when chatting with his parents after the funeral when they'd come back to reminisce that Chris suggested his sister not go into the ward because we had German measles, that the mum mentioned the child had already had measles when she was expecting Johnny. All these years they had denied themselves another baby just in case. There was a happy ending and they did have another child. I was so fortunate that despite testing positive for measles when pregnant with Kathryn that she was fine, my absolutely perfect favourite only daughter.

At Forteviot we had two domestics, Annie and Mary. Both had been there many years. Annie had come straight from school and after some time her sister was released from a mental hospital where she had been confined because she had an illegitimate child. Mary was not quite the full shilling but worked well, lived in and would have been perfectly able to live in the community. Annie was married and had one child who was more or less a resident and when he went to school, it was to a school nearby. From a large and very poor family, Annie was going up in the world. At that time, she, her husband and the child lived in one room. That room was immaculate and nothing was out of place and everything had a place. Under the bed was a work of art. She cooked on a black range which was as shiny as a guardsman's boots. They were getting near the top of the housing list and in that cramped space under the bed was all the new things she was buying ready for the move. Annie learned from Chris Edgar and was a loyal retainer forever after Forteviot. When she had a proper house and her husband didn't need his wife to go out cleaning, she 'did' for Chris and her partner.

Chris Edgar's partner was the hospital dietitian and they met over a feeding programme and spent all their weekends together. If Chris was on call, Miss Mack, her partner, would spend the weekend at Forteviot. Sundays were very special in that I still had my morning proper coffee, coffee break, with her and Chris but the difference was the crosswords. By evening we had to have completed both Times and Observer. One Sunday I was on my last round with the night nurse when I thought of the answer to the last clue and there was a little ceremony where we actually rang Miss Mack to make due pronouncement. The answer was 'thematics,' I don't remember what the clue was.

Chris Edgar was prone to bad headaches and while I was doing my General, she had a stroke which finished her career. The stroke left her quite handicapped but with Miss Mack's good job, her sick pay and what there was of a pension, they lived very comfortably for the rest of her life. I used to visit them every time I came to Edinburgh and in time took a growing number of little Mitchells with me. They were my first ever experience of a same sex couple which of course were considered only as friends.

When I was doing my general, I met the second pair and what a kerfuffle that caused. A student nurse fell in love with one of the night sisters. Her parents were brought in and all sorts of barriers introduced to bring this to an end. It didn't work though because the night sister moved to London and the nurse used to fly down for her days off. She came from a very wealthy family. When she finished her general, she too went to London to do her midwifery near her friend. As soon as she was twenty-one, there was nothing anyone could do about it.

Time was passing and I could not delay going to do my general training and I went to the Western General Hospital when I was twenty-one.

12 General Nursing

I had my 21st birthday just before I started at the Western General to do a two year post graduate training to add RGN (Registered General Nurse) to my RSCN. My birthday fell on 31st December and, as was my habit if possible, I worked Christmas to have New Year's Day off. The build-up to Christmas began at the end of September and was in full swing by Hallowe'en. At the Western you could say it was low key and nobody got over excited or demanding, whereas at Sick Kids there was the fierce competition between wards for the best theme and the most elaborate manifestation. The Western made do with a few streamers put up by the porters, who came with their long ladders.

By the time Christmas came at Sick Kids, we were all weary of it, and on the day itself after three months of dressing pipe cleaners in themed costume and building scenery, we had, unless you were already on-duty, to meet in the front hall at 5.30 a.m. Once in the place from which we were normally banned, Fish, the Assistant Matron, led us – our cloaks worn red side out – singing carols to the children. Always glad to get to Hogmanay. Well usually, with the exception of the year of my 20th birthday. I was 'floating' which meant I got sent to where the action was anywhere in the hospital. Nine times between Christmas Eve and Hogmanay my first dispatch was a ward where a baby had been rushed in after being found blue and cold by their parents. They called it Silent Pneumonia. Every morning I was sent to arrive just as life was pronounced extinct and went straight from the mortuary to breakfast at 9.15.

Back to my 21st and comparing with the events of now, it was so dull, uninteresting and utterly boring. Was I ever so lacking in fun? I was on till late the night before and didn't rush home – I've never known my mum so excited. The front room was laid out as for a wedding present showing. I got pearls from my parents, a leather writing case from my god-mother and a dressing table set from Auntie Louie and Uncle Neil. I got a pocket fruit knife with a mother of pearl handle in a little leather case and a cigarette lighter. The party was very genteel since I was only permitted to invite four people and they had to be on my parents approved list. That put a right kybosh on proceedings as most, well none of my available friends qualified. I ended up with my teetotal church friends most of whom I saw very rarely because being a nurse I was never off at service times. Seven females, Dad and dinner at a hotel. It was a proper dinner though with coffee and after-dinner mints.

So, early in January me, my trunk and my added extras like the dressing table set and writing case moved into the Western. It was only just up the road from home but living out was only just becoming permissible for nurses and was considered unusual. The Western is a large teaching hospital. The nurses' home was a custom-built barracks, but generally, a lot less institutional than Sick Kids. In 1956 the shadow of the workhouse still hovered over the main hospital and in no way was it well endowed. It was not necessary to get into full uniform to go to the common room. We not only had the equipment to boil a kettle, we could also make toast – bread and milk provided. Though not open to the public, the dining room was accessible to us in or out of uniform. All down to very large numbers and to the hospital being at 4/1d per day, per person, catering. Food at Sick Kids was interesting. The food allowance was 3/11d a day (19p). and there was no menu. Coming from a 'take-it-or-leave it' institution, we were amazed to find a choice of starters and three mains. The cauliflower cheese was in a class of its own. People who lived out supposedly paid for their meals and the off-duty timings made it unrealistic or unnecessary to take the long walk to the dining room. The reality was that nobody was on hand to take the money so presumably if you were strapped for cash at the end of the month, nobody would notice you were not a resident.

The corridors of the nurses' home were not policed in the same way. We had to sign in and out. Talk about easy come, easy go, signing in was up to 11 p.m. and late passes a mere need to write in the book that you would not be getting in till a specific late time and the reason. I don't know whether the illegitimate birth rate in such an easy-going regime, was higher or not. Being more of us, we tended to be larger gangs going out. Whereas, at Sick Kids, maybe a couple of us would go to the local chippy for egg and chips, bread and butter and a cup of coffee for 1/3d (7p), Western could be up to half a dozen of us getting on a bus to town and descending on a café for coffee, a Kunzle cake and a fag or two. Unlike Sick Kids there was no handy chip shop or greasy spoons around the corner. Our neighbourhood choices were Comely Bank, Craigleith or Blackhall all on the posh side or the new build Corporation Houses; none of which had the kind of places we patronised.

Generally, more relaxed, the slave labour ethos was alive and well and we were just as exploited but in different ways. We thought their probationers didn't know they were born because so little was expected of them. They didn't do as much deep cleaning and they had ward orderlies who made a contribution, doing things like the flowers and water jugs. The deep cleaning brought long ladders and chaps and the sluice throughput much diminished. Whereas we were accustomed to ward cleaners who ruled their roost at Sick Kids, orderlies were a new breed in a dictatorship where they reigned supreme.

This extra layer added interest and a learning curve in hierarchy. The ward cleaner remained queen of the kitchen, but lost her power in the ward itself. That led the kitchen power struggle into a tripartite regime where there was conflict between cleaner and orderlies, but they joined up against nurses. Alternatively, cleaners might side with the nurses on occasion just to ring the changes. It was wise when going to a new ward to establish who was in charge. It could be sister in charge in name only while the power lay with the longest serving orderly. Policing in the ward was an orderly role. They were anti most activities which patients indulged in which might impact on their sovereignty or result in their doing something all over again. There was no disease, condition or syndrome that a well-entrenched orderly could not diagnose or pontificate upon and be prepared to discuss with authority and understanding, with patients, other patients and relatives.

Anyone reading this will already know an awful lot happens that does not directly involve patients. Orderlies didn't do dentures or sputum mugs, which have always been a job for a professional along with bedpans and sick buckets. We were useful in ways that were money-saving. On night duty if the Post Graduates were managed well, the hospital could reduce the number of night sisters required and rely on the PGs to check drugs. That way night sisters avoided having to travel miles in the middle of the night to oversee DDAs (Dangerous Drug Administration) and injections. It was fine for them, but not so fine for us. Wards were in batches and they put one PG in say a group of five. That meant all night you could be stopping what you were doing and going somewhere to check drugs. That in itself was not straight forward. Night sister might give you a list of provisional sorties you'd have to make. During the night wasn't so bad, but first thing in the morning was a nightmare. All five of them would want their insulins checking so they could give the correct dose exactly 30 minutes before they plonked breakfast in front of the patient. What about **my** beds and **my** breakfasts?

A real iniquity was the exam marks. At Sick Kids training was undertaken in your own time, at the Western, it was done in blocks. You attended lectures all day every day for a month at a time then sat exams. They were so relaxed and easy on students; the pass mark was 45 per cent. Well to a clever Tom like me, who since the debacle that was the nursing exam, had never been other than first in the class, this was a culture shock. I'd passed all right, but only above the Sick Kid's rate of 65 per cent. We began to chunner and I became appointed spokesman. I was chosen because one of the papers was Materia Medica and I only scored seventy-five per cent, I knew I had 100 per cent. Sister Tutor was very open about it explaining PGs were automatically deducted 25 per cent so as not to demoralise the first timers. Now we understood War was declared and we ensured that 25 per cent or not, we always headed the leader board.

One of the ward sisters was very keen on in work training and every afternoon after handover she held a short tutorial, which going and coming staff were expected to attend. I was asked how many reasons there were for carrying out a procedure and I gave the number. Looking sceptical, she threw out – how many functions of the liver and I spat it back. How did I know? Because that is how I learn. I learned a big lesson over my Sick Kids nursing failure and thereafter I wasn't only awake, but my notes were made to a system of numbers so I could recall at any time. How many for almost anything so if the question asked how many or how much, I could give a number. That left only for me to recall them and write down the answer. It worked for me. There are 14 functions of the liver – maybe they have discovered more now, but that was then. If the question was what is the function of the liver? I knew there were 14 and just had to list them by seeing the list in my head. I think that is why I really like the Criminal Case game on my iPad.

It was at the Western I created my permanent reminder of my career. It was only a 12-inch wooden ruler, but it was carefully carved with dates of where I'd been and what I'd done. I only originated it during the repetitious classes, but when I left, I knew I would have it for ever. Sadly, it has since been lost. Colour coded and very neat mini text, it would have been something to leave in my memory box. We did the usual kind of immature things we did at Sick Kids but at the Western, medical students joined in making them more ambitious.

At the main entrance of the original hospital was a pillared entrance guarded by two very large stone lions. These lions were the source of a lot of activity. One very early morning, I sat astride a lion having a cigarette before starting the wake up of patients and my companion said, 'How is it you are so high up when your lion (lying) sitting down'? I suppose you had to be 5 a.m. night duty silly to find it hilarious, but 'how we laughed.' The lions were kidnapped. These were proper stone lions, not plastic and likely never moved since they were put there when the workhouse was built. The night staff claimed to have heard nothing but a ransom note was received. This was followed by a series of anonymous tip offs suggesting they dig at such and such a number of paces north and east from the cross way. Sweating porters were seen digging up flower beds to no avail. Then, one of the lions appeared on the skyline. It had travelled all the way to the new Radiotherapy building. Once there, up three floors before the roof. Unlikely to have got there via the lift, but again nobody saw or heard anything.

Next day the second lion turned up outside Casualty (open 24 hours) covered in Gentian Violet and wearing a very professional frog plaster. Tempers were rising and the university hierarchy and the police began to take an interest. An amnesty was offered and on the third day both lions were back where they belonged. They were still adorned with laurel leaf, plaster of Paris and Gentian Violet, but back where they belonged. Who and how, we never heard. Block and tackle would have been essential and that meant a vehicle of a significant weight bearing capacity, but nobody heard anything. It is extremely unlikely, that something like this could happen today because no matter what time, night or day, somebody is outside a hospital having a fag.

We didn't get hungry like we did at Sick Kids because the patients were unanimous and competitive in feeding us with goodies from their nearest and dearest. We never ate unwrapped sweets proffered from beneath the draw sheet, but anything else was acceptable. Naturally we accepted sticky toffee as we'd hate to offend, but just didn't indulge. The harvest on night duty was always a good one. Once when I was living at home and came off nights and started to empty my pockets Mum was amazed at what I laid on the table. We had a lot of pockets; the bib of the apron, the uniform dress had two and inside the cloak was one large. Some things were undoubtedly a thank you gift, but much was to ensure there was nothing left in their locker when next nearest and dearest came and found the patient had failed to value their offerings. Meals now come in little plastic packets and the recipes have been created by chefs of renown, but hospital food in the 1950s was really quite good. It was still a time of austerity following the war and the range of food available limited, but people tended to stick to the simple food we had when rationed.

My first adult experience was on male genito-urinary and a baptism of fire it was. Every one of them was a Water Lily (a rude generic name for men with problems with their water works), and the variety of willies extensive. We were allowed to 'dress' them, but not catheterise. Catheterisation was strictly a job for a doctor or male nurse. Female doctors could catheterise, but female intervention led to rising expectations and apologies. I came across my first male nurse there. Jimmy was my mentor and his kindly jocular way made things easier. I was very green regarding male bits and I hadn't realised that a classroom joke wasn't really a joke. A student nurse said to a staff nurse, *'the man in bed three has LUDO tattooed on his penis.' Later the staff nurse said to the student, 'It's not LUDO, it's LLANDUDNO.'*

Jimmy was one of only two male nurses over the whole site accommodating hundreds of patients. My first job after breakfast was cleared, lockers done and dust settled, was a dressings round with him. The only way I could see to 'get over' this was to follow his example and apply his script. Phrases like 'let's get his hat off' or 'let the dog see the rabbit' and variations. Other parts of the day were no different than any other in a male ward. A place where it wasn't unusual for the person you were using two hands to roll over for someone else to massage his pressure areas, to poke his hand up your skirt.

There are nearly as many things can go wrong in the male reproductive system as the female so we had variety. Hypospadias were common. This is a congenital disorder where the opening of the urethra in on the underside of the penis. As always you have to gauge that against the fact that this was the only place where these people would end up so not really common. Some of these men were being dealt with for the first time in their twenties. Born at home then hidden from sight, the ones I met tended to be odd, shy and furtive. It is easy to see why as a wee boy who had to sit to wee would be a joke. Mostly they were being given a man-made penis which was grown before being attached to where it should be. They'd start off with a little tube of skin grafted into a pedicle on a leg, then one end was cut off and moved to near where it was going to end up and allowed to develop a blood supply. It was now time to cut it free from the leg and attach to the urethra and again develop a blood supply before freeing up and having a dangly bit. The dangly bit was usually assisted in the cosmetic process by having a row of beads sewn on to create pleats and discourage shrinkage. The job was finished when the beads were removed.

Though the Western had grown, and enormous departments built on, we still had to go to other hospitals in the group to gain different experience. The Western had the first in-house Radiotherapy unit and much was made of the width of the walls to screen the machine. The care and safeguarding were specific, but not as much as there is now. We had to wear heavy lead aprons in X-ray and in treatment areas, but when managing the carboys of radioactive urine, we didn't have to wear them.

One medical ward admitted patients with Hyperthyroidism who were given Radioactive Iodine to drink. The drink was delivered in a lead box by a suited and booted radiology staff member who took out the little conical flask and the patient drank it through a straw. The errand boy then left us to it. All urine passed had to be kept and then properly disposed of. This involved our having to pour it down a funnel in the sluice that took it down to the cellar and into large carboys which were later removed by the atomic energy people. All the staff on radiotherapy had to wear little Geiger counter badges to measure if they were getting any more radiation than was normal. However, off site on the medical wards, all they did was come around with a Geiger counter while we had patients being treated to check on the area round the bed.

When children from Sick Kids had radiotherapy, one of us would accompany the child to the then only radiotherapy unit at a general hospital. One Sick Kids nurse had been going in to the treatment area with a child too young to lie still and only after she'd been every day of the treatment did anyone notice she had not been given lead protection. All Hell was let loose and she got six weeks holiday at a summer camp. Mostly the child would be left to lie completely still while a tiny area would be blasted. We could chat and encourage.

When I did a stint at the Northern General, I was on a male medical ward wholly given over to chests. All these men were quite unwell, coughed, spat, gasped for breath and smoked. Only if on oxygen was smoking forbidden. For these chaps it was a case of mask off, visit a fellow patient or make for the bathroom. Unable to work and very likely for a long time before they were admitted to the Northern, it is unsurprising the wives were not well off. Sickness benefit was payable, but in order to access it they had to have been working previously or the family could only get a form of public subsistence benefit. They were a tired little bunch waiting to be 'let in' for visiting. Belted raincoats and head scarves, shopping bag dangling; they purposefully made their way to the bedside. The minute the bum landed on a seat; the bed occupant was hanging out of bed making overtures to 'the bag.' A pack of cigarettes was first out, then maybe Lucozade, Lemon Barley or a wee bottle of Mackeson's Stout, all before the clean pyjamas were put in the locker and the dirty ones put in the bag. While the patient did his heavy breathing, the wife sat with hands locked onto the bag with some little conversation and definitely no laughter, till the bell went. The minute the bell went, she was up and ready for off. Some money was placed on the locker and she departed till tomorrow. The money was for his paper, bets and more fags. The chaps came alive out of visiting hours.

They would bet on anything. Nurses were set up to do wheelchair circuits timed and odds given. A kind of in-house activity. The paper boy did a roaring trade in papers and cigarettes. Spectacles on and pencil poised for the most serious business of the day, marking winners. The porters came and took the stake money for outside betting. I can't remember any big wins, just the poor women's money down the drain. There was a theory that 'chest men' were extra highly sexed, but I don't think they were any worse than any other male medical. You'd no sooner lay hands on them to help turn them over or give them their meal tray, anything that involved both your hands and they were free to grapple up your skirt.

There was a chap there who was going nowhere other than the crematorium who had legal aid to fight for custody of his children. Screens would go up when a bunch of lawyers arrived and as soon as it got tricky, he'd have a turn and the lawyers would flee and huddle outside to wait and see if they could continue. Usually not and they'd come another day. This cast a pall over the whole ward so we decided to brighten up Christmas. I put a sputum mug on the table and as people came onto the ward, they were confronted with a sign, which said, 'Please cough up for the Christmas fund.' Sister made me take it down.

His children visiting didn't help as they were dirty and neglected and the oldest girl looked careworn already. They were fetched by authority but clearly uncared for – snotty, sniffing, feral and far too much for the girl to manage. If that had been 1951, they would have been reported to RSSPCC and gone to a children's home. Families like that often went to

Quarrier's Homes at the Bridge of Weir or Barnardo's, where families were kept together in units. I'm not clear if the legalities were to get them away from their mother whom he was endeavouring to have found unfit; we never knew. He was a desperately sick man, but just as desperate to find a way to keep his children. To this end, beyond the lawyers, he was frantically making felt stuffed animals to sell to raise money. He wasn't well enough, but he would not give up. We bought them and marketed them around to help but I don't think any would go to a good home. Kapok-filled, they had lumpy tummies, unstuffed joints, squint eyes and long loopy stitches, where bits hung out, but we bought them. He was an escape to the bathroom smoker.

The next-door ward was female chests and while I was there not one of these women smoked. They likely couldn't afford it and any cash would be for their husbands' little pleasures. The bookies runners didn't go there either. The women kept busy with knitting and chatting as much as their restricted breathing permitted and kept the library trolley on overtime with their need for true romance.

Patient choice isn't new; we had it in 1956. Waste was another result of being a 4/1d hospital. Food didn't come in little plastic compartmentalised trays with impossible-to-open cellophane packs. It came in heated trolleys and was served in the ward according to patient choice. Regardless of menus, we were still hungry and would hoover up leftovers behind the kitchen door. Behind the kitchen door, the place to find a nurse any time anywhere. *A nurse entering heaven was reassured by the keeper of the gate that there were other nurses about. She returned to complain she was unable to find any and the doorman said – 'have you looked behind the kitchen door'?*

An older married nurse was always keen to take bits of meat home for her cat. That cat was well fed. She began to bring a shopping bag and a storage jar. It was suggested maybe she didn't have a cat. One fine day she filled up the storage jar with mince. The sceptic – an orderly of course, took it out of her shopper and added cascara. The cat nurse was off work for three days. She, her husband and son were all struck down with nasty diarrhoea. It apparently floored all of them at once.

13 Eastern General

General training was undoubtedly a culture shock to us superior post-graduate students. The probationers were having new experiences but for us learning to apply economy of scale. A lady of enormous dimensions was to be admitted. We were forewarned and a special bed was unearthed from the tunnels. Her weight was beyond the 40 stone maximum of our equipment. Charged with carrying out the practical aspect of admission, usually a one-man job turned into an all hands-on deck. The combined services of fire and ambulance had achieved the deposit from platform to bed and over to us for the admission undress, check for pressure sores and a bed bath. How could you re-assure the patient, then gently and kindly and conversationally bathe this mountain of stinking flesh? I was a novice, no way could I pick her up and deposit in a soap flake bath, introduce a wee duck and engage in dribbling waterfalls for fun. A few years ago, a nurse told me nursing was all about shovelling shit and smiling while you did it. I set my trolley, set my face and remembered what Jimmy had taught me when dealing with wonky willies and joined by a full supporting cast and patient participation it was to those hearing the behind screen laughter, an Oscar winning performance. The patient despite being bed-ridden for years was social and fun despite the sorry and painful state of her body. It took two people to lift each breast to see the extent of the ulceration underneath. When we got to the turning on one side, the human hoisting was three each side. A kind of push and pull to achieve the position then three to hold it and three to be there if there was any wobble of fear of toppling.

The Western wasn't well endowed and there were many examples which caused us PGs to be derisory. At Sick Kids we were referred to as nurses – no names just Nurse and if anyone felt cross enough at your indolence or mistakes, nurse Whatever. A name badge was issued with uniform to be worn on your chest at the Western. No lanyards, no picture just a metal pin bar with your initial and surname black on thick white Perspex. The Sick Kids silver with blue enamel badge was the most important item we wore. Perhaps wear the badge on the other side? Oh no. Unless presented by royalty, badges were worn on the right. The Western hospital badge once you'd earned it, had to be paid for. Paid for? It was a large gun metal round with four spikes, perhaps like a sea mine and it hung by a few chain links on a matching bar. Honestly, were you to hang over the cot of an infant, you could clout it; this was only one of the reasons we never wore it. It looked cheap and had been copied from a prestigious London hospital badge, but so modified with its bar and chain and the spikes replacing elegant crenelated towers. Making matters worse, we were required to purchase it. Spend money on tat like that? Our Sick Kids badge was free, classy and expensive and, in fact, more expensive than the insurance value of an MBE. My group held out to the last day for being able to have your name engraved then reluctantly coughed up while vowing not ever to wear it after presentation.

While there was still a lot of non-patient contact due to domestic duties, significant interaction took place and our role was akin to that of a hairdresser. Nothing was sacrosanct, but most useful were the things they told us they never mentioned to the doctor. We had a little woman being investigated for a massive weight loss, but nothing else. She wasn't fair, she wasn't fat nor was she forty and to date no tests had shown anything up. She mentioned this bit of a pain in her shoulder she thought was 'arthritis' and bingo. Fed back to the report then the medics she was quickly transferred to a surgical ward for a cholecystectomy.

The vicar's wife was a lovely lady, who, by virtue of her role in society, was given a bed in a small side ward when she came in to 'have her veins done.' Actually, these were called 'amenity beds' and people who disliked the thought of mixing with common people paid to occupy them. They didn't get much for their money. A tray cloth and a china cup and saucer were as privileged as they got and we were not overzealous if they were the 'sit-on-the-bell' kind. I received her back from theatre. She treated me to an erudite, articulate, abusive, blasphemous and foul tirade as she came around. I mentioned it to a colleague, who said she'd had a priest, who was worse and that the clergy were noted for it. Many years of meek and mild clearly led to loss of inhibition, but we didn't mention it when later I got her settled with her china cup and an extra for the vicar himself.

I used to worry about quiet men. To me that was the clue there was something really the matter. There were absolutely no mixed sex wards. It wasn't even permissible for a man to be admitted to a side ward adjacent to a female ward. Male wards were always full of noise, whereas in female ward the propensity was for little special interest cliques to form. I've never known a betting syndicate in a female ward. Once a chap left me an accumulator as a leaving gift. Till then an accumulator was one of the things I used to fetch back from the ironmonger for my Granny's wireless. However, my grateful patient-cum-turf expert explained I could expect my winnings from race one to be automatically placed on race two and the winnings from that on race three and the porter, who had placed the bet knew to bring the £45 directly to me. One fell at the first fence, two didn't run and the third was an also ran. I'm better at raffles.

I just happened to be on the ward to which a close friend of my aunt was being admitted. I was informed, when I bumped into my aunt and another three of her mob in McVitties. They regaled me with a wide and very amusing account of all the ailments which had preceded the admission. I left knowing she had been admitted with 'her feet' and that she had been wholly reassured by her chums that now it had got to her feet it couldn't go any further and there was nothing else could possibly ail her. When I did go on-duty and met this raving 'hypochondriac,' I knew immediately she was a dead cert for the epitaph 'I told you I was ill.'

We did not do palliative care well nor did we approach the provision of information well either. There was a kind of standard response to a patient suggesting they felt ill and might not recover. A brisk, of course you will. Once you've swallowed this, had a lovely cup of tea and I've plumped up your pillows you'll feel much better. Then the dying itself was a kind of routine. Once the Brompton Cocktail was prescribed the patient was moved near the door and free visiting allowed. Brompton, a strong morphine-based mixture which while reducing pain and inducing sleep caused foul smelling breath and perspiration. Screens were pulled round the bed and an

Airwick or two pushed underneath it. The light was covered with a yellow duster to shade the bed space. We were vigilant in mouth and pressure care but the good deaths which can be achieved today were rare. There was no aftercare for relatives. We performed the last offices but shrouds were readymade and porters took over at that point. We took pride in the appearance of our laying out and once complete we invited the relatives to view before alerting the porters. The relative comments were usually appreciative and they clearly took comfort commenting on the peacefulness or the age having left them.

My aunt wasn't the only person to consider hypochondria as a diagnosis of a terminal condition. A plump spinster lady about 45 was admitted for a breast biopsy. I admitted her and before I'd got beyond her name and date of birth, she had become hysterical forecasting her early demise. I didn't get much support from the doctor who reckoned it was a milk cyst and certainly not worth Largactil when a cup of tea would do. She went to theatre next day and had the biopsy. The following morning, she got the early cup of tea followed by a basin of warm water, towel and washbag placed on her overbed table so she could freshen up. I'd no intention of performing her ablutions. A biopsy. I had the patients who had had serious operations who needed my help to drink and then wash. She laid there like a beached whale and wanted to know when I was going to help her. I suggested she do it herself but sat her up and put everything within reach. Next thing I hear a yelp and 'I'm drowning' and quickly respond to see three yes three drops of water on her chest. Her biopsy was negative. I met her six weeks later, I was on days and she was admitted to die. She was not the same fractious nervy lady she had been but had reached the stage of calm and acceptance. She was easy to care for but had no relatives and few visitors.

One of the sisters at the Northern was very strange. She dusted. The staff nurse took the report and did the rounds and the rest of us did as she instructed. Sister kind of flitted round always with a duster in her hand making occasional flutterings on things. She didn't say much or do much else just a kind of presence. We wondered if perhaps she was allergic to patients because they didn't interest her at all. One afternoon we admitted an unconscious and very obese woman. She'd had a stroke except we didn't call them strokes. The generic Scottish term for a stroke is 'a shock.' The hospital term was Cardio Vascular Accident (CVA). If someone told you the person next door had a shock you knew they meant a CVA. As the lady was transferred from trolley to bed, sister was caressing the window sill with her duster. No words were spoken as I moved in but sister swooped in to the other side of the bed and began to partner me in the process of assessing and positioning and spoke. She accompanied her actions with a succinct lecture on the possible cause, present situation and possible outcome. She could well have been a lecturer and a good one. Things happen in hospital that have no rational explanation.

You might go on night duty and be told the patient in bed 4 was unlikely to make it through the night. Your mind picks up and decides, not on my watch, I haven't got the time and they do make it not only through the night but out of there altogether. One lady in particular I remember because it happened like that. She was very agitated and medication wasn't helping. Having settled the rest, I took her hand and spoke to her and suggested a cup of tea. The tea went down a treat and she spoke of her sons and became calm and I tucked her up and didn't hear a cheep, till morning. Sometime later my father asked me if I remembered a lady called Mrs something or other. Well of course I didn't till he went on to tell me what she'd told him. She'd introduced herself to him at a Presbyterian event where he was the speaker and asked him if he had a daughter a nurse at the Western? She told him I'd saved her life. She told him she knew she was going to die and her mind and her heart were going crazy then I came along and cared for her and made her a drink and all the screaming in her body just went away. Amazing what a cup of tea can do.

I only remember one old lady with dementia and her confusion was exacerbated when the lights went out. She kept calling out for Jean and all she got was me. 'Have ye wound up the timepiece?' I must have agreed about six times till she suddenly came back to now and said – 'you're no Jean' where is she?' and bit me. The day staff got 'Jean' to fetch in the timepiece and her Westclox was on her locker next night and I left her light on – problem solved.

When I went to the Eastern General, I got great experience. Again, making use of our existing skills I got Theatre. Theatre is daunting for anyone unused to working with gloves on and having to be careful not to bump into any clean person etc. All surgery at the Eastern was thoracic. Thoracic surgery takes many hours. They were leaders in the field for cardiac, lung and oesophageal surgery. The year following my stint, Ethicon introduced surgical needles with the thread already attached. This had many benefits. Thoracic surgery and particularly in the oesophagus, requires many internal stitches of the very finest thread with the eye of the needle just enough to get the thread in. In theatre as well as swabs, our afternoons were spent preparing threaded needles for stock.

Not when they found me though because I could assist an oesophagectomy with three needles. Internal stitching needs to be watertight so the stitches need to be very close together and not have big entry and exit holes. Before atraumatic sutures each needle used, and they didn't do continuous stitching, had to be threaded and clamped to a pair of forceps before passing to the surgeon by an assistant. They would go through dozens of needles and forceps because few people could thread the needles and keep up with him. My previous plastic surgery experience meant that rather than have up to 50 needles to thread to replace, there were only 3. Needles with eyes the same size as the thread to go through, I could do with my eyes shut. This was reminiscent of plastic surgery at Sick Kids. That was what I did. It was all down to how you cut the thread, where you positioned the thread between finger and thumb and how you drew the eye of the needle over the thread. Not even the theatre sisters there could do it! I became famous and taught them all. Unfortunately, it is a dead skill, and even with a large eye and thin thread I can't do it anymore.

Without exception, the surgeons were all over six foot tall and irritable. The registrars were randy. An operation could take between four and six hours and there was no break. The surgeon got the occasional sweat off his brow wipe, but that was all. At five feet four and assisting as his left-hand man, the table would be pumped up for the convenience of his six feet four, standing on the floor. I had to stand on tiptoe just to see what was on the table. The solution was a little stool ten inches high with four legs and the platform the exact size of my two feet clamped together. There I was for the entire performance;

an immovable object except for my hands busy threading needles and creating mini-mops.

The start was a bit like a ballet. We all got scrubbed. Sister taking the case and assistant surgeon on one side of the table and me and the high heid yin on the other. Once the patient was in situ, me and mine approached the table, which was pumped up to Sir's required height. I step on my stool and with my gloved hands pick up a dressing towel – a bit of cloth about a yard square. I waft it open as Sir turns his back on me and I place it over his shoulders. He stands still while with exaggerated care I pick up towel clips and use them to fasten it to him. Once a careless assistant picked up flesh. She left the same day. All this because as we worked closely together and he was able to freely turn this way and that, with his gap filled (like all hospital gowns, they cover the front, but leave nothing to the imagination at the back) so that HE did not dirty me. These operations were initially dramatic when after a systematic cover up and a nod from the anaesthetist, and scalpel raised, a sweeping incision was made in a perfect arc. A short interlude while he freed up the ribs then sharp snap as rib or ribs were whipped out and discarded. They were not thrown to waiting dogs, but that was the kind of theatre we had. Though the next five hours were tense, the end was always sudden and unexpected. Sir would suddenly throw down his instruments and thrust the sheets covering the patient to the floor. This completely discombobulated both sister and me as she had to recover for audit his hardware and swabs. I stumbled off my stool once when he walloped me with the covers and his unkind one liner was – 'You should take up tennis.'

The randy registrars were kept on a very tight leash and never got to actually do any real operating. They were in training and even for the pre-op gastroscopy or thoracoscopy, they were mere bystanders which gave them absolutely nothing to do with their wandering hands. These procedures were carried out in the dark. Again, my pre-experience made me Sir's Number 2 of choice. Part of my role was to position a narrow bright light at the end of a 24-inch wire into a groove then, holding it in position, carefully swing the other end of it into Sir's hand so he could slide it down into the depths to see what was going on. Randy Reg (RR) is ostensibly looking and learning over my shoulder, but his hands are up my skirt. I kicked, my hand shook and Sir bellowed – 'What are you playing at?' Afterwards, as I came out carrying an armful of dirty linen and swung the swing door into the place it got dumped, I did it extremely viciously. The resulting backswing hit RR on the head and threw him onto the massive mountain of dirty linen. He lay there dazed as I and another looked through the round window smirking. Sir looked over our heads and said, 'I see.'

The student nurse experience here was not good. The surgeons were irascible, demanding, impatient and disinclined to teach. They expected and were granted instant gratification. Students were never, while I was there, allowed to be left-hand man assisting. However, they had to scrub for oscopies. They were a constant source of irritation and incompetence from the minute they scrubbed and set out their trolley. Not fast enough, not ready, wrong instruments. Stupid was a mild epithet. I came on at the end of one newbie's first case and she was a trembling, weeping wreck setting her trolley for the second time. There are always ways and means and the dark. I armed myself with a couple of sterile Cheadle forceps and as she was wavering with her drapes, I was undoing the safety clip on her towel clips and placing them one at a time in her hand. For the entire procedure I remotely acted as a left-hand man and we got to the end with no further tantrums.

14 Foot Loose and Fancy Free

A strange choice of title made by someone with rigid feet and a lifelong prisoner of circumstance, but anyone can dream. Somebody had the great idea that we should have a hospital hockey team and initiate a Hospital League. What a pathetic turnout. It was obvious, my once only turn out as goal-keeper for Gillespie's first eleven made me a player of choice. Other hospitals rustled up teams to play with us. I can't remember any being up to much and certainly there was no money in the kitty so we didn't have a strip. We didn't even have shin pads. We'd dug out our old hockey sticks and light canvas boots with any padding provided by a folded Daily Express down the socks. Being a natural goal keeper I had little use for the stick and relied on my feet which were assaulted many times down to the opposition always being in my inner circle. I limped, but carried on even after the high shot that fractured my thumb. That was the Western, always in the forefront of everything.

Dancing was alien to me when I started training and not much more than a passing acquaintance by the time I finished. Apart from the one year I attended the Gillespie's v the Royal High School dance, I had no experience. There were two dance halls in Edinburgh; the Palais de Dance and the Plaza. Maybe because it was in Morningside, the Plaza was the one patronised by student nurses. The lower echelons went to the

Palais. I believe the dance floor was heaving after 10 p.m., but that wasn't something I experienced as we had to be back signed in by 10 on weeknights and 10.30 on Saturday. Being the product of a girls' school, I hadn't known any boys since I left primary school so I was a 'cold case' so to speak. Before 9 p.m., there was nobody there. So, till around 8.45 p.m. we'd 'get ready.' Getting ready always involved a bath. Having a bath before you went out, more than washed away the malodours of a day on-duty, but saved having to have a bath when you got in.

Having a bath when you got in meant a potential loss of a quarter of an hour sleeping time. Sleeping time and off your feet were then a student nurse obsession. If you didn't get the requisite number of hours, you'd be dead the next day. Our PTS (Preliminary Training School) did a bit of research on how much sleep people like us needed. We rigorously followed a Daily Express feature on how to work out how much sleep you as an individual required to function. Mine was seven hours 21 minutes. On night duty I could never achieve anything like my quota. After my bath, I'd be out cold in minutes and stay that way for about four hours then wake up. Getting back to sleep was really difficult so I'd spend the next two hours desperately trying to get off. Then I'd drop off just before it was permissible to get out of bed. I've been a martyr to 'morningitis' all my life, but on night duty it kicked in about 5 p.m. I usually explain it using the excuse that I don't believe in life before 10 o'clock, but that's not true. Once the children grew up, I frequently used to get up at 5 in the morning and work very happily all by myself till the phones started about nine. It's just I can't stand chat in the morning. In the years I used to go to conferences or holidays, my first question on checking in is – 'what time does breakfast start?' I've been to breakfast, done the crossword and am ready to go as soon as anyone else turns up.

There were issues with night bathing because of lights out by 10.30 and the queue building between 10 and 10.30. Never a shortage of hot water, just not enough baths. Each cubicle was provided with a dishcloth and Vim. Well not Vim exactly, a cheap and grittier version of it. Without exception nurses scour the bath every time and the more it is scoured the more like a beach the bath becomes. The excessive scouring more than habit, is just to ensure it has been cleaned because after years and years of Vim the baths are all discoloured and disgusting to look at and you don't take a chance in places like that. In all the nurses' homes I've lived in we had privacy in the bath. By privacy I mean, the plasterboard went above waist height to about a foot off the ceiling and the baths were in blocks of three. You could chat or enjoy someone's radio, but it wasn't a spectator sport. In Bechuanaland, I stayed in a hotel where there was no privacy and it was mixed bathing. The screen between baths was so low you could ask next door to pass the soap. Also, historically, nurses only ever sat down on their own personal toilet. Matters improved when it was proved that STDs only transmitted if the seat was wet. How many suffered chronic thigh cramp from habitual hovering? But think about it. We were never free to go all that often. Drinking five litres a day wasn't promoted then, but the opportunities were limited. It was absolutely forbidden to use a ward toilet. In Sick Kids there were no public toilets and needing to go would have meant being excused from duty by sister to return to the nurses' home. In theatre there was no way you could go unless you were 'dirty.' Even dirty had heavy responsibility in being in charge of counting instruments and swabs. The titchy weeny dabs used were a nightmare to account for. References were made about having to 'haud in and spit oot' or they think I'm a fairy, what are you? I'm a bloody fairy too.

Back to the Plaza where soberly-clad musicians played for waltz, foxtrot and quickstep for a number of ladies sitting at tables round one side of the room. A few lads leant on the wall at the other paying great attention to where the ash from their cigarette was landing on the floor. They could have a half pint on a table they were not sitting at. The tango and samba were reserved for later when there just could be one or two people actually dancing. The ladies favoured drink was orange squash or lemonade because ladies did not buy alcohol. It was acceptable to approach the bar and purchase soft drinks but never alcohol. A few couples would get up and dance cheek to cheek then retire back to their table where the lady had left her 'wrap,' i.e. cardigan, because they had come together to dance. For everyone else it was a pick-up joint.

The brave lads came as near to closing time as would allow them to be admitted to the Plaza. There were neither 'pass outs' nor 'pay to enter' after 10 p.m. Whereas those leaning against the wall were usually fairly tidy, the inebriated were more casual in the slipped tie knot and silly grin, but all had a greasy pocket comb to sweep back the hair before they sauntered across to say something like 'Are ye dancing?' A few forward girls, tired of clutching their one drink might get up and dance with each other to show the other side what they were missing, but never more than one dance. Another, 'come on' was a trip to the ladies the long way around. Going that way meant the chaps could get a good look and ladies bestow a few 'Excuse Mes' where there was a chance it could be productive. I went to the Plaza a few times. I don't know why, I couldn't dance, wasn't interested in learning and wary of men. However, the thing was if you got properly picked up and you weren't keen, when asked what you did, you said, 'I'm a midwife.' This was passed down from PTS to PTS and it worked; midwives were unacceptable. I've thought about this and why, not then because it was applied learning, but now. Midwives would be over twenty-one and to say District Nurse would date you even older. Was it the age? Or was it that they knew that midwives know what happened when bodily fluids were exchanged so were not easy meat? Personally, I don't know anyone who met their fate at the Plaza.

The 'fancy free' is daft as well. How could I, the product of a restricted United Free Church of Scotland (1929 continuing) Presbyterian upbringing, have the opportunity? The Free Church of Scotland, known as 'the Wee Frees,' was worse. They stood to pray, sat to sing, but had no music, just a dour chap with a tuning fork. We sang fine, but not rousingly like Methodists and we'd graduated to Hymns Ancient & Modern, but were still hooked on psalms. Though there was no drinking or dancing, we did have 'socials.' I still have my Dad's book of Party Games. I tell you now; these were only coming into play when I escaped. A social was usually an occasion for families to come out together bearing tins, in which were the food offerings to the gathering. Nobody could fault these offerings. It was a fight to the end to have the best sponge, finger sandwich filling or brand-new different kind of cake. The event was predictable. Always in bleak, draughty church halls or huts. On arrival, tins were taken to whichever ladies were in charge of catering. Small boys slithered about the floor and little girls wished they could. Older children huddled and spoke in low voices so as not to 'draw attention' and were made to put out chairs or hymn books. Oh yes, hymn books. Because it was a 'social,' chairs were set out theatre style and school dinner trestle sort laid out round the sides of the room. Had it been Church of Scotland, they had small tables because they had whist drives, but we did not play cards – well, not there anyway. No whistle was blown, but quite peremptorily we were told to 'sit.' The minister and other important people would sit at a table at the front and we opened with prayer. This was followed not by a sermon because it was a social but there was a speaker and because it was a social the speaker was to entertain us.

The speaker could be a minister from say the Highlands or an island to tell us of the beauty, the birds and beasts of where he hailed from. My dad was session clerk and on occasions such as these when the speaker came from afar, we would have to entertain them for high tea at our house. Such entertaining meant the house being spotless, the tins full of a wide variety of home-made cakes and the best china. All the towels in the bathroom were freshly laundered and a new cake of soap provided. One time my mother went off on one of her more spectacular meltdowns because either my sister or I had 'washed our hands on the clean towel.' We both denied having laid hands on any towel during the time frame. The next time he came the threats preceded him, but my dad was next in the bathroom after him. When he'd gone, dad told us that it had been the reverend and not us, because when he went in one of the towels was crumpled and had filthy hand prints. Perhaps in mitigation we should have accepted he'd come a long way and trains are dirty things, but ever after he was referred to as Mr Blackhands.

More often the speaker was a missionary on home leave. These poor sods got to come back to Scotland every five years for three months called 'furlough.' For the entire time they went from one UF Church to another telling of the poor little black children and the privations of Africa or India and melting our hearts. So emotive they were, we gave them all the money we had on us to take back and do what they did for the next five years. Very much in the way sales staff targets must first meet their own overhead with enough left over to feed the company. I knew many missionaries as we tended to accommodate them when they were in Edinburgh. A lot of Dad's disposable income went to these people. My mother, in later life used to regularly explain how much better off they would have been had she looked after the money. She lived her entire life in the belief she was born to be a lady. She dressed to impress.

There was never much talent at United Free Church events. It was mostly down to geography and no people actually living near Martyrs and St John's attending. It was adjacent to Greyfriars Bobby, and just down the road from the Children's Shelter. I think when the split from the Church of Scotland happened in 1929, that Martyrs was perhaps a kind of missionary outpost. Slap in the middle of Edinburgh's worst slums, the core membership was from the suburbs of Edinburgh and could easily have attended a UF church nearer home. While I was at secondary school, Martyrs reached out to Craigmillar. Craigmillar was a sprawling housing estate and home to the first of the major slum clearances. Sundays became different then. Instead of Church in the morning followed by Sunday School, home then back for evening service. We had a more church intensive day.

We did church and Sunday School as usual. After church my mother and wee Margaret would go home on the tram. Dad and me, plus any without transport would set off in the car for Craigmillar. On arriving at the school, we unpacked ourselves and various boxes and tins and just had time for a quick drink from a flask before hordes of children were banging on the doors to be let in for Sunday School.

Afterwards, and before the evening service was quite an occasion. All the tins, greaseproof parcels and flasks came out and we had what I learned later in England was a Jacob's Join – you bring along to an event enough food for yourself but once you get there rather than eating your own 'picnic' it is all set out on a table and people help themselves. On these occasions people tend to make something they are 'known for'. Not really the kind of event for me since my specials are fish pie, stuffing and trifle but I can always be relied upon for decent sandwiches. The providers were so competitive, it was as bad as the social events with admiration of efforts high on the agenda. My mother's contributions were always quickly snapped up. I didn't care as I was more interested in other people's cakes and sandwiches; I could eat my mum's any time. Conversations would go like 'Jim are these new? I'll have to get Rena to give me the recipe.' She was inventive and her tins were always full. You could call any time, except you didn't in those days, and be amazed at what was in her tins. One of her inventions was Pearlies. The mystery ingredient was liquid paraffin replacing butter or cooking fat which were rationed. No idea where the name came from but I can see them now. In a little Beeko baking case it looked just a wee bit like a rough cast fairy cake. The rough cast being Brown and Polson's Cornflakes and there were one or three sultanas as well but where the name came from, I have no idea. The post war version was OK too.

After our feast we had a quick clear up and rearranged the seating for an evening service attended by a goodly number of adults. Children attended willingly because of the annual Sunday School Picnic and Christmas Party. As time went on there were Brownies and Guides and my sister became part of the Craigmillar packs and made some lifelong friendships. Missionaries have not always been for the common good as time has told, but I rate Craigmillar a success. Two of Margaret's friends, identical twins, first came to Sunday School, lousy, feral and filthy. Both grew up to be good at their jobs and married well. One never lost her broad Craigmillar accent despite her husband becoming a high-ranking civil servant and secretary to a minister. I don't suppose anyone at Westminster would realise it was anything other than Scottish. I recall an American saying to a girl from another recognisable sink estate, 'I love your accent.'

I did venture out with a couple of boys from other churches, but can't even remember what they were called. My second cousin Douglas strangely enough was smiled upon and I even went to the Plaza with him. Strange really, when account is taken of his mother having a learning disability and his father unknown but thought to be a Norwegian sailor who took advantage of her down at Leith Docks. Another acceptable was a son of the Manse from some remote highland place. He was at Theological College and was offered our hospitality because he was so far from home. I had a blind date for the Sick Kids Ball, but blind would have been an advantage. What a drip. He couldn't dance, he was shorter than me and still had teenage acne. Despite the pressure from Enid, whose boyfriend's best friend he was, once was enough. Let's make no bones about it; Ronald who married my sister was on offer, but not for me. He hovered around at Martyrs and St John's all our young lives. His parents were strange, remote people with high ethical standards and a very narrow outlook on life. He was an only child and they were a tight knit-unit. Wherever Daisy, his mother, went, his dad and Ronald were sure to follow.

Our early acquaintance was when he and I were both being walked round Inverleith Pond in our prams looking at the ducks. High coach-built prams and side by side any time they met up, Daisy and my Mum would promenade. Mum had many stories regarding the family and her intercourse with them. An early one was Daisy's refrain – 'Now Ronald, don't be wild.' One tale, I was standing up in my pram tethered by harness throwing stuff out and generally rocking around when Ronald, tidily tethered with neat pram rug, reached out his wee hand to pick up his rattle and Daisy came in with her 'Now Ronald, don't be wild.' Just after the war, when we'd moved back to Comely Bank, I would meet Daisy, Tom and Ronald in McVitties on a Saturday morning. They always shopped as a family and this was a special outing so they could each 'choose' a cake for Sunday. Obviously, Daisy must not have had tins because a McVitties' cake was a treat we were never indulged in. I'd be queuing for bread, which was rationed then, and my Mum had no coupons to waste on shop cakes. They were special though and such a treat if and when, as a nurse we could afford it, we had one with our coffee when out on the town. Though Ronald and Margaret, my sister, were nearly an item for years, he did have a short, very short, one-off interlude with the daughter of the new minister. It didn't last, but I think in the eyes of Daisy and Tom, she was a step up from wee Margaret. The said daughter of the Manse regaled me with the tales. Ronald had asked her out, not to go anywhere, but home to Daisy and Tom, where they had very delicate meat paste sandwiches and a shop-bought Victoria sponge. The clincher was the quantity of meat paste. They had apparently walked from wherever they met and when it was time for Ronald to 'see her home,' Tom dug in his pocket and handed over a silver sixpence so they could take a bus, but he wasn't to forget to bring back 'the change.'

All of Ronald's oddities manifested in dementia and can only be blamed on his strange upbringing. His father, Tom was a fairly regular patient at Morningside mental hospital and indeed Ronald himself was a customer for quite a while himself, when first he went seriously 'off piste.' Daisy as far as I know was never actually confined; just barking all her life. When Ronald got his first pay cheque as a teacher, he bought her a washing machine. She made him send it back as 'only lazy people have washing machines.'

15 What Next?

I was in the second part of my General at the Western General and their sub hospitals. The nurses' home was the same, but different. We were not as deceitful in relation to food as it was allowed on the premises. A bit like midnight feasts and Enid Blyton's Mallory Towers, but not covert as at Sick Kids. Although the nurses' home was a fair way away from the hospital and wasn't policed as closely, you could still be locked out if you were late. I don't know what they've done with all these rooms now that nurses no longer have to live in. There were the usual escapades, but being a bit more grown up not to the same extent for us PGs. One evening coming off at 8.30 with another, we met a couple on their way out to somewhere and said, 'Wait for us,' but they didn't. We created a dummy and removed a light bulb. On return as they turned into our corridor there was the gently swinging body of a nurse hanging from a cross pipe. How we laughed. We pinned a little verse to it. "Ye wouldnae take me wi ye, ye said ye hadnae time. Ye left me here tae hang masel, ye dirty rotten swine." It was possible to get really silly without alcohol. Being bone tired had a lot to do with it.

Being silly still goes on today, but I'm sure our very grounded silliness like sitting out on the windowsill three floors up singing in harmony wasn't a better way to offload. I invented a cure for burning feet I still pass on and people are amazed at just how effective it is. I discovered it in theatre first time around. I'd been standing for hours taking a list, and about to start all over again with an emergency and the red-hot pain was taking over my head. I picked up a bottle of methylated spirits and poured some into each shoe. Eugh! It was horrible and because my shoes were thin on the sole and cracked though shiny at the sides, it leaked out. Then the most amazing thing happened the eugh turned into pure cold anaesthetising bliss and lasted for ages. It really does work.

The no alcohol deserves a mention. On my dad's side, my Grandpa had been a heavy drinker, but now retired, living with my Granny and the aunts who had eyes everywhere, he had limited opportunity except on the occasion when he went to the library. I heard one of the aunts saying he was on his way home 'stotting.' I thought he just staggered because of his advanced age and poor balance. Granny, the aunts and my dad were teetotal, not just Band of Hope. It was because of the awful example of their youngest brother, who had to be sent to Grandpa's half-brother in America during prohibition to wean him off alcohol. It didn't work and his lifetime leisure was given over to alcohol. He was a grand chap and always held down two full-time jobs to feed his habit and the genteel aspirations of his wife. The other brother was a social drinker. During the war he sustained a serious head injury which involved surgery leaving a long deep scar. Granny thought it was a war injury, but apparently, he fell off the back of a troop lorry when he was drunk in Tobruk.

It was my maternal uncles who took it upon themselves to educate me. My mum's brother was a self-made man and professional social drinker. My aunt's husband's parents ran a pub in Portsmouth! Horror of horrors, she didn't only marry a sailor she met at Donnie Bristo, a naval base in Fife; he was English and as you would expect being brought up in a dockland bar, drank. During the war everyone did war work. My aunt and some friends went all the way to Fife to help out at the naval base. They apparently helped out in a canteen! The uncles had a confab at a family party and decided I needed to know my way round drink. There were two schools of thought. Upwardly mobile uncle along with his wife took me out for drinks. This was a kind of posh pub crawl. Just the once. The merits of whisky as a 'clean drink' were promoted along with brands. Dressed in my best and after my second, this time a Vat 69 with ginger ale in the North British Hotel my head was swimming and I needed to go, but couldn't find the ladies. I asked a waiter – there were loads of them just standing around – he wasn't a waiter; he was one of a crowd of similarly suited men. The born into drink was a different experience. I used to visit them at their home when I had an evening off. They'd always feed me so it wasn't that I was drinking on an empty stomach, but I always had to exercise serious caution getting on and off the buses back to the nurses' home. My uncle's idea was that I try out different drinks and each time he would have a few samples for my edification. Later when I was a landlady myself, I could see the effect a large small sherry had on an elderly abstemious relative at a funeral.

A perk at the Western was the opportunity to attend a matinee at a couple of theatres, the Lyceum and the Pleasance, for free. I saw some really good plays and some of the early Fringe theatre. A surprise was to find the brave probationer who had dared to bring her knitting and hot water bottle into class before she left to become an actress. Always at the back of your mind was what you'd do if you got kicked out. I knew

I could always get a job washing the steps at the Kings Theatre. That was a show on its own. The lady had a mat to kneel on, a bucket and a large cloth. She dipped cloth in the bucket and lightly wrung prior to splatting it across quite a wide sweep of marble step. Having dipped and wrung out the cloth properly, she repeated step one and moved down a step to do it all over again.

I'd look at that and compare with the Children's Shelter system for their front steps. They hadn't even one per cent of the traffic. You started without kneeler, but bucket, scrubbing brush, industrial carbolic soap and the cloth. Once you eased off your aching back at the bottom of the steps, you very carefully made your way back up keeping to the sides so leaving no footprints and down to the cellar to empty your bucket, rinse out the cloth and collect Cardinal red, dusters and buffer. By now your steps were dry. Time now to paint them red – a brighter red than that you'd just scrubbed off. It wasn't difficult, but energetic. You applied the Cardinal red polish with a cloth then rubbed it in with your buffer and then polished it with your fluffy duster. You can see why I knew I'd easily fit into the Kings Theatre with the skills I had.

There was also half price at some cinemas in the afternoon, but just as the evening timing was out of sync, so was the afternoon. In the afternoon you got the start of the film, but not the end whereas at least in the evening there were two showings and you could see the end then the beginning. Never bothered me at all that I'd be depriving some late showing person still queuing to get in who'd be left hanging when after God Save the Queen, the only way to find out what the ending was to ask the doorman.

I had one unique selling point that made me popular. I and a few friends could get into the Edinburgh Military Tattoo free. My uncle was MD of a Military Outfitter. He was the one with the television. Officers' uniforms were tailor-made, and they had different tartans at different times of day or occasion. That gave him lots of military contacts. During the Edinburgh Festival he was on call all the time as the source of anything that might be needed. One-night, Prince Philip's valet rang him at home because he had forgotten to pack the regimental tie required for the following day. Another night it rained so hard that the small flashes on the side of the busbies were ruined and had to be replaced for the next night. He was also an expert on regimental uniforms and was involved in creating the new uniforms for the Amalgamation of the Regiments. When he retired, he declined the invitation to be advisor to the War Office as my aunt was unwell, but they purchased for a very goodly sum his personal regimental records. He also created pseudo army dress for films because they could never accurately portray a real regiment due to red tape. Anyway, he was close friends with the brigadier who masterminded the Tattoo. So, he gave me his business card and written on the back was 'Introducing my niece,' and signed Bob. All I had to do was avoid the queue slowly snaking up towards the castle esplanade and address myself to a sentry. I'd hand over my card and ask him to take it to the brigadier. He'd return shortly and escort me and my friends to seats and always good seats. We once were even lucky enough to get in the Royal Box. What I had to be sure to do was reclaim Uncle Bob's card to use again.

I haven't any proper recent experience of what nurses have to do, but I know they don't clean and I see them clustered round a desk. When you see hospitals on the TV, the screen is full of nurses on computers and not a patient in sight. Is it human rights or confidentiality that keeps the patient hidden? It certainly doesn't sell the overworked and understaffed they talk about. I worry about things like that. If you are on-duty you need to keep patients in sight. I'm sure they never have to worry about masks and feeders and sterilising instruments. I don't take exception to the reduction in cleaning, but the level and distance patients are placed disturbs me. The suggestion that some caring action may help a patient feel better is no longer permitted. Rather set language is applied requiring patients to give informed consent to a person standing at a distance. Phrased like that, any chance of therapeutic touch is obviated.

Many tasks, which took up time, could never have been cost effective. Making swabs in a range of sizes and ply before counting and packing and sending for sterilisation took ages. If you hadn't completed the task by the time you were due off-duty, you stayed till it was done. Masks were a nightmare. We made them and the preferred style was the one with a wide front and narrow under chin and they need two different sizes of tapes – one over your ears and under your chin and the other the back of your neck. Washed in the ward, they got grey quickly and offended. They were always boiled, but often that wasn't enough and we'd resort to soaking in bleach. Once a very zealous bleacher overdosed and when I came to remove them, with forceps of course, prior to rinsing, they came out in clots. There were twenty in that pan. I couldn't make that many even with the help of my junior, overnight. That was 120 shapes to cut, then hand sew into forty pieces, then sew together to end up with twenty shapes waiting for the eighty individual tapes to be sewn on. Not tacked on – people yanked these tapes and it was supposed to be tiny stitches round four sides. Masks with missing tapes ended up in the mending. By the time I got to the Western they were using flat masks with a bit of elastic round your ear for every-day use and the proper jobs came ready-made. Some people just hadn't the patience to undo a knot – yank it off and snap the tape. Feeders likewise: get in a knot, out with the scissors and cut it off without a thought for the poor sod who'd have to ruin her eyesight sewing tiny stitches in the dark.

Instruments were boiled for twenty minutes after each use. A district nurse came to my house to attend to a friend who was staying after a minor operation that required a dressing renewed. By that I mean, a piece of sticking plaster ripped off, wound admired and patted with a swab and new plaster applied. The nurse arrived with her black bag, a folder and a massive parcel. Before the grand unwrap, she needed to take particulars, which extended to me. How old was I and were we safe together and eating OK and a lot more that took up twenty minutes? Then the great unwrap. A plastic apron, gloves, sealed packs of forceps and scissors, a variety of sizes of swabs, little plastic pots and dressing towels. Separately were little sachets of stuff like you get vinegar and ketchup in in cafes. Once set up and her hands sprayed, gloves donned, nothing was touched by hand at all – just like a scrubbed-up heart transplant assistant. She was with us for forty minutes. I don't remember infection being anything other than a warning of what could happen if you failed to follow the no touch technique. Different transferrable diseases were treated in the same ward through barrier nursing. Syringes were used time after time and to break a syringe was tantamount to criminal damage. The first time I came across a disposable syringe was in Africa. Our children leave home at the level of the attainment of their parents. When I left home, it was a transistor radio. When my children left home, I had TV & video player, car, freezer and microwave. I had not quite reached dishwasher level. In Africa we were years ahead in terms of modern equipment.

While on one of the teaching blocks, we were told that 'if' there was a normal delivery during class time we could go and observe. There was. First four out of the room! We sprinted from the classroom across the concourse and into maternity, upstairs to delivery, grabbed gown and mask and puffing and panting were lined up agog at the end of the bed. It was a bit like *Call the Midwife*, but I never saw Nurse Phyllis or Sister Julienne launching themselves onto the bed to further the process like this midwife did. I decided there and then I'd adopt and might give midwifery a miss. A messy process.

I'd begun to toy with the idea of maybe being a doctor. One of my mentors was very supportive and could see me fulfilling her lifelong sorrow that she hadn't taken the plunge. I had the necessary general subjects, was very proficient in shorthand, typing and bookkeeping, but short on a science so I signed up for a pre-entry science course. Then while at the Eastern, I picked up a very virulent bug and ended up back at the Western via an ambulance in isolation with Haemolytic Streptococci. I was kept in for a bit then discharged home to convalesce because I was a bit run down. Before I got back to work my joints seized up and I had rheumatic fever. That put paid to my course. After I got back to work and considered my options, I decided to give midwifery a miss and do further theatre training at Birmingham Accident Hospital. I really fancied that; you could specialise. I already had general, thoracic and plastic surgery experience and I thought to add neuro and trauma. After the rheumatic fever, I had my tonsils out for the second time, but was still on prophylactic penicillin.

They offered me a place at Birmingham, but I had to wait at least twelve months before they'd let me take it up. That's when I decided on a gap year in Inverness.

Having my tonsils out for a second time was because I never got rid of the infection despite being permanently on penicillin. The thing about it was that I had to have it done in the ENT department, where adults were seldom admitted. The pre-operative mockery from colleagues was vicious, but I made up my mind. I ordered scrambled egg and 'starch' (three spoons coffee, three sugars and made with milk) for my post-op tea. They didn't believe me so I showed them. Next morning, I further demonstrated a long-held, thought-to-be-apocryphal statement, generally cascaded by ENT consultants, that the best thing post tonsillectomy was toast, was true. Not easy, but I had my principles. It is actually and such a good example to the poor little kids wailing and doing everything they could to avoid swallowing anything at all. It was a successful procedure.

In 1956, we didn't have TV yet in our house and I used to visit an aunt and uncle to watch *Emergency Ward 10* and *Take your Pick*. They had friends staying from Inverness who were keen that I go back with them as they were absolutely sure it was just the thing to get me on my feet again. I did and really enjoyed my stay. I came back not just fit, but with new experiences. Visiting with my hosts, it was remarked how small my hands were and I was introduced to a ewe with a lamb in breech position. They were not a bit upset that I had no midwifery certificate; it was the size of my hands that mattered. By the time I returned, I'd repeated my live delivery success a couple more times.

The outcome of the holiday was their suggestion I get a job up there while I waited to go to Birmingham and I could live with them. I finished at the Western, reluctantly paid for my badge and I was ready for the off. I never wore that badge, but I still have it.

16 My Gap Year in Inverness

My two-week convalescence was not like my usual holidays. Since I began nursing, holidays were primarily to catch up on sleep and read if not actually studying for something. I did take reading material and revision with me but can't remember unpacking it. This was a different kind of life. After a couple of days of being a guest I got stuck in, served breakfasts to guests and helped Anne in the dairy. Once she was finished, she was free to go and we'd go places and do things. No car, but we had bikes and visited and picnicked and did a bit of pony trekking which Anne kind of fancied, but hadn't tried. It wasn't exacting as the mounts were docile and slow moving. What was a surprise though was the way all my 'bits' screamed in agony the next day. I hadn't realised just sitting there and chatting was actually exercising muscles I never knew I had.

I wasn't utterly sold on jazz, another of the things she fancied, but couldn't actually participate in because of going alone. We did a Young Farmers' dance as well, a great improvement on the Plaza. It was in a hotel ballroom which looked quite salubrious with the lights on. Anne knew loads of people so it was more like a party. We went to a football match as her dad was a director of Inverness Caledonian (Caley). Another new experience in a truly action-packed fortnight. I got caught up in the spirit of company rather than the game and the pie and Bovril at half time were an antidote to the freezing draft up my skirt. Trousers were not the thing. It had been OK during the war when you could wear a thing called a Siren Suit, i.e. warm pyjamas, to go out into the air-raid shelter. Women working in munitions wore trousers and Land Army girls wore breeches. Along with headscarves and curlers, trousers were common. HM the Queen wears a head scarf when she's out shooting and fishing and riding, so why can't we commoners?

I fitted in and they suggested instead of hanging on staffing at the Western until my twelve months were up before being accepted to Birmingham Accident Hospital that I get a job in Inverness. Even though I could have fitted in midwifery in the time, it just wasn't for me. So, when a job cropped up in the Nursing Mirror for a staff nurse in the children's ward at Raigmore Hospital, I was successful. I sallied forth just to fill in until I could go where I thought my future lay – specialist theatre.

I've very fond memories of Raigmore on and off duty. The Infirmary in the town centre was like all old hospitals – workhouse style. Raigmore wasn't a proper hospital in that way. It could have been a temporary army hospital during the war or thinking about it, a POW camp. There was a main block – some Nissen huts joined together, but the rest was randomly sited huts without joined-up corridors. If you went off the ward, you went outside. Taking children to x-ray or theatre was an outing.

The preparations were as involved as a day trip. If your child was of an age to carry, we didn't bother the porters. We'd make sure the child was warm enough and rainproof, tuck the notes underarm and we could go. A trolley trip was more complex. Being warm enough and ready to go was just the start as we then had to wait until it was our turn for a porter and his trolley. The rain proofing was Heath Robinson and involved tarpaulins. When it came to removal of bodies, there was a covered cradle that fitted a trolley disguising a corpse and keeping it dry but totally unsuited for children going strange places to have things done. We had to go against the golden rule of only feet first if dead. There was no other way around it. The nurse ducked under the tarpaulin joining with the child for the trip and blind to any hazards like puddles. We didn't really get out much, but those such as porters who serviced our ward got a lot of exercise.

I've Googled Raigmore today and it is an amazing place and looks bigger than Royal Blackburn. If you want to look, there are two pictures from my era on their website. You can tell by the rusty metal windows and the lack of screen tracking. We had the proper screens that you dragged to the bed and with a skill born of experience flicked and kicked till they either screened the bed or fell over. That was the last job I ever had an interview for. Then I gave it all up for Charlie.

My Mum wasn't over keen on this move. My hosts were friends of my mother's brother and his wife. She, the sister in-law had humble beginnings coming as she did from a railway background. Her dad was a shunter and they lived in a cottage in the yard of Haymarket Station. When she was child sitting me, no doubt to 'give my mother a rest,' she'd take me there and I learned to make toast. There was a very shiny brass trident and you hacked a slice off a plain loaf and anchored it on the prongs and addressed it to the fire in the range. It needed a lot of looking after and checking to see it was done. I wasn't very good and it kept dropping off into the ash pit, but no problem, my aunt picked it up, blew off the ash and stuck it back for me. Her dad loved my toast and clearly a kindly man like my Grandpa, who would taste my made-up recipes and exclaim in delight. Despite working in a specialist embroidery emporium, my aunt, being a shop assistant, was a bit low class. My mother's family were white collar. Her sister worked in the office at McVitties. You could pick them out, when the whistle went at McVitties, and the workers streamed on to Slateford Road, the clerical staff stood out because they didn't have curlers and head squares.

My hosts, doing farm bed and breakfast tells you something about my mother's brother. Mum thought he exaggerated his standing in the community. We didn't do bed and breakfast, we never had. We'd outgrown boarding houses and were into boutique hotels. Number 1 middle class Edinburgh snob my mother – 'they canny be as weel off as they think they are,' still going B&B.

In fact, it could even be about now, in 1958, that my dad had his first pre-prandial. When wee Margaret was at her first job she went out to dinner with her employers. They had drinks before the meal. Dad asked her what she had and she said 'ginonet.' What a thing to start off with – one slug (Scottish optic) gin made up with three Martini Rosso. It makes my learning look feeble. I don't remember any wailing and gnashing of teeth when she went to Southport as a nanny. She trained as a nursery nurse and applied to work with a family with two small children. The elder girl had Down's Syndrome and the younger girl 'mentally retarded.' Not for long after Margaret got there she wasn't. Her milestones had caught up and exceeded within three months. It was all down to lack of stimulation because she lived in the shadow of her disabled sister. In next to no time Margaret had them both skilled up and doing things to the delight of their parents. She stayed there till she returned home to marry Ronald. She maintains contact with the family still. The mother was a Jehovah's Witness; that could have made for serious problems in the household, but it never did. She'd be out and about door-stepping but never a word at home. They all came to the wedding and every year thereafter she'd come and stay with Margaret and Ronald while she went to a conference at Edinburgh's Kingdom Hall.

Disapproval oozing from her pores and prognostications of it not being the right thing to do, my mother was unrelenting in her protestations against the move to Inverness, but I did it. Puberty at twenty-four? I packed my trunk with the requisites of living in a nurses' home just in case I had to move into hospital due to weather or any other of my mother's worst case scenarios, my bike and a suitcase of mufti. I never unpacked the trunk seeing as I was at the farm, until the day I left to go home to Edinburgh for the pre-nuptial preparations.

The bike was an improvement on my original; it was my sister's cast-off. When I got a bicycle, we still had wartime conditions and it was a black and dull metal sit-up-and-beg and the bell and pump were extras. When Margaret got hers, it was a blue and silver Raleigh with gears. She was now disposing of it as she had no need of it and surprise, surprise I didn't have to buy it. My sister has always been very good with money. She normally claimed not to have any. Say we were going somewhere for a certain time; we'd set off for the tram stop. She'd keep going as it was 1p less if we walked two stops further on. Almost certainly we would end up being late. Not just bone idle, but a stickler for being on time I'd say – 'I'll pay.' If there was a good film on she so wanted to see, but couldn't afford – 'I'll pay.' Mum said to me once, 'You are a mug; she's mair money than you.' From the farm to Raigmore would be about six miles and I worked the usual shifts – so more often than not did the trip four times a day. Sometimes, if it was very wet, the farmer himself would be dispatched to pick me up and the bike got thrown in the boot. It was always a lovely surprise to come out the ward pushing my bike round to the road and see the green car waiting. It wasn't only the farm car though, because I'd become an ardent fan of Inverness Caley. My shifts never allowed me to get the supporters' bus to away matches so, I would be picked up by others in a similar situation. They never made any secret of their arrival. Armed with rattles and a two-tone horn, they'd screech up to the back door. By this time ambulant children would have been looking out for them and telling me. We travelled fast nourished by a constant supply of a munchy chocolate bar. I forget what it was called and what I think it was isn't because Lion bars weren't invented till 1976, but that's the kind of texture.

While training I, and most of my mates, were permanently tired. It wasn't a bit like that in Inverness. On my days off I was up early to lend a hand vis a vis B&B guests and when off afternoon or evening there was always something doing in the activity line. Quite early on my small hands were in demand for lambing, not just at our place, but across the neighbourhood and for relatives as well. All had sizeable farms and prime stock. They had lots of twin lambs and well-fed ewes have a habit of delivering large lambs. All parties would fetch me and sometimes fetched the ewe to ours. Losing a lamb was upsetting. My first stillborn wasn't ours. The chap who fetched it had been guddling about himself for too long and the ewe was dry and exhausted. The audience was supportive and assured me that If I hadn't got it out, he'd have to send for the vet and by the time the vet polled up the ewe would be dead. One day, a visitor coming in to the ward said there was a chap looking for me. There was, but he wasn't there to take me to a sheep, he'd brought it with him in his boot. Fortunately, I was going off so it was OK to go out and deliver on the spot. The children were all lined up at the windows to see the 'wee lambs.' It wasn't long till I was elevated to calving. I might just as well have done my midwifery exams. I settled easily into the job and on and off-duty I had one of my very happy times.

A member of the extended family had a brother called Charlie. Charlie was something in Africa and due for a long stay. We were introduced as soon as he arrived. Charlie had no farming blood and had worked for the Water Board before going to Northern Rhodesia and working for the Government Utilities. I don't know exactly what he did, but it involved living out in the bush and coming into town for fun in a government Land Rover. Fabulous ex-pat lifestyle and the ideal place for a nurse. From the day we met, we spent all my off duty together. It wasn't long before we began to plan our idyllic future. I was completely absorbed into the extended family. Charlie reluctantly went back to the then Northern Rhodesia, and I would join him in the spring, when we would be married. He could not extend his leave to get married before he left, but he met my parents, who approved and I had a very respectable diamond engagement ring. It was all announced in The Scotsman, and as soon as he was gone, my mum went into planning with missionary zeal.

I can't remember there being any suggestion of this being the wrong thing I was doing. It was favoured on all sides and everyone joined in the planning and arrangements. There was never anyone less prepared than me. I'd been to an all-girls school then nursing and a few trips to the Plaza, no sign of any eligible doctors and my dating experience was limited. Although I'd lived away from home from seventeen it was always in Edinburgh or thereabouts. Nurses were always skint and holidays were either with the family or going home with someone who was used to coming to our house and her parents were returning hospitality. One friend used to visit an aunt who was head teacher at the village school in Killiekrankie and I went there with her a couple of times. I went to Llandudno with another and we practised for a talent show on the pier. It involved a mouth organ and her singing with me joining in with a bit of harmony. We chickened out.

I had no real-life experience. Always in a group of nurses, I'd have a meal out once a month at one of the British restaurants and the other three weeks it was 1/3d for egg and chips, bread and butter and coffee at the chippy round the corner. I didn't even have my own money. I had to hand over my pay packet and I got 10/- a week back and I had to buy my own stockings and pay for shoe repairs as well as the one proper meal out and three chip shop outings. The places we had our splurge at had to provide quality meals at a price and I think it was 3/4d for three courses.

The British restaurants were set up in 1940 for people who were bombed out, had lost their coupons or had some other disaster thrust upon them. After the war they were assumed by local authorities and while rationing was still in place to provide healthy eating at an affordable price. During the war the cost was 9d. Anyway, the one we patronised was in Lothian Road and you got there via a door between two shops which opened straight into a staircase. Reaching the top of the staircase you queued. The tables were set with starched white damask and heavy hotel silver service cutlery. There was no menu, once seated, a waitress came to tell you what you were having. Soups were hearty. Nothing like broccoli and stilton, just lentil, potato or Scotch broth. Offal was often the dish of the day and tripe and onion or liver and onion. Haggis and mince were frequent flyers. Pudding was heavy-going treacle sponge or suet pudding and custard. There was no coffee after, but the option of a cup of tea was extra. Coffee was not the popular drink it is today. Post war this was good food. One day we overheard a rather posh lady say to the waitress who had just informed her 'potatoes are off' – 'Oh dear I feel just like a potato today' – you had to be there or just accept, that nurses laugh at the stupidest things.

I wasn't to be trusted with money and I owed my parents for all the school fees. Raigmore was the first place I got my wages to myself and I also got the living-out allowance – I was rich. My hostess was not for taking anything, but I was well brought up. Soon as I got paid and handed over my board, she'd have a bit of an outing or some retail therapy for Anne and me. This was a whole new life experience. To be fair, when we went on holiday it was 'all found' and certainly way beyond anything I could have afforded myself. I dived into romance and had a wonderful time with Charlie. Once he'd gone back, we wrote to each other every day. Wrote so much in small writing and up the sides of the Airmails as well.

Not even the ward sister at Raigmore was RSCN. Bit of a rare breed we were. She came from Skye, left there to train in

Inverness and had not been any further south. Being a Gaelic speaker was handy because many of the children who came had parents only really comfortable in that language. We had a paediatric consultant and he was spread very thin as he covered all the Highlands and Islands hospitals. Sometimes it was a bit like Africa and children were brought in and wouldn't see their parents till discharge and sometimes even then they'd be collected by someone who just happened to be on the mainland for something. There was never any shortage of girl's names but it wasn't uncommon to have wee girls called Duncanina or Donalda or Davida

We had one little girl who was not for this world and both parents would visit, but the father couldn't understand why his wife was so upset. "It's no as if we dinnae have ony other bairns." She didn't drive and he brought her every day, but I wonder how that eventually turned out? The death of a child often wrecks a marriage due to unbalanced bereavement issues and there was certainly no help then. They would be unlikely to divorce because it was uncommon and certainly not in the narrow lives of crofters.

We had a little girl with Hirschprung's disease and her parents had accepted that additionally, she was backward or mentally retarded as was the term used. Having my McDuff experience, it wasn't rocket science for me to realise she was deaf. I mentioned it to the consultant on his round. He had never known of a Hirschprung's being deaf. Well I had and she was and he was so chuffed and I have to say the parents were delighted. He of course got in touch with Mr Robarts at Sick Kids and he said they were going to write it up for the BMJ. I was able to help the parents get started communicating and every time they came down, they could see a difference in her responses and participation. Clapping hands for attention, Balloons and bbbs and they were really keen to get things moving. They brought Granny who was also chuffed, but 'she'd aye kent that bairn wisnae daft.'

We admitted a beautiful child under two. Sometimes you see children with an internal light and the face of an angel. She lay there smiling, with her golden curls and wide-open sparkling blue eyes. That was all. There was nobody at home. She was admitted from a children's home where she lived with her now fifteen-year-old mother. It was not generally known in the home of the relationship, but the big girls helped with the little ones. She was a 'father unknown.' The young mother disclosed an incestuous relationship to a social worker, but unfortunately unwitnessed. So, no action could be taken. How long have we had DNA? The child was admitted because of a swollen lumpy tummy. She went for an exploratory operation, a laparotomy. Immediately they opened her up a mass of cauliflower floret tumours burst out and kept pouring out like a rip tide. They couldn't stop the flow and with great difficulty and strong stitches closed her up. She never cried, just lay there smiling while her abdomen swelled and her little arms and legs grew like twigs until she faded away. The mother's parents visited and it was easy to believe the father was evil. He was dirty, smelled and had a nasty wee moustache. He wore a shiny suit and was creepy. The mother also smelled, but she was just a shilpit broken little woman, who had had her daughter taken into care because her husband was a 'kiddy-fiddler'.

My first experience of junior alcohol case was at Raigmore. On night duty we had an emergency admission from A&E at the Infirmary. Two years old and staying with his granny he'd got into the sideboard and drunk her medicinal sherry. They'd done a stomach wash-out, but he was flat out and remained so the rest of the night. He was a right bonny wee lad with black curly hair, who looked as though 'butter wouldn't melt.' I was standing at the bottom of the cot when he suddenly opened both eyes and sat up. Like a flash, both hands flew to his head and he slumped back down with a howl of pain. His very first hangover. I don't know if granny was ever allowed to look after him again.

Time passed and Christmas approached and there was no mention made of themes. At the Western decorations hadn't been anything to do with nursing staff, but when I asked what the system was, it turned out 'we'd have to make some.' I served a long apprenticeship at Sick Kids so I suggested we ask Inverness Caley Football Club to do it for us and get themselves a bit of benevolent publicity. Asking was easy and they were keen to do it but – time passed. I began to worry. Sister kept forecasting they wouldn't turn up and I was feeling the same way. Then all at once a mob turned up with expensive and very fancy readymade decorations such as they had never had before. Flashing Santa and hundreds of fairy lights and the ward looked amazing. They also brought a sledge load of toys. Sister was fair taken away with it all having never seen anything like it. They didn't even have electricity where she came from.

The time came when I was ready to leave and I don't remember any regrets at all and certainly no worries. It never crossed my mind that anything could go wrong.

17 The Long Journey

Edinburgh Waverley station: hissing, smelly, holiday-exciting smelly, big Menzies (now W.H Smith) – bliss to people like me. On a damp, dark Monday night, 16th March 1959, is where it began. I was being seen off from the Waverley by a respectable crowd of family and well-wishers as I set off on the sleeper before embarking in Southampton to travel to Lusaka in Northern Rhodesia. In Lusaka in almost four weeks' time I would be married. I'm a bit ahead of myself; the journey began about a fortnight earlier when I left work in Inverness and returned home to Edinburgh. I went home to do the things that respectable families do when a daughter is getting married. Even before that, there had been some early planning regarding 'ultra-modern' clothes suited to my new position, a wedding dress and THE CAKE.

One of my mother's friends was married to a master baker and confectioner: not just any old craftsman, but THE Master Baker and Confectioner at McVitties. Nothing to do with my mother ever bordered on ordinary. She chose the cake decoration to match flowers in the hairband/tiara that would hold my veil in place and the lace of the veil was reflected in the flat bits where there were no sugar roses or frills. I never saw it till the Queen's official birthday in June 1960. It had to be baked to the same recipe as the master baker and confectioner had used for the wedding of HRH Princess

Elizabeth; matured, iced and then placed in a sealed tin. Not a cake tin – a massive, sealed tin, the size of a tractor tyre. It became part of my hand luggage. No way could such magnificence be consigned to the hold. That bloody cake haunted me, stalked me and smirked at me during its lifetime.

Even if you are leaving the country to do it – getting married is no picnic in Edinburgh. The engagement notice appears in not only, the Edinburgh Evening News but in The Scotsman also. Congratulation cards are received and letters thanking people for sending cards dispatched. The wedding notices – invitations – are sent, as if anyone could afford or have time to travel to the venue. The outcome is presents – not easy when they have to be chosen for a foreign country, a warm climate, wild animals and natives. So, we moved then to the showing of the presents. That has to be brought forward because they all have to be packed – professionally packed and shipped for 'not required on voyage' with a deadline of a week before I leave. So, the presents are unpacked and displayed all around the sitting room like a market stall. That is unkind – an upmarket shop – placed on pristine hand-embroidered cloths. Invitations are sent with the thank you letter to all donors who duly turn up on a choice of dates to admire, criticise and price compare. Having made the right noises, they are treated to tea, scones, pancakes and about eight varieties of home-made cakes. Naturally the jam is home-made too and the china – fine bone. We do things properly in our house. My mother was the model for Mrs Bucket. She believed she was born to be a lady, but when she grew up there were no vacancies. She lived a life of terminal disappointment.

Perhaps now is the time to mention the 'ultra-modern' clothes. I was 24 years old, dressed by my mother and her friends who knew what was right – there were only two items in the whole trousseau I liked. Everything matched – suits, blouses, shoes. I was allowed one coat – a camel coat – I liked that and wore it until it got totally out of shape due to frequent pregnancies. The blue dress was the other – I shared it with others in the sisters' mess; it was just so right for all occasions. My mother had friends in the 'mission field.' These women know what you need to live and socialise in Africa. I tell you now – the blue dress must have slipped past the sentry. Now, hair permed, possibly a Marcel Wave, dressed in a – can't remember the brand, but all fashionable ward sisters wore it – suit, with my camel coat perched on my shoulders I reached the Waverley. Three crates professionally packed should by now be in Southampton – Not Wanted on Voyage. In the guard's van, two trunks and two cases. One of my trunks is blue, brass fittings and brand new for the occasion and the other my battered, about third hand when I got it, hospital trunk. In with me is the cake, holdall, handbag with wallet, tickets and passport. The goodbyes are low-key, we don't do emotion in Edinburgh and to be honest the last two weeks have been so action-packed they're all worn out. Surprisingly my sister – two years and ten months younger – was a wee bit upset. She should have been celebrating – all my clutter gone. When the UF missionaries went back to the field we always sang at a slow tempo '*God be with you till we meet again*,' but clearly not for weddings. I've waved and gone back into my sleeper.

I love travelling by train – always a treat. Part of my yearning to be common. We always had a car; my father had his first personally-owned car after the war. Being in the motor trade there were always a number of demonstration cars for him to choose from. He decided according to the occasion. When I went with him and my mother for a last holiday before I went away – Skye, I think – he took this massive ungainly Austin something or other and encouraged me to drive. I think likely because he wanted to be sure I was safe in a foreign country without supervision. I complained and he said, 'I thought you'd like a big car.' Well I would, but with narrow winding roads with passing places, I could never be sure if my big end was tucked in.

Anyway, on the train there was not a lot of room for me, the cake and bulky travel clothes. Do you get undressed? Of course, the jacket, blouse and skirt – no trousers for ladies yet. I wish I could remember the brand of the suit, but I do remember the colour. It was Air Force blue with a narrow brown stripe. I remember lying on my narrow bunk with my book and when I woke up, we weren't travelling any more. The sleeper gets shunted into a siding till a reasonable hour when the attendant brings you morning tea– on a tray. You choose when to rise and I planned mine with the time of the boat train in mind. I'd been in London before but not like this. I had to get a porter for the cases and trunks and the cake then change platforms – check the departure board – not flash digital – then ask at least two people in railway serge if I was on the right platform for the right train for the Union Castle sailing.

The boat train slid into a siding on the dock and this time it was easier – they take everything to your cabin. Against all dire warnings about not letting it out of my sight, I let go and trusted them to take the cake as well. Twenty years ago, I was in the very same departure lounge and it hasn't changed – the very same Union Castle ship pictures and settees. I can recall checking my crates had been stowed and then standing in a very small cabin, no porthole with my trunks, case and cake, thinking – something's not right – this is not an outside cabin! I found a man, and got moved to something much better. With what I needed unpacked, trunks stacked and only missing the travel rug that would have disguised them in the nurses' home, case and cake alongside, I sat on the bottom bunk to read the letter I received when I boarded.

It was from Charlie and included a ten-shilling note; he suggested I get myself a drink as I might be a bit homesick. However, first I had to book a hair appointment for two weeks today – the day we would land. I would do this at the purser's office. Following that, I had to locate and tip my bath steward to ensure I got the best bath times. I sallied forth. The purser was far too busy to deal with my hair appointment and when he wasn't too busy, I was too late to get landing day. Bath steward, I managed. They draw your bath, inform you they have done it and then hover – not looking just skulking because that's what they do. The baths are in a small cluster but, on board they were in proper cubicles. In Bechuanaland they just had waist-high partitions in bath and toilet and it was dead friendly – pass me the bog roll! I didn't go for the drink because they were tannoying for people not sailing to go ashore so I went to the rail and watched.

Quite a crowd on the dock and the deck – waving, boat hooting, throwing streamers ship to shore and as the engines took up power, the strains of '*God be with you till we meet again*' reached us on board. You can't get away from it, so I knew there must be a load of missionaries on board. I felt then a bit lonely. Not for long. Ship life is amazing. No entertainment in these days, this was a voyage with a purpose, not a cruise. Hundreds of civil servants going back after long leave and missionaries after furlough mixed up with odds and ends like me going for the first time. Some nurses going out for their first bash at adventure, travelling free on a three-year contract courtesy of the Government of Rhodesia and Nyasaland. I later knew the right name for them was 'sunshine girls.' Nurses are elitist, but in Africa, definitely not the only ones. They got free passage, more money than they earned in the UK, local holidays then three months paid long leave every three years with free travel to and from the UK.

Our table got on well and we played a lot of cards. We did deck games and talked a lot. Everybody but me drank a lot. I was brought up teetotal! Of course, my uncles had done their bit in a practical way. Uncle Bob's advice was stick to whisky, it's a clean drink. Uncle Benny really wanted me to try lots and his were fancy like Tia Maria and yellow sticky stuff that had a bush growing in the bottle. The first beer I had, as recommended by Charlie took about three minutes to go to my head and five to overfill my bladder and worse, so I took things very slowly on board.

When we passed another ship, there was a tannoy announcement and everybody rushed on deck cheering and waving madly. Apart from the feel of the engines under foot there is no commonality between sailing then and now. We stopped off briefly at Madeira and as all the other places the locals danced or sang or dived for money to entertain us and make a living for themselves. I only learned about Sail Away Cocktails when I did my first and only cruise as an old lady. Considering my pathetic tolerance in the 1950s, they may have affected me even more dramatically than SA Lion beer.

We socialised with those we ate with and only three of us were Lusaka bound. Alma, the only other female on our table, was joining the Northern Rhodesian Police and the chap, John, did hypnosis as a side-line. Now that was an experience. He was only wholly successful with Alma and me which he explained was because we were both used to 'doing as you are told.' He had us clasp our hands together tighter and tighter and despite my engagement ring gouging a lump out of a finger, I did. We were at that time in a very hot and muggy climate and everyone was lethargic. John told us that when we woke up, we'd have boundless energy for the rest of the day. We did. Later in Lusaka John had a private practice providing hypnotherapy for all kinds of ailments and phobias as well as party tricks. This bothered me and some of my colleagues because there were women among his clientele unable to go to sleep at night unless he snapped his fingers. The personal experience for me was useful when in 1998 when the idea was run past me that hypnotherapy had a role in treating the side effects of chemotherapy. It made it easier for those who were looking to me to support their ambition to include complementary therapies in palliative care.

Two weeks flew by and we occupied ourselves with what the Union Castle Line provided such as the swimming pool, deck quoits and volley ball. There was of course the ceremony of Crossing the Line. The pool was emptied down to about eighteen inches and a rope slung across. First-timers, crossing the equator, had to queue up and be lathered with shaving foam by one of Neptune's minions prior to its being scraped off with a sword. Next, two sailors grabbed the unfortunate and dipped them once on each side of the rope. For this you received a certificate. There was a lot of jeering and cheering and Neptune himself was a nasty old rabble rouser.

When we reached Cape Town, it was the reverse of Southampton. I had to sign for my crates and say goodbye to everything – even the cake and we were free to go until we had to report back to the railway station in the evening. It was good that the cake was guaranteed safe storage until train time, because not only was it in a small cage with the trunks and cases, having signed it over, it would stay there till Lusaka. We'd not seen Table Mountain as we came into dock because it was misty which was usual according to the been-there-got-the-T-shirt people. We used to have the same thing in Scotland in a lot of places. If you can see it, it is a sign of rain. If you can't see it, it's raining. It wasn't raining; there was a kind of heat I'd never experienced before; I think suffocating describes it. I felt a bit not well, dizzy and my feet kept climbing yet the terrain was flat. I'm not always slow, but I didn't know that this was normal; you don't get sea legs when you come off the ferry at Brodick from Ardrossan.

A state of emergency had been declared and there was a sullen silence about the city. Police of all hues carried guns – something I had never experienced. They used to have these periodically and they made headlines in the UK press, but this was just how it was in South Africa. Apartheid was tricky; we had to be careful where we went. Signs were in English and Afrikaans, but it was odd to have to think about which bit was available to us. Northern Rhodesia was multi-racial to a degree in that the Africans could shop where they wanted, live where they wanted, eat where they wanted, have medical care where they chose as long as they could pay.

Apartheid in South Africa made sense to me because there was animosity and discrimination, and without 'parallel development' there would have been more trouble than there was. On a ward – which bell do you answer first – which accident do you send the ambulance to first – that could be trouble and that is what they tried to avoid. It wasn't scary. Maybe if foreign interference had been less aggressive things may not have got as bad as they did. The foreign press encouraged examples of discrimination. An example which made headlines in the UK was of some African children rummaging in a bin, for food. What was wrong with the picture was that it was not taken in South Africa, but in a recognisable compound in Rhodesia where the photographer threw a large bag of sweets into an upturned bin and encouraged the children to forage. However, they really never did live up to the meaning of the word apartheid and blood was shed and the rich got richer and the poor more downtrodden. Would it not have been better had they been truly able to live side by side as equals?

Cape Town was my first experience of realising that underdeveloped countries are far more developed than the UK. A store in Glasgow had an escalator – we had to travel from Edinburgh to Glasgow to experience this modern marvel – all the stores in Cape Town had escalators. The stores were air-conditioned and up to the Patrick Thomson department store standard. Everything on sale was the same as in the UK, the only difference being language. The logos were the same, but the wording in English and Afrikaans. However, when it came to edible items there was no similarity as they were made in SA and the taste poor in comparison or to our conditioned taste. We had a full day to spend without luggage and all these shops to go at. Because of the emergency we stuck to the city centre. We took a long time figuring out signs as we had been pre-warned to do. Always the niggle that since there was a 'state of emergency' in place any small infringement on our part might kick off riots. The Cape Town shops were well worth our leisurely inspection because we were seeing things not seen in the UK since before the war. Colour was one thing and not just the people, coloured glass, coloured china ranges of fabrics, it was a wonderland to us. The sea legs were still catching us by surprise when it was time to make our way to the station. I'd think – it's gone then suddenly for no reason the pavement would tilt. Alma and I were travelling together to Lusaka, where she'd join the police and I'd get married a week on Saturday. We would travel on by train for the next five days.

The station in Cape Town was similar to Edinburgh, but different – the body language of the porters and their demeanour was different. When someone doesn't speak English, we raise our voices, but people talking to the Africans not only raised their voices, but also changed the tone of voice. My son refers to this as 'colonial ways' and though not accused of this personally, a friend was. Apparently, though I didn't live there long enough to be branded 'colonial,' I have a 'servant's tone.' The station was the first time I experienced the smell of the native African. They do have an odour particular to them, but to them we smell of 'dead people.' Very soon I ceased to notice it except when they were anxious or afraid and then the scent becomes more apparent. I put it down to 'relish.' Relish is special food, delicacies that the well-off and aspiring to be well-off African can afford. Seeing 'relish' in weevil moving sacks outside stores never recommended any of it to my pathetic taste buds.

Because railways in Africa don't have a common gauge, we had to change trains at the border, and that meant the whole shebang. They lied, our belongings were not to remain caged till Lusaka, they were liberated and redistributed in another cage on another train. Back at the station on the dock in Cape Town we had to identify ourselves and our baggage before being shown to our cabins. Much more commodious than the Scottish Sleeper. We had washing facilities and an arm chair. During the day we moved to day carriages, which doubled as dining cars. We played Canasta all day, every day and watched the dry and dusty veldt pass. We had sight of herds of animals racing the train. I recognised zebras and wildebeest right away and added impala and duiker as we moved north. We stopped a lot at 'halts.' 'Station' was far too grand a word; there was no platform, just a long drop to the dry earth. People got off and porters rushed – sorry, moved about slowly dealing with the luggage. We were the rushing idiots, the African preserves his strength in the heat. Just like at Madeira and other places we'd stopped at, but were never allowed off. The natives came and sold us crafts or the children were sent to beg. At each halt, we'd hang out of the window and see wildebeest or zebra or skinny cattle minded by little boys with big sticks. Once at a game reserve in the future, the men did a dance, grinding mealies i.e. maize, for flour, but that was just show. In the bush, men wear little and don't do much apart from talk, smoke and drink Kaffir beer. The women are mothers and wash and cook. Babies in a sling suckle and when the next one comes along, the sucklers are handed on to grandma who then takes over and weans.

Things improved when we changed to Rhodesian Railways. First thing, the cabin bunks had sheets – proper white ironed sheets. Africans are very good washers – even with the horrible muddy water they seem to somehow get whites that look like as though their mothers used Persil. The food was better – we had a lot of sausages and silver service. Things took a down turn when we crossed the border from Southern to Northern Rhodesia. We'd produced passports and tickets in Cape Town then in Bulawayo without any problems. Customs came on board at Livingstone and checked us all. I did not have a visa or a work permit. I don't know why. I'd been injected against everything from Yellow Fever to Bubonic Plague, but I did not have a piece of paper that allowed me to travel. They didn't put me off the train, but said I had to report to Immigration in Lusaka on Monday. I don't recall being over anxious and the time began to drag as we travelled north on the last lap.

I remember looking out on the Zambezi at Kafue and was amazed at such a wide flowing river in such a dry land.

I recall getting a bit dithery as Lusaka drew near. I had such a lot to look forward to. We'd stay in Lusaka until we got married. We'd have a short trip to see the sights like Victoria Falls on our honeymoon then make for Fort Jamieson where Charlie was stationed. Up near the border with the Belgian Congo it was a long road journey or plane ride away. The planes weren't exactly canvas winged, but primitive – very primitive. Once there and acclimatised I was to work at the hospital in town and commute to the bush station where Charlie did something with or about water. That would just be until I started spitting out the six little Frasers we'd planned. Even then, I'd still work, but we'd move into a P3 in the town and Charlie would commute if we were still stationed there, but we could really be anywhere in the Territory of Northern Rhodesia. In fact, I could even be Director of Nursing and Charlie the Chief Engineer for Rhodesia and Nyasaland and we'd come back to UK in retirement with all six children privately educated at the expense of the British Government and live as ex-pats with mega government pensions.

We steamed into Lusaka – not a station – a halt – no platform – just the ground a long way down. It's six days since my hairdo and it's been a bathless five days on a train. Not many getting off, but just me and my travel mate un-met. We jumped to the gritty ground. We watched and checked the two trunks, suitcases and the cake off loaded and kept looking round as did my travel mate. The train was grunting up to steam off north and there was all Africa and us – no porters – just us. We panic quietly before an NRP Land Rover pulls in and a policeman gets out for my companion. Then a car pulls in with two young women in it and I'm all that's left. They introduce themselves as Elaine and Lucy and huff and puff over why Charlie's not there. Elaine, I know by name because I'm staying with her and her husband Bill and family until the wedding. They used to be stationed in Fort Jamieson, but with three children and the eldest coming up to secondary age and a promotion for Bill they've moved to Lusaka. Also due to his promotion they've moved up in the accommodation and they have a P3. Very few people own a house in Northern Rhodesia as most are employed by the British Government and housing comes with the job. It's a very parochial kind of 'know your place' is Africa. Even the civil servants have cliques. There's education, health, PWD – sort of council workers known as Procrastination, Waste and Destruction, then there's the people in the High Commission, they're posh, and of course health. Within all these are subsections and some people have feet in both camps. The foot-in-both-camps are people who have been on a posting and when they moved met up with their past and renewed acquaintance. That is a very handy thing as I found out. Seems Charlie's not very well. My travel mate came across and asked if everything was OK, then leaves.

Well of course it was OK. I'm thousands of miles from home with £105 to my name, no work permit or visa, not met by the guy I am marrying in three days' time and I have to report to Immigration on Monday. The ground is rough sand and my trunks, cases and the cake are just plonked down. Lucy seems to know a man who knows another and an African came with a pickup and took away the trunks, but we loaded the suitcase, me, my holdall, tickets and passport and the cake into a Ford Anglia and we drove away to God knows where. Not really streets, there are areas and plot numbers and they all look alike in a way because they are sort of little campus' of assorted Ps. You don't need a street address because you don't get mail. You collect your mail from the post office from a box you pay for. Mail arrives on the days after there have been trains or flights in. We'd arrived and I'd met the children and been give tea before the facts emerged. My fiancé is drunk – very drunk. They have been trying to sober him up since Friday. They had hoped it may be possible to get him to the station, but even after the lads hosed him down – no chance. I would see him in the morning.

18 A Rabbit in a Room

It was mid-afternoon on Monday, April 6, 1959. I was sitting on a bed, in a room by myself. The door was closed. I was alone. No stranger asking questions, sympathising or making suggestions. My brown trunk, not my new one with the brass fittings, the grey suitcase, with the soft top and my initials on it which I got for my 21st, the green canvas wooden-banded suitcase, part of our family set since the war, now generously donated for my purpose, a holdall which was green as well. That luggage was our first ever 'set' and my mother's pride in reaching matching luggage status. All these along with the great metal sphere that is 'the cake' occupied the floor space.

The assistant matron, Grace Pullen, had shown me my room. This is the sisters' mess in Central Hospital, Lusaka. She didn't ask me any awkward questions. The wedding cake was one of the things in the whole saga that rocked my boat. She explained that a boy would bring me some tea. I could unpack and meet everyone in the dining room at supper time. She said she would see me in the morning; and that one of the other sisters would collect me and show me the way.

The boy wasn't a boy, but a barefoot African man and there were lots like him. They wore scruffy trousers like theatre scrubs in grey with white tunic tops. They all answered to 'Boy,' but they had names – interesting names some of them, like Kaiser, Sixpence, Albatross. I called them by name, but the colonials didn't, they just called any African male – Boy. What I learned quickly was, they all answered to 'Boy.' However, say you called a boy, Ticky and he wasn't Ticky because he was Tuppence, Tuppence would play dumb unless I called him Boy – no way would he say – I'm not Ticky I'm Tuppence. Looking back, it was an easier way to communicate directly with the person you wanted than the way it worked in my family. It could have been conducive to lowering my blood pressure. I'm not saying the boys answered quickly because they didn't – Africans are never in a hurry and go to sleep when it gets dark. Despite that, they sweat a lot more than we do so effectively don't suffer from the heat as badly as we do.

It seemed a long time since Saturday. So much had happened with so many people and no escape. We had supper on Saturday after the children were in bed. After sundown we'd sat on the stoep (a South African veranda) and had drinks. My plate was piled high and that's where the problem began – I just couldn't swallow. To this day a hefty portion induces anxiety. The light was yellow to keep away the insects and the sounds were strange and I felt lost – at sea? I escaped to my room after supper and I must have slept. I'd met several more people seemingly a bit put out about Charlie, but on reflection none of them seemed more than 'he picks his moments.' Morning came and Elaine did my hair – she's a hairdresser and I'd had a bath so I was sanitary. I was supposed to send a cable home to announce my safe arrival, but you can only do that during post office opening hours and on Sundays that was 11 – 12 noon. With a pretty frock, make-up and heels, I was ready and waiting, waiting and waiting.

Eventually Charlie put in an appearance – what a wreck. He was a pathetic sight. He was wearing smart pants and a clean shirt, but he was shaky, sheepish, shambling and furtive. I can't recall the conversation, but I know the cable said – 'Arrived safely – wedding postponed – letter follows.'

We went back to Elaine and Bill's and Charlie was taken elsewhere and a load of people – well several people polled up and things began to happen.

I think I've mentioned the rigid ex-pat hierarchy by service and the subsections therein. An exception was people who'd been stationed elsewhere – usually bush stations and on transfer the links were maintained. The Fort Jamieson link was clearly evident. The guests from the previous evening returned as well as others. A couple of guys came with wives and children and while the party started, they took me to one side and sort of interviewed me. The women had broken it to me that Charlie was a really nice guy, but had a serious drink problem. Fine in the bush and good at his job, but the minute he hit town he drank till he had to be hospitalised. I don't know how we managed to spend nine months seeing each other without it happening but we did.

He did keep popping into pubs where women don't or didn't go in Inverness and Fort William or wherever, but he was never drunk. It was always just to say hello to an old friend and never longer than it would take for a wee. He didn't have a car. We always had a driver. The driver was an old mate from school days, Lachie, who 'wisnae workin.'

One of the Lusaka guys was Railways and the other High Commission. Once they'd got the information they required, they made a call and another couple arrived with offspring – Hugh, a medical director at the hospital. He asked a few questions and then they had a plan – railway guy would sort out my luggage, High Commission would deal with customs and immigration and Hugh had given me a job. It was fortunate they had a children's ward with an isolation unit attached. There was not another RSCN in Northern Rhodesia. From being a staff nurse at Raigmore I was going straight into being a Departmental Sister. I would be paid more than I'd even been paid before and because my first qualification was RSCN and I had a post graduate RGN, I got the double scale payment.

Now that was sorted, Bill and his mates sorted the Braaivleis (pronounced Bryfliss) – and is a barbecue and big in life in Africa. –A UK barbecue is pathetic compared – more the meat than anything. Castle beer or Fanta to drink. Crickets chirping and all the other sounds that are Africa at night, I was sorted. I was to be picked up first thing. ──

Hugh's 'Boy' brought a letter which confirmed I had a job. Bill and I set forth for Customs, Immigration and the station. It was so easy. All in spitting distance of each other, once Immigration had stamped whatever it was I should have had, but didn't, we all strolled over to see my luggage. Customs couldn't release the crates. However, since the brown trunk contained my clothes, we could take that. What's in the blue trunk – mostly wedding presents – no that'll have to go back with the crates. Is there anything in there you might need? Well, yes there was actually – my dictionary and thesaurus. 'Have you got the keys?' They went about some other business while I rummaged in the blue trunk. I don't remember what I dug out. I remember I knew exactly where everything was in in the trunk. Years of changing rooms in nurses' homes, I'd packed so often I knew where everything would be. I had a very dinky travel iron and of course the dictionary. When Immigration and Customs came back from wherever they turned their back on me to go, I left with Bill, the brown trunk and my extra bits.

Back at Bill and Elaine's, there were two cables for me. One from my dad requiring more information and telling me he had contacted Alfred Merriweather in Bechuanaland. The second was from Alfred suggesting I travel to Molepolole. I cabled back telling Dad not to worry, I had a job and was absolutely fine and letter following. I told Alfred the same. That's how I came to be holed up in a little room, all by myself in a foreign country, my money diminishing, but with a job, accommodation and time to make up my mind what to do.

Going home is not an option. Apart from my stricken state there was my mother – don't call me Mum – mum is a deodorant. At least at a distance I wouldn't be a captive audience for her anger, shame, embarrassment and her strap lines – you are a disappointment, you're letting me down, you don't try, you should've known better, I don't know what I have done to deserve a daughter like you, bone idle, left to yourself you'd spend your life buried in a book, after all we've done for you, the sacrifices we've made. Well not her, my Dad, yes – he pleased everyone except himself, did his best, but he too was a lifelong burden she bore – not quietly, but a bleating martyr.

Getting married – I can't – I'm supposed to be thinking about it. I'm not thinking any more – I can't. I wasn't thinking of all the little Frasers with a hard-working mother and a daddy who drank. I was thinking about me. The dreadful sickening picture of him drooling in the bath having evacuated from all orifices and a stupid grin on his vacant face did it for me. I'm a nurse and I know what it means – you shovel shit and smile while you do – never let the patient see or feel anything they do is distasteful – losing control of bodily functions is the worst thing that can happen to anyone – my role is to make it something that doesn't matter, is easily sorted and make them clean, dry, sweet smelling, comfortable and laughing if possible. I'm in despair – I can't do it.

I thought about going to Molepolole, but I'm not really missionary material. I smoke and like dirty jokes and I've been taught about drinking and quite like it – in moderation – I read a lot, but not scriptures. Scrap that.

Stay where I am, wait and see and make the best of it? I'm a snivelling mess and that bloody big round shiny cake tin is leering at me. How I felt is hard to describe. The nearest I can get a frightened rabbit.

I'm a displaced person. Deposited, I will wait and see, what to do and where to go next. My room in Rhodesia was a normal utility type nurses' home cell. Perhaps a wee bit bigger and I had a walk-in wardrobe that fits all the baggage except the cake. There is a light outside. The curtains are inadequate with the rail and the fabric being the exact window width. The reason for this economy is that too much fabric is fodder for bugs. The light hits the shiny surface of the armour of The Cake and it glints. It's laughing at me. I throw a towel over it; one that I rescued from the blue trunk. The tea was on a little tray with a doily and a teapot. They didn't do mugs – mugs were definitely non-U (not upper class) in Africa. Neither did we drink out of bottles! Third World, but the niceties your granny lived by. I wonder now what briefing had been given to the other residents of the mess. Dymphna's dead now so I can't ask. It was a two-storey building – it wasn't over large – most staff lived out. There was a downstairs dining room and sitting room and a couple of bedrooms. Not a Nissan Hut exactly. I was downstairs at first. Later I was elevated to the corner room on the first floor – two windows and a bigger walk-in. –It would have accommodated the cake, but that was no piece of luck. I hadn't quite stiffened my resolve sufficiently to make my way to the dining room when, there was a bang on the door and a cheery chubby girl bounced in to show me the way.

The dining table was set for six. Chubby produced me with a grand welcoming gesture introducing two people already seated. Betty, middle-aged, twinset and pearls, clearly refined and from Aberdeen and Muriel, a pert and posh with attitude in uniform minus cap. Chubby, about my age and a Sunshine Girl on her second tour, was from the Midlands, engaged to a guy in the BOMA i.e. higher end Local Authority, her name escapes me but started with an E – Edie or Enid – I'll stick with Chubby, but the chap's name was Eric.

Eric was the person who was the butt of Colin's self-reported humorous side. I'm not sure in which service Eric did his National Service, but his mufti was always a bit despatch rider/pilot. In an oft-repeated anecdote Colin would ask if I remembered when he'd said to Eric 'Just dropped in then?' Sorry, it's an age thing – mind wandering. Colin actually had two jokes over our life together along with his ability to get drunk on one bottle of Castle beer. The inebriation led to his party trick which was a floor level demonstration using furniture, books and elaborate uncoordinated gestures on the Battle of Culloden Moor. His favourite film of all time was Zulu.

At the head of the table – well one end – you will understand later why I am not sure which end is the head at this time – I'd not met Dymphna then, is Betty. Betty Keith – twin set and pearls from Aberdeen – is in charge of Maternity. She has been in Africa for many years and there are few ex-pat children she has not delivered. She has a wide circle of friends and lives a very staid existence. She had principles my mother could applaud. Muriel, pert and posh, another Sunshine Girl – second time around has a fiancé James and he works in the High Commission. That means she can already have delusions of grandeur. I think she had them before she came.

The food arrives and thank goodness it is self-service in silver dishes so I can suit myself. As I now know – if you suit yourself, you know you're suiting somebody – Mrs Ireland coined that phrase. Muriel is on the female ward and Chubby is on the male ward. Outside the trees are pretty, but the earth is dry and all round we have a six-foot plus deep moat. It is actually a storm drain – they surrounded all houses so they didn't get flooded when the rains come. It wasn't raining at this point as it was –winter, but it was warm. Then, there is a swoosh and a flurry and a woman in a short floral dressing gown with pink ribbon ties flowing at the neck, sweeps in and takes her place at the other end of the table. She waves an arm; a boy approaches and she places her order. I'm introduced to Dymphna Aherne, who has had malaria, but was convalescent. She's just down from Abercorn and will be on male ward. She acknowledges my presence. My daughter recalls when she took us both out for a posh afternoon tea and clearly Dymphna thought she hadn't the necessary gravitas to summon a waiter, she stood up calling out, 'Young man young man.' At least it wasn't 'BOY.' Well there I am, life in ruins.

19 Central Hospital Lusaka

The hospital was 'managed' from Salisbury, Southern Rhodesia, and periodically we had a visit from the Chief Nursing Officer (CNO). Though we had more responsibility and much less red tape than in the UK, there were regulations, official ones, particularly in relation to uniforms and correspondence. Locally we had common sense and some accepted variances. In the UK it was customary when on holiday, to write to matron prior to your return to say you would be returning on a certain date. In Africa you wrote to her to say you were going, when you were to return and where you would be while you were away. We hand wrote the letter which went to admin to be typed. Once typed, it was returned for your signature. A bit like the cleaners in the nurses' homes, the boys in the office had standards. Regardless of what you wrote or to whom, your closing line was 'I am, Sir your obedient servant.'

Uniforms were stipulated. Simple, but strict. All the sisters wore white dresses with metal buttons, which we transferred each day to a clean dress. Sister in charge wore a veil – a nuisance of a flowing thing, otherwise a 'back of your head' Sister Dora cap. Footwear was brown leather lace ups; belts again were standard. However, we dressed to suit ourselves. Nurses wore hospital badges and belts with silver buckles won after three years hard labour. I never wore lace-up shoes after PTS; brown was OK by me, but flat slip on only. I was not alone; matron and assistant matron, Rose and Grace and everyone else, wore their own personal interpretation of uniform. The only time this was ever a problem was on the day when the CNO inspected and a back-door exchange system was in full swing.

Cigarettes were cheap: fifty for a shilling. A fifty-pack was a perfect fit for the top left pocket of uniform dress. Of course, we took them out and put in desk drawer on arrival. Rose told me early on that we couldn't really afford not to smoke. I smoked Life king size.

Central Hospital, known as the European Hospital, was purpose-built. The only other hospital in Lusaka was the African Hospital. The African Hospital was free. European Hospital was free if you were a government employee or family of. Otherwise it was pay as you go. We didn't have a large turnover of African patients as upward mobility status made referral to specialists in Salisbury desirable and essential. There is no elitism or snobbery to equal the height of African rising stars towards the lesser aspirational of their race. While I had some little Africans, usually too unwell to travel, my very limited experience of adults was confined to two ladies.

Both my ladies were gynaecological emergencies. The first admitted to isolation so she had a private room post-operatively. The experiences were very different. The first lady had been assisted to abort in the compound and had just needed a D&C to clear out retained products. The wives of high-achieving men often lacked formal education and found social interaction outside the compound intimidating. This poor girl was terrified and totally unable to allow a white person near her. Not even one of the aides who spoke *Chinyanja* could uncurl her from her foetal position, cling-wrapped in a sheet. However, she did respond to the nanny and only to her. My other lady could have given Mrs Bucket a ride for her money.

Mrs Mokono was the esteemed wife of a high-ranking civil servant. She had miscarried due to venereal disease and required to be isolated. I was not privy to how the GMO dealt with Mr Mokono, whether prior deliveries had brought forth syphilitic babies or whether this was a recent infection. For her entire stay we were at the mercy of her call bell. Bells were always answered promptly by the nearest person free. The bell only alerted and directed to Isolation and only once you had entered the unit, was the source highlighted. Not only did Mrs Mokono require instant gratification, which, if not met, meant a permanent finger on the button, but only a sister was fit to meet her needs. We had a further contention as we had a Sister Patel whom Mrs Mokono despised as any aide or nanny. A delicate situation in not just the limited number of white Europeans, but compounded by the time lapse between someone answering the call and after having gowned up and being dismissed, disrobing and seeking a replacement. The time between could be further extended as on the arrival of a suitable practitioner, the lady now being able to voice her requirements might well mean a further gown off, trip to base then gown on again to meet the need expressed. All because her husband's position entitled her to first-class treatment by not only the top white woman on site, but also the very best of white man medicine. The African belief that an injection superseded any other treatment meant she refused any tablets. It would have been reasonable to suppose that the massive doses of very thick penicillin being pumped into her plump bottom would have been sufficient to reassure her. Unfortunately, headache, or any kind of twinge would only respond to an injection. She was unpleasantly demanding of everyone who attended her and completely lacking in dignity, in requiring us to perform the intimate personal care nurses turn themselves outside in to deliver discreetly to avoid patient embarrassment. Because she lived in the bush, it was decided the penicillin course must be completed before she was discharged. For the entire ten days she remained bedbound by choice having full nursing care. We were glad when she went and unsurprised when she didn't leave us a box of Milk Tray.

The entire perimeter of the hospital was surrounded by a six-foot storm drain which had some extra runs just to confuse the unwary who'd suddenly discover they'd have to reverse and start again. There were three main wards, Male, Female and Maternity, Outpatients and usual offices in one wholly connected building then Children's Ward with Isolation. Main wards had three or four corridors linking the six/eight bed units and a screened veranda with more beds running along the gully side. On the inside corridor were the utilities, duty rooms, sluice, stores and theatre and delivery blocks. Outpatients was exactly as any other I ever knew; clinic rooms, waiting rooms, trolleys in corridors. There was a car park outside the main entrance which accommodated visitors, ambulances, staff cars and boys' bikes. The children's ward was attached, but if you entered from the main entrance, you'd been everywhere by the time you went through a set of swing doors and up a slope to our doors. On the way up the ramp there was no veranda, no fence, just the steep drop so not surprisingly, our children never went out unaccompanied. A trolley with a dodgy wheel could have caused a catastrophe. On entry, straight ahead was the entrance to Isolation. Turn left and you'd find yourself in a small hallway with a linen cupboard, first on the right and the duty room next, back door with kitchen opposite and the ward.

I had twenty-four beds in the Children's Ward and ten single rooms in Isolation. Not only was it mixed bathing, but medical and surgical was all in the same place. In the adult wards, mental health, rehabilitation and alcohol poisoning were all in the mix. As well as the GMOs – Government Medical Officers – there were twenty-three GPs who worked across all wards. We had several consultants. All these medics looked after their own admissions. There was no ward doctor. The facility to ask a resident or registrar was not available. The questions I would have addressed to them were up to me and when assistance was required you had to wait – and wait because their practices were widespread. Patients were admitted from places far from Lusaka. No mobile phones. Some places relied on radio. A GP might ring and ask for a bed, give the particulars, explain the reason for admission and the treatment and unless there was any reason to contact him, I might never see him. I also was in charge of my own budget and staffing. Nursing there was different. If I was a bit dependant when I arrived, it didn't last. I grew up fast.

The system worked, I was in-charge, but I had to take my turn covering nights. Two weeks out of eight was night duty, but after fourteen nights, you got five nights off and we always used the time to go places and do things. Staff complement was sisters, ward aides, nannies and boys. Sisters were graded; the grading identified by uniform differences and the role a combination of, sister, staff nurse, junior doctor, police/security. The aides were essentially kindly women, all European, who did the lesser tasks student nurses would do in the UK. Maybe if we delivered this model here now, we could fast track the 2015 delayed and stymied Transformation Agenda designed to end fifty-five years of unrest, acrimony and outright war between health and social care. Nannies were African women who sort of cleaned, fetched and carried. Orderlies would describe them in the UK. Though, interestingly, some 'boys' were nannies; lines of demarcation, between a 'boy boy,' and a 'nanny boy' were distinct. The cleaning was done by nannies and boys. Our standards were high, but the time to complete extended throughout the day. They never seemed to be finished and always 101 reasons why and ninety-nine of them down to minor altercations between nannies and boys.

Most cleaning was done just like in any other hospital, except the floors. Once the polish had been applied things were different. Our floor polishing was the pilot-show for Strictly Come Dancing. The buffing was not done with an electric floor polisher such as at Raigmore, nor with a bumper as at Sick Kids; the whole performance was carried out by pieces of blanket on barefoot boys. It started with one man and his feet then the nanny would join in. Swan Lake it wasn't, but they'd get quite animated and turn up the radio. The children loved it. Please understand, we had the tools for the job, but using the bumper was for sissies.

I only ever had female nannies at night, but they conform to habit and failing daylight brought on yawning. They succumb quickly to deep sleep. Immediately the evening tasks are complete, the nanny vanishes to the linen cupboard and you are on your own. The shelves were slatted and there was a decent gap between each to allow for the 'piles,' except the bottom shelf which was close to the floor. Under the bottom shelf, tucked up with a blanket off the shelf, is where they put themselves – a tight fit. They hear nothing and when there is a need for assistance, you have to make a real effort to arouse them. You shout and poke, but do not give in to the temptation presented by a fat bum. The reality was that it took longer to wake them and motivate than it did to feed a baby or deal with wees and drinks of water.

Hospital equipment was far more up to date than we ever had in Raigmore. The first time I ran out of oxygen tents and had to borrow from the African Hospital, the one they sent me was a revelation. So simple. No more zips to get in to tend to the patient and no more tucking in all round. When it was time for me to order, I knew I wanted one. Our respirators were advanced as well. A patient with polio was not required to be sealed in a box with just his head sticking out. We had one of these (Drinker), but I only once had to use it. The new positive pressure was much better and of course now these are all museum pieces. One night a new-born prem with disabilities had been transferred from maternity and occupied a very modern incubator which was not one of ours. The nearest description would be that it looked like the stainless steel and glass fittings in a chip shop complete with the lift-up swivel top to get to the chips. The poor little thing died shortly after I came on and I switched off the power. It was a much more complex machine with lots of dials and moving parts than I'd been accustomed to and immediately the power failed, lights flashed and loud bells rang which kind of delayed things a bit.

Africa was a revelation. I'd thought it would be grass huts, wild animals, black men in loin cloths and women with babies at breast in slings doubling as a kind of frock. Towns, I thought, would be on the lines of the Wild West with saloon bars (it was in Bechuanaland), and shops that sold everything out of sacks into paper bags. I was amazed to find Lusaka had a wide main street with angle parking. It's so easy, I don't know why it has never caught on in the UK. I'd brought supplies of things like deodorant and shampoo and Blue Grass because I'd been advised these were hard to find or not available. Though it wasn't quite Princes Street in Edinburgh, it wasn't far off. The perfumery counter was on a par and there were department stores. Just like home, the stores served different classes of people. There was a Jenner's, the Harrods of Edinburgh kind, and a John Lewis level and Co-op and C&A, but they had South African names. The stock was branded as in the UK; just the language wasn't English. Unlike today, there was no option to choose from about a dozen languages. You recognised the item by the packaging and the text was in the language of the country of origin and Afrikaans.

Most things made in England were also manufactured under licence in South Africa and bore the stamp Pty SA. That was the source of one of my disappointments. Cadbury's chocolate or Rowntree's or anyone else's did not taste the same. I loved Cadbury's Marzipan and seized on it with delight only to be cast into despair. No branded chocolate or sweets tasted like they should. I did mention it in my letters – had to talk about something, so I got little parcels with Cadbury's Marzipan and Fry's Chocolate Cream and Rowntree's Fruit Pastilles. The taste difference wasn't confined to confectionery What they did to Heinz beans was criminal, but we adapt to change. It never occurred to me then that the UK flavours were based on the wartime recipes which wasn't something that had affected Pty SA. Off Cairo Road, the Bond Street of Lusaka, were the Asian-owned stores selling fruit and vegetables and materials of all sorts. I'd no idea, brought up as I was on carrots, swede and garden peas as standard vegetables and apples and oranges as almost the only fruit, what these exotic looking fruits and vegetables were called or how one ate them.

A delicious breakfast treat was paw paw (papaya) with orange segments. On our days off we breakfasted in bed. The night before the event you convened with the Mess cook and designed your breakfast of choice to be delivered at a specific time. Orange and paw paw weren't always possible as he may not have sufficient oranges which would be a disappointment. At the appointed time I'd have unlocked the door, done what had to be done and be sitting up poised to accept the tray – a large heavy tray, with milk jug, sugar bowl and condiments, coffee pot, toast, poached egg and on lucky days the paw paw. No newspaper, no crossword. It wasn't the newspaper I missed; it was the crossword from the Observer. I didn't go long-term cold turkey, though, as my Granny used to send me the Sunday Post and my Dad would cut out the crossword and send them in batches. The papaya in the UK doesn't taste like paw paw and I think the small juicy oranges must be the wrong size for exporting because I've never tasted any like them since.

Despite all the preparatory advice, my clothes were all wrong. I did wear the dressed-up clothes in my trousseau when we were entertaining or being entertained. Otherwise we wore uniform or loose-fitting dresses. Out of doors and travelling which we did a lot, we wore shirts with long sleeves and tight cuffs, trousers tucked into socks and sturdy shoes. I lacked the long-sleeved shirts and loose frocks so was directed to the bazaars where the Asian shopkeepers sold really good quality bright cheery prints and checks very cheaply and we made our own. Believe me, I did. The high neck long sleeves and trousers kept our skin from exposure to the sun. We never sat in the direct sun, but we sat out and never wore factor anything. I never heard about sun screen till Costa del Sol package holidays became affordable. We wore sunglasses for the light, but hats were unusual. Dymphna borrowed a sewing machine – now that's a chapter on its own – and helped with the long seams but I did both of our button holes. I still have a dressing gown I made on night duty – lot of fine hand stitching.

I was settling in to this new life – not like any of my previous lives at all. Everything was new and strange, the same but different. Work, lifestyle, people and place and I too were different. The 'me' bit was difficult. In one way I felt free in a way I never done before. Inside I felt the guilt about the anxiety I had caused and the embarrassment and shame of the situation I'd put them in. I got very little mail from my mother, but Dad, after a flurry at the start, wrote to me every week. The very palpable anxiety and fears about distance, danger and potential for future disasters he relayed as emanating from my mother could only be assuaged by her receipt of regular letters of reassurance. Initially, I wrote every day, guilt-inspired reports of hour by hour activity and assurances of security, avoidance of risk and introducing all the right sort of people I came across. Once I realised mail only went out on plane days, I cut back, but I kept this up until I landed at Turnhouse in December 1962.

20 Matters Arising

I met Dymphna the night I arrived at the hospital. It took a while to establish her name was not Dippner. She was a person of great interest because she had what was rare for a nurse, albeit a midwife. She had a new car. A pale blue Volkswagen with grey seats! Not even Betty Keith had ever had a new car. If I introduced you to Grace or Rose you would understand that even they were not the sort of people who had new cars. Betty, however, looked as though nothing she had would be second-hand. The pale blue Volkswagen raised the status of the mess to previously unreached heights and maybe a hint of consumer envy because shortly after Betty took the plunge and bought a brand-new Morris Minor from the local dealership. When I did achieve personal vehicle status, it was a Morris Minor, more rust than bucket, worn seats, not quite a see-through floor. It was known as Hesperus i.e. 'wreck of.' My dad was horrified that I'd bought a car for so little and said so. Being in the motor trade, his view was that buying a second-hand vehicle meant buying someone else's troubles. In his next letter he said that maybe it wouldn't be as bad as he thought because I would not have paid purchase tax. The engine was reliable and it never let me down.

Dymphna had great skill with money – she never carried it. When she spent, she was the most generous person on this earth, but unless essential it stayed where it was – at home and out of the way of temptation. She saved, and her world travels are testament to what you can do if you do not fritter away your money. She saved enough during her first tour and worked out the cheapest way to buy a car. She bought it ex-works in Germany thus saving UK tax and import duty. Then she had it shipped at ex-works price and travelled with it as luggage in hold to Cairo. By travelling with it and having a work permit, she was not required to pay import duty.

I don't know how she persuaded the government to change her ticket to travel this way. We were ranked as government officers and free travel to our home address. If you were permanent and pensionable, you had a return ticket every three years; it was one of our perks. Permanent and Pensionable (P&P) was a status symbol and did not apply to the Sunshine Girls brought out on a 'suck it and see' basis by the Crown Agents. P&P, you travelled directly from your posting to your registered address in your home country and returned from your home to your new posting fully paid for. She didn't do London to Southampton to Cape Town then train to Lusaka. Her actual journey was Ireland to Lusaka via Germany and Cairo. She had to fund the petrol from Cairo to Lusaka so it may have been an arranged accommodation.

From Cairo she drove 4434.55 miles to Lusaka, her new posting. Going through customs in Cairo the officers couldn't believe she not only intended to drive all that way, but by herself, alone. A woman, unarmed. Such lunacy they had never encountered before. They had a confab and did a lot of huffing and puffing before they produced a panga. This was a scimitar; a sabre with a curved blade. Africans use pangas for cutting grass and scrub although they often also chop bits off each other with them. Confiscated from someone else as a 'dangerous weapon,' they presented Dymphna with it for her protection. With my experience I'd have been in melt down and absolutely known the car was about to be impounded. But then, I never had the serene aplomb that took her through customs in many lands. Her brother tells the story of her arriving in Australia with, as always, more sundry assorted luggage than a moonlight flit when he met her at customs dockside. Waving her hand vaguely she told the officer that two of the boxes contained elephant feet. He laughed with her and chalked the boxes. As they moved onwards, Dan said, 'You haven't really got elephant feet, have you?' She did. She carried the weapon under her car seat till she married Ted. It then became matrimonial property and was replaced by Ted and his revolver. For the journey stops in Africa are Government Rest Houses, where again you were accommodated free when the end route was anywhere on Government business. Somewhere on her journey, she'd been bitten by a mosquito and contracted malaria, from which she was recovering.

Her mother was a Kennedy and had a dowry! Dymphna was the first of their very large family. I can only recall eleven, but I may be one short. I never met her dad who was always referred to as PW. My perception of him is of a kind of Captain von Trapp from the *Sound of Music*. He had the large family and by all accounts, ran it on military lines. Her mum, always referred to as Mater was a small plump lady, who was very old when I met her. A very relaxed lady who allowed life to take her there. They always had help in the house, but PW controlled the spending and there was no waste. That's likely why Dymphna would eat an apple core, pips and all. It never seemed to do her any harm. I was brought up to believe that swallowing an apple pip could cause appendicitis. I imagine their house had several floors as PW bought in bulk and stored in the cellar. Including butter which apparently arrived in hessian sacks and she had to undo the stitching to get at the butter. Dymphna always made butter curls – no dumping of the butter from fridge to table on a dish. In all she did, Dymphna was exact, economical, precise and efficient.

The pale blue grey seated vehicle was a 'motor car' and anyone referring to any passenger vehicle as a 'car' was withered with a look. Just as calling a telephone a 'phone was considered a lazy abbreviation. She had serious issues with people who were 'lazy, idle and indolent,' and frequently applied the term to all of our children. I used to feel embarrassed for Hesperus and imagined him shrinking with his little orange indicators over his ears when he was referred to as 'your motor car.'

Dymphna had been posted to Lusaka following long leave. We were in a similar discipline to police and armed forces in that we went where we were told. Previously she'd been stationed in Abercorn, a bush station, where she had delivered thousands of babies of all colours. The parents of the ex-pat babies, and these babies themselves now grandparents, have followed her all the rest of her life. The 300-plus Christmas card list is stand-alone evidence of the work she did.

In all she did, Dymphna was exact, economical, precise and efficient. Dymphna could start and finish an out-patient clinic while the rest of us were passing the time of day with our first client. Troop carriers polled up one afternoon and dozens of soldiers spilled out for yellow fever inoculation and cluttered the waiting area. She directed them to two registration desks then required them to form an orderly queue.

They were to line up, facing the door and roll up left sleeve. They all reacted in military fashion bar one chap who approached her and was abruptly directed to the line. He seemed to be protesting, but after a couple more 'excuse mes' gave up and joined the line. A boy with a tray piled high with syringes led her train as she moved swiftly down the line. Swab, jab and discard in the bin of a following boy. She came to the lad who had dared attempt to step out of line. His face was swollen and one eye was an angry purple, pulsating mess, she jabbed him, looked at him and said authoritatively 'You want to get that eye seen to,' to which he replied, 'That's why I came.'

I never saw Charlie again after the Sunday after I arrived. We cancelled the wedding, but I did hear of him, more than once after that. Returning to Elaine and Bill's, there was a kind of swop, where I was drawn in and he was taken away. There was no apology, no goodbye, just a bloke needing somebody to stop him falling over. I wasn't much better and had no idea what I was going to do, but fell on my feet. Nobody condemned him, but the thread was, 'He's a really nice guy but… and he's unlikely to change.' There was a warning that by my working in the hospital at Fort Jamieson he'd be in town regularly and exposed to drink. Once he's back in Fort Jamieson, he'll be overcome and in touch. Well he wasn't and I didn't do anything either. I gave in first and wrote to say how sorry I was not to have heard from him but with regret, I was not going to sign up for life with a drunk. I said I would return the ring as soon as I could get to the central post office. I'd thought about my fare, I was then still a bit vague about who paid for the voyage, but I couldn't afford to refund it till I got paid. Anyway, it turned out to be a bit like the railways, families travel free. That was the piece of paper I should have had on the train, but didn't. Even later I discovered that my ticket was stamped Territory of Rhodesia & Nyasaland, which indicated I was sponsored anyway. I could have kept the crates and the blue trunk! But I couldn't and I wasn't. My sponsored status became invalid when I failed to marry on the Wednesday after arrival. Charlie responded to my letter and said he hadn't paid the fare and to keep the ring. I shoved the ring and its fancy gold stamped, leather box to the back of a drawer. I'd no intention of ever wearing it again. Every time I began to feel as though the nightmare was over something else would crop up and I'd be thrown back into the tumble dryer.

In the scheme of things, the next little hiccough was just that. The friend who had sheltered him and housed him was irate on behalf of his wife who had incurred excessive spending during his stay. Not only comestibles, but household items which had to be replaced. He wrote to Charlie suggesting he should reimburse her. That wasn't what Charlie thought and forwarded the letter to me with a footnote suggesting this was for my account. Just a little embarrassing as his hosts were not my hosts and I had not even met them – yet. Now it all seems very insignificant and just good training for the much more serious issues and matters that seemed to follow me.

Then, out of the blue, a courier delivered an embossed document of intention to sue for Breach of Promise. My one and only ever, complete meltdown. Can you go to prison for Breach of Promise? Even more shame on my poor parents and all who were associated with me. This time the sisters' mess rallied. First Chubby then the rest followed right up to Rose and Grace when Hugh was summoned. The poor man was medical director for both hospitals. I must have been a problem he could well do without. In short, my shift was taken over and Hugh whisked me off to a solicitor. I had to deposit the ring with the solicitor who would discredit the writ. When all the nastiness had been set aside and Charlie was dispatched back into the Bundu after being detoxed, the solicitor would return the ring to him and require him to have no further contact. What I had not known was that my colleagues had been keeping his admission under wraps to avoid upsetting me. Breach of Promise? I didn't contemplate suicide. I have since, but not then. On reflection and on the scale of things it wasn't as drastic as many things which took place in later years. All these things pouring over my head like custard because my plight was all down to my betrothal.

The ex-pat community was once again showing solidarity. I did have the opportunity to repay Hugh when he and his family went on long leave. They were going to Edinburgh so that he could complete his FRCS. He needed to find rented furnished accommodation for six months so my parents didn't just send a few addresses, but inspected and organised it. When they landed at Turnhouse my parents met them and delivered them to their flat. My mother had been apologetic about the twin beds, but that's no problem to ex-pats. It's easy to shove them together and rotate the mattresses so the join is somewhere about waist level. She saw immediately that by lending them some double-size sheets and a wool blanket as a mattress pad, all problems were solved. My Dad being in the motor trade was able to first lend Hugh a Demonstrator then a one-lady owner trade-in which he bought back when they left.

While I was engaged to Charlie, a couple called Tina and Tubby used to write to me, so I'd know people when I got to

Fort Jamieson. Well, Tina did regularly so I had in my mind a good idea what she and her husband Tubby were like and looked forward to meeting up with them. I wrote to Tina and explained matters and regretted we wouldn't be neighbours. Although we'd been places and done things and shared experiences by airmail, we had not exchanged photographs. One night when I came on-duty, there were two strangers sitting in the corridor. The person I was relieving said, 'these two are here to see you from Fort Jamieson.' Bewilderment. Who on earth are these odd people? I did both ward rounds, hands behind back like you do, passing them between Children and Isolation, I nodded and smiled. All the time, I'm scrambling my head as to who they were and what on earth I'm going to say.

The day staff left – now what? I invited my guests whom I had decided could only be Tina and Tubby to join me in the office. After the initial pleasantries I offered tea which was accepted. The wards were quiet and the nanny was my sole sleeping partner for the night. I went into the linen cupboard and called, then poked the nanny who was asleep under the bottom shelf. In her own time the nanny delivered the tea on a tray with doily and teapot.

Neither T lived up to the picture I'd built in my head, during the earlier correspondence. Tubby wasn't in the least robust. He was certainly short, but not tubby at all. He was stunted, skinny, dyspeptic and visibly squirmed while Tina lied through her teeth. Tina wasn't teeny either, she overshadowed him by almost a foot and he would be totally eclipsed if he were behind her. Plastered with pan-stick (combined cream and face powder best applied with a trowel), she had bare legs and coloured nail varnish on her toes!! Please know that heat or no heat we all wore stockings. Tights and pop socks are a lovely modern invention but not then. In my Scottish Presbyterian perception, she looked like a barmaid and no better than she should be. I could see why she and Charlie were friends – liked a drink. That was partly the tone of the petition – likes a drink. Stilted on my part, hers was an emotional plea around Charlie's heartbreak. His being tired through overworking to add his days off to his local leave so we could have a honeymoon resulted in his being not well when he came to Lusaka. Charlie's unconfined joy while waiting for me wrecked by his having a drink. There had occurred, an unforeseen, unexpected, unusual and unfortunate blip. Tubby wriggled; I was sufficiently unaffected to think of asking if he 'needed to go.' I never let slip the recent episode which necessitated admission, nor did I bring to their attention the Breach of Promise case and the combined settlement and non-molestation. We parted amicably. I would be thinking things over and in complete agreement as to what a lovely life we'd have if we were all in Fort Jamieson together. I knew she knew and Tubby was visibly relaxed that I was not about to think at all. My mind was made up. I did not raise the matter of the failed troth plight.

I was on yet another night duty stint when –Charlie was admitted to be sobered up again. I did not know till the last morning when I was putting my gear into the boot of Betty Keith's new car. We were off to Salisbury. Betty never did night duty – supreme seniority, but she had the week off too and was taking me to meet some friends on a farm where they grew tobacco. One of the doctors stopped to pass the time of day and said in passing he'd discharged Charlie back to Fort Jamieson. A regular customer, but one who always pays his bills! I don't recall it ringing a bell then, but that meant Charlie was going private for his alcohol treatment – he should have been under the GMOs. I heard nothing more till back in the UK when news filtered that he'd bought a pub in Salisbury (now Harare). Sobriety was mentioned. Last I heard was he'd died and left all his money to his nieces – I could have been the merry widow of a drunk was the message that accompanied the news.

21 Broadening my Horizons

The sisters' mess immediate social alliances were with the police and Army. Once Dymphna got together with Ted, education was open to us. Muriel having James in the High Commission brought invites to better-quality events. We made friends with patients and their families who although not of our circle, invited us to a 'thank you' braaivleis (barbeque). Anything was an excuse for a get-together. The Olympic Flame in 1948, was not my sole public performance – I did ambulance duty at the airport when the Queen Mother came in 1959, and got to do my stuff when the Lord Chief Justice ricked his knee getting out the plane; not her plane though. If you ever saw the film with Alistair Sims – *The Best Years of our Lives* – that was what could happen to us and did. It was about a boys' school evacuated to a girls' school and a need for neither parent to know their precious child could be morally corrupted. So, rugby posts were swapped for goal posts and all sorts of joint activities had to become single sex for the short period. Mayhem. Royal visits are the same. The Queen Mum leaves Salisbury and is seen off by the Lord Chief Justice and other dignitaries with a full Territory of Rhodesia and Nyasaland remit. The minute her plane takes off, they sprint to another and manage to land in Lusaka before her. When she sweeps down on to the tarmac the very same line up, she left in Salisbury is waiting to be introduced again and shake her hand, again. She came on the Queen's Flight – a lovely red plane.

I wasn't really all that chuffed about having to deal with the locked knee of the Lord Chief Justice (LCJ). I was there with my ambulance and as was customary and in order to ensure a good view, I sat on the bonnet. The dignitaries' plane landed and we were being summoned to the plane steps when he injured himself and my pressing thought was not the great man, but that I'd miss seeing the Queen Mum. I think her plane must have been made to circle a bit. In the time before it landed, I'd summoned James MacPherson, our orthopaedic surgeon. He did a twist-and-click and I was back on my perch and the Lord Chief Justice was first in the line to be introduced as she swayed down the plane steps. They had one more stop before they left the territory.

Anyway, the Police and Army. I think we were sort of regarded as escorts, although we were very carefully looked after. When an invitation came, those of us who were free would accept and be picked up by a uniformed escort. While both Army and Police required the blue dress (my only really suitable trousseau frock) kind of get-up, our return fights were much less formal. On arrival you were announced and a chap in full dress ushered you away and offered you a drink. Expected was a small sherry. Clearly, they didn't know whisky was the only clean drink. Stilted small talk and limited mingling was the order till dinner was announced. A very formal, four or five courses with wine meal. There was always a toast to the Queen. White gloves were worn for dancing. After dinner things relaxed a bit and we could mingle. I was never formally introduced to the man I later married because he did not attend the dinners because he did not drink. He did not drink, not because he was teetotal or anything, but because if a drop of alcohol crossed your lips in the mess, you had to pay a full share of the bar bill. He was saving up. I encountered him when involved in a later incident.

Rivalry was rife, and an incident had taken place during which Regimental Colours were ripped from the flagpole, unseen and unheard. The Police were suspected.

An Army WAG (Wife and Girlfriend), not one of us, was charged with locating it to avoid consequences. Once the spirits had risen, careless talk revealed the location. It was necessary for the party to spill over into the living/sleeping quarters where apparently 'the flag' was in a sock drawer. Chubby and I were delegated to act as decoys. She got into clinch on the stoep with the owner of the sock drawer, while I had to watch out for anyone approaching.

One man, Colin, had obviously been for a shower – very damp, bare-chested, wet towel round his neck. I'd never met him, but he had to be stopped and the best I could think of was to suggest he walk off with me in the opposite direction and show me how to get back to where I should be. Just at that point the WAG shot out from the bedroom and she and I shot off leaving Chubby canoodling and the half-naked chap bemused and went back to the party. We heard about the incident next day.

The Army retaliated and a pair of green frilly knickers was seen flying from the Police flagpole causing unrest in both camps. Actually, it was a great deal more than unrest as in both camps, the flagpole and whatever it was dressed in was totally sacrosanct and could invoke serious punishment. Only if the perpetrator could be apprehended, of course.

At the hospital there was much rejoicing, somewhat dampened by the possible suspension of these events due to lack of supervision and inappropriate behaviour. It all blew over though as such things do and normal service resumed.

Hospital parties were not a bit like the barrack ones. We were due a return bout in both directions. Chubby asked Grace Pullen, who, as assistant matron, managed catering, and knowing we'd have to pay, asked 'What's the cheapest way to feed a lot of people?' Mince and jelly. That's what we did – spaghetti bolognaise, cheese and beer. Informal and fun, we always got a good turnout, but never the man I would marry.

Sometimes individual party members would invite us out to the cinema. Known as the Bioscope, always old films, the entrance looked like the foyer at Sadler Wells. We really did dress up to go to the pictures. A rarity, the Bioscope had air conditioning. I learned fast. You entered the foyer from the heat of the day in your off the shoulder finery to be thrown into a freezer. I used to throw my camel coat over my shoulders so that once inside I could breathe lovely cold air but not get frostbite.

I discovered Founders' Week was a bit like Thanksgiving in the USA. In July, it was a pageant, party week and Grace was doling out ingredients for it one day when I passed through the kitchens. The kitchen boys were to make fruit cakes for the wards for the festive meal.

"Stop – lock it all up again – I have the very thing," I said. I offered them the cake. Once she was sure I meant it, two boys removed it and were to set to with a tin opener.

Its absence made my room much bigger. Cecil Rhodes was never feted with such a lavish cake, nor anyone else before or since. I gave not a thought to the master confectioner or the art work, I just felt light. It was a lovely cake – moist, with perfect marzipan and many people enjoyed it. The tin opener didn't work. Ticky cut his finger and Grace had to deal with the drama so she sent for PWD (AKA Procrastination, Waste and Destruction) and it took a hammer and chisel to get started, but the cake was undamaged. I was asked if I wanted to have a look. It felt like an invitation to view the late departed. I hadn't seen the cake before it went in the tin so I'd never properly known it. The nearest I got was a picture of the wedding cake of Princess Elizabeth and Philip of Greece as made by my mother's friend's husband. I declined. For three months, that cake in its silver casket, had followed me, leered at me, and tripped me up. Sometimes I felt it was reproaching me, disapproving and condemnatory – Cecil Rhodes week was a good cause.

Special occasions were frequent. We were a mixed bag and every country has a national day and we picked up on most of them. The Queen's Official Birthday was a very high holiday. I don't think I'd noticed it before Lusaka. That was one of the better-quality events in that we were entertained at Government House. It was a lot of mingle, very little munch, but a wide variety of alcoholic beverages. We were in the run up to Independence and there was a gradual assumption of roles by African civil servants. The 'boys,' wearing a fez and white gloves, bore silver trays set out with a variety of drinks. Wine of various colours and spirits of all sorts were on each tray, but no beer. As they sort of dipped and swooped into your little conversation group, you checked they had what you were drinking. If the tray on offer didn't meet your needs, there'd be another along in a minute. The wife of a newly-promoted African mistook the proffered tray as a delivery, sat down on a sofa, drank the lot and fell asleep. It was all over when I got there except for the spectacle. The woman had what had been an elaborate headpiece. It still was, but no longer on her head. With her legs akimbo, she was fast asleep on a sofa. By her side, on a colonial-style beaten brass occasional table, was a silver salver with over a dozen dead lipstick smeared glasses. Another wrong thing we did – too fast and too soon – our way not their way.

The first African train driver was reported as saying that £80 a month was far too much money. He had more than enough money for food and already had a bicycle. You might think he was going to be prudent, but that is unlikely. They were not used to money and had no idea how to spend it after they'd paid for 'scoff' (food). Our boys were a perfect example. Every penny after basic food supplies and 'relish' went on Kaffir beer to the extent that they would be unfit to work for days. Kaffir beer was drunk out of buckets. Not real buckets, but large pottery vessels of the size of a bucket. Relish was a supplement to the staple diet of mealie meal porridge. Relish was on offer in the Asian stores.

Although they bought tins and packets from the shelves, most of their purchases were in open sacks. Open sacks on the ground outside. Handy leaning posts for roaming dogs to lift a leg. No relish ever appealed to me; it all looked mouldy, maggoty and smelly. Biltong was strips of dried meat much enjoyed by Afrikaners. Quite a lot of Europeans developed a taste for the brands sold in the more up-market establishments. Sacks of little fish like whitebait from Lake Tanganyika, buzzing with flies, were another. Dried fruit, sometimes glacé and others just dehydrated were relish. African staff were paid monthly. However, even the government didn't pay just once

225

in a month. Salaries might be say, £6 a month then £1 or £2 a week depending on family size, for scoff money. On pay day they bought scoff then Kaffir beer so they were strapped for cash before the end of the week. They had desperate need of next Friday's scoff money. If during the month they might have come by some extra dosh and had even a small amount of beer, it was virulent and you could tell straight away.

White women, being a minority, were much sought after for entertainment purposes. Police and Army events were good to go to as were receptions in the main, but international journalists we only did once. There was a Summit Conference in relation to the coming Independence when Northern and Southern Rhodesia would become Zambia and Zimbabwe. Matron was asked if she could provide partners for the big-name journalists and six of us were duly collected by limousines. Matron thought we were to partner them at the official dinner, but we weren't. The journalists had not been invited to the dinner. Journalists, when abroad. apparently expect ladies to be provided for their entertainment and pleasure. The cars did not, as expected, take us to Government house, but to the Ridgeway. The Ridgeway was THE hotel and watering place for anyone who was anyone in Lusaka, black or white. Introductions were made and drink taken, but soon it became clear that the bedroom was the next stop. Stop it dead and the cars were recalled to take us back to the mess. Dymphna in her usual forthright language made it clear that we were a courtesy not courtesans and it may well be that their editors could hear of their behaviour. Shifty probably describes the group who saw us off. As our spokesman, she duly provided Matron with a full unexpurgated report and we heard that as a result Matron contacted the High Commission who were responsible for the invite. That was not the end of the matter and apologies flowed and a further invitation extended for a day out to see Africa. Urged to forgive and forget and not cause an international incident, off-duty was switched, and we had a mini safari day a la posh.

22 Children's Ward

Being given the children's ward was pure luck, but for my experience, ideal. I had six years history of working with children against only two of adult care. At Sick Kids we were loud in our views that a six-week secondment as part of general training was insufficient exposure to children to give the nurses any kind of competence. They could not be thrown into the deep-end. They were all in their final year of training and in terms of superiority theoretically in a place slightly short of a staff nurse. We felt they were nannied too much and got to pick and choose. They were certainly cared for ahead of us.

In our sluices we had a very heavy drop-down foot pedal operated bedpan washer. Sometimes inadvertently when counting out dirty linen for the clip holder checker, your foot would hit the pedal. Seeing as how you were bent double anyway, the weighty drop down suddenly connected with the back of your head. It only happened to me once and knocked me out. You do see stars. No further mention was made once I'd been castigated for being so clumsy and warned to avoid doing it ever again. I had a lump and a headache and my friends were sympathetic. Three days later it happened to a nurse from the Royal on her six-week fast-track Sick Kids training. Though she didn't knock herself out, the ward came to an immediate standstill. She was wheelchaired up to sick bay. Staff returning from visiting later reported that she had been X-rayed, had an ice-bag on her head and hospital transport would return her after twenty-four hours to the nurses' home at the Royal for convalescence. Cosseted is not the word for it.

Comparing my general experience, it was abundantly clear to me that I could never have been entrusted to be in charge of an adult ward. Just as the nurses from the Royal were treated to a short sharp introduction to children, ours had not been significantly different with regard to adults. The two years I spent between Western, Eastern and Northern hospitals, in different specialist areas bypassed the grounding gained as a probationer. As PG student nurses we had an average of four years practical experience and the usefulness of a State Registration. Particularly on night duty we were useful because just two sisters oversaw several hundred beds. Management were making the best use of our skills, but to the detriment of our practical patient interaction.

In Lusaka then, we were the mini-doctors of today. In the hospital itself there were clinics run by the GMOs, but off site we were on our own. Though we did little blood taking, anything else was on our list. Bloods needing more than the doctor's DIY had to go to Salisbury so it was a procedure timed to coincide with plane days and a courier system comparable to organs being transported for transplant. We cross-matched and measured haemoglobin, but nothing else.

We had disposable syringes in Africa. In the UK we boiled needles and syringes for twenty minutes after each use. The UK Dangerous Drugs Act 1959 (DDA) applied to syringes in Africa. Syringes were issued by Pharmacy, signed for, used, returned and signed for. We could not carry stock on the ward. Our emergency stock was locked up and part of our daily inventory. The returned and signed-for was draconian. There was no delay between handover of a used syringe and mass destruction with a blunt instrument which pulverised it.

Despite this, local nurses and orderlies did a brisk trade in £1 injections. The ordinary African set store by 'white man's mootie' (medicine) and had absolute faith in an injection. All they required to provide this service, was an empty penicillin bottle and a syringe. Off-duty they ran clinics and quickly graduated from bicycle to car owner. It was apparent when on the African hospital campus that there were more cars than at ours. Sisters not resident in the mess were collected by hospital transport and delivered home again afterwards. Two car families in the ex-pat community was rare.

I'm glad I never had to work in the African hospital because I really didn't like the workings of it. I'd poke my nanny to wake her up when she was asleep under the shelves of the linen cupboard during the night, but never kicked her. The disdain and casual cruelty meted out by the African nursing staff and orderlies to patients and relatives I found abhorrent. More of the African hospital was veranda than ward and under the beds on the veranda were the relatives who had accompanied the patient to hospital. Approaching a bed to deal with a patient, any adult or child lurking underneath would be kicked sharply. I don't think Africans ever suffer from insomnia. As the sun goes down, so do they. Even when it's daytime, the ability to sleep overcomes them if they are not on foot. They were equally supercilious within the hierarchy. During my time in Africa, no African doctor worked in the African Hospital. I was told that no self-respecting African would ever take such a post and elsewhere they had only private patients. The nursing staff didn't do much nursing either as personal care was wholly the remit of the relatives and lower-class Africans.

During the day our association with the African hospital was fairly normal. They might ring and ask if I could lend a cot or some piece of equipment and I'd send a boy or a driver to deliver. At night the only contact was in person. I ran out of oxygen tents so I rang and I rang until I gave up. I woke a driver and we went. There weren't even any scavenging dogs. He knew better than I, and went straight to their sleeping place. There he did his 'I am superior; get up and serve me' act. And I got the loan of the new-style German oxygen tent of which I was so envious. A very positive thing in Lusaka was that when you indented, within your budget of course, you were not confined to one UK provider. The world was your oyster. My first splurge was one of the German tents and an incubator. In the UK, our incubators were little more than a glass case with a lid containing the baby, a warm mattress and a gas pipe from cylinder to the corner of it.

Children's Ward in Africa, had children of all ages, medical and surgical, brown, white and mixed race, but few African. The long-held belief that the Devil spawns' twins, despite all the missionaries, colonisation and education thrived. If by chance twins were delivered by community midwives, arrangements would be quickly made for one or both babies to be placed out of harm's way. In the bush a common way out was for the mother to deliver both and leave one behind for the Devil to reclaim. In other cases, they just ignored one until it died. When twins were born at the African hospital, a common outcome was that the mother, with one or sometimes no babies, fled back to the bush. These and other spare babies were discharged into the care of a foreign mission establishment. Lusaka had fourteen established religious varieties with a membership sufficient to warrant at least one meeting place in town and outreach stations in the bush. The fourteen I am sure about because within the staff complement that is the number the drivers who provided transport to and from them on Saturday or Sunday.

I had only one African twin baby and her survival was a testament to our determination that this baby would not die. The malnourished twin was picked up at a bush clinic, discovered by the nurse running the clinic because she remembered delivering the mother of twins. She was presenting one baby for vaccination, but where was the other? Where was Granny? Something wasn't right. After giving birth the mother breastfed until she was about ready to give birth again. Granny stepped in, took over and weaned while mum started the process all over again with the next one. Mum was defensive, but an older child, pointed her out. Granny had a tiny skeletal infant tucked into her dangling flap of a dry breast – the other baby. This little scrap was fourteen months old and moribund. She came in directly from the outside clinic.

I'm never comfortable watching the television appeals for help to rescue starving babies. I'm like that because the assumption is that once we've donated sufficient to provide the nourishment delivered by pipette that they'll all live happily ever after. It isn't that simple. If you do manage to minimise the pain and distress and achieve recovery, it is a long journey and normality is – the luck of the draw. My treatment plan of choice would have started by maintaining the skin-on-skin contact with Granny which was scuppered because Granny scarpered along with mother and the rest of her brood. I needed a doctor, but immediate action was necessary if he wasn't to have a wasted journey. No matter how small, soft and cosy a cot, the fear and anxiety, strange smells and foreign voices could have ended her life. I initially hijacked a reluctant nanny as being the nearest smell to Granny and subsequently bribed her to replace her. There was a kind of 'hands-free' contact system between mothers and grannies and babies. A mother with a child in a sling with free access to breast at all times, carrying a heavy gourd of water on her head while her arms swung in time to the swaying of her body as she walked from well to home was a common sight. The African superiority to those of a lesser standing for nanny was a barrier and while she would deal competently with a white nappy, what we were asking was way beyond her comfort zone. We didn't rush into any invasive and hyper-active intensive care procedures, but started with parenteral hydration and planned introduction of nutrition. We called her Mary and baptised her just in case. Once she was stable, we weaned her from the nanny who had warmed to her role and brought her into the ward with the other children. She left us when she had graduated to bottled milk and Farex, smiled and chunnered and could sit up, supported. She went to a mission orphanage in Chilanga, but never came back to our clinic so we never knew how she developed.

I was called in on my day off to fly to an outstation to bring in a toddler with diphtheria – he'd had an emergency tracheotomy. I had never flown before. I'd never even been to the airport. I didn't know it was a kind of part-time affair. I was dropped off at the entrance with all my kutundu (baggage). The place was locked up and deserted and the driver had gone. When I eventually found a boy watering the surrounding grass, we had to part sign, part English, part kitchen Kaffir exchange. The outcome was that the only plane going anywhere was parked in the distance. A bit of a remote speck. I had to cart my oxygen, suction and sundries for quite a way from the runway. Hot and bothered, I found the pilot polishing his windscreen. He was a really kind and helpful chap. He explained about the airport only being open on plane days and any other time air travel was by charter. I had no idea where we'd be going. Rose had told me, but it meant nothing apart from it being the furthest away we covered. Though it would be a long flight, still in the province, we had to cross the Belgian Congo, one of the current trouble spots. The plane was a four-seater but two seats had been removed to make room for the gear. Apart from my stuff the only equipment was a wire stretcher.

The pilot never asked if I'd flown before and there was no pre-flight safety information. I was strapped in and with full co-pilot gear of shoulder webbing as for a back pack, which required adjusting to size; the buckles were not clunk- click. My pilot had headphones and I just listened second-hand to the chat between him and air traffic control which took place once he had switched on and revved up. Cleared for take-off, we kangaroo hopped – this was not No. 1 runway – and then I saw the ground fall away. We were airborne. Once airborne, the pilot took off his headphones and kept his hands off the controls. I dared to ask how far and how long the journey would take and he explained it depended on wind speed. He said the Congo was more ground than air missiles. Safety gear for if we crash landed in the bush? Apparently, he normally carried webbing so that once landed you could spell out an

SOS, but he hadn't room for any of that when it was a mercy flight. He hadn't even brought his lunch. I worried quietly.

I could see quite a lot of wildlife. He asked if I'd ever seen 'crocs' and as we suddenly went into a dive, death stared me in the face and my stomach hit the floor. He only wanted me to get a good view. I'd kind of got used to this as over the hours he showed me all kinds of herds of animals. A herd of zebras was grazing and then a herd of buffalo thundered along and seemed to keep up with us. Why was I not cock-a-hoop at getting a free safari? Still you can get complacent and nearing our destination, losing height and circling suddenly and without any warning the wings began to jerk up and down as little boys do at weddings. 'I'm just letting them know I need petrol.' My bladder was causing me severe tonsillitis, it was so full by this time, wholly due to sheer terror. A bit of empty bush and a lot of bumps and we were down.

In Africa, you can have wide empty spaces without sign of man or habitation, some minor activity occurs and there are more people than Wembley Stadium. This is one of the amazing things that take place anytime and anywhere in the middle of nowhere. One time, Chubby and I were returning to the mess when an ex-pat child on a bike fell off some way ahead. We did an emergency stop and approached on foot. She later said you had to be sure to be a long way off or you'd be lynched for knocking the kid off. There was no habitation in sight, back, front or either side, but as we reached the scene and I picked up the bleeding child, men women and children were approaching from all sides. We legged it back to the car where Chubby threw the bike – not a large one – into her boot and we screeched off to casualty.

Avoiding attracting a crowd was always forefront in our minds and Africans on bicycles were a regular hazard. What Africans can transport on a bicycle is worthy of a chapter, but I will contain myself and tell you about the double bed. Africans do not have lights on bicycles so in the dark any glimmer of red from a reflector and you make a wide detour. This night I just had a feeling, could have been air speed or flow sounding wrong, but I crossed to the wrong side of the road. There was no back reflector, it was obscured by a frock. When my headlights did their job – oh, for a mobile phone and a picture – a small girl was standing on the saddle, arms held high to support a double bed while the cyclist stood on the pedals taking them wherever.

Back to the mercy flight. By the time the engine stopped there was a crowd commensurate with an independence rally and a few Land Rovers. I stretched my legs and asked where the toilets were. That was pre-supposing there was one and was directed to a locked shed. Oh yes, but the shed only opened on plane day and that was not today. My pilot was very blasé and waved an airy hand towards the bush, indicating I had the whole of Africa to choose from. He had a word with the petrol chap and I got a lift to somebody's Picaninny Kaya– (little house i.e. toilet). I was back and my equipment in position when the jeep with the patient arrived. We then had to re-arrange as the mother was coming too. Not even a drink and we were on our way.

Crouched on the floor, mostly on my knees, the distressed tot was very wet and the next two hours were not comfortable. The stretcher was metal mesh and that is bruising. The mother was an enigma. She wasn't helpful on the journey – try balancing on your knees and managing a manual suction nozzle and swopping to oxygen and dabbing drips. To be fair, we didn't do any swoops for animal watching on the return journey. Our arrival time was radioed ahead and an ambulance was waiting. I unwound myself – no safety harness this time – and got myself and patient to the ambulance along with our gear so we were good to go, but the mother had already gone. I thought perhaps the friends who picked her up would bring her to the ward. They didn't and we never saw her again. She did not fill in the admission form and nobody enquired after him and nobody visited. He was three years old. We know she returned home because there was a bit of activity regarding infection control. He did well and I sent her handwritten (I used to write very nicely) updates every plane day. But she never came back and he was returned like a parcel with a stranger.

23 More Children

I'd only ever learned about rabies in class but not experienced it. Few people ever do. In 1960 playing in their garden, some children spotted a dead dog in their swimming pool. Alerted by his children, Daddy did what daddies do and lifted it out. The children were warned to stand well back while the body was wrapped and sent for a post-mortem and the pool emptied. There had been no bite so he didn't start anti-rabies shots, just in case, as most ex-pats would have done. When the family was contacted with a positive result, it was too late, he was already sick. The outcome was inevitable. Had the Ebola protective suits as seen on TV in 2018, been invented or the materials created, that was the level of infection control required to protect against rabies. Nobody with as much as a healing pimple was allowed to take part in his care. The whole family, their cook, garden boy and all with whom he had contact at work commenced anti-rabies injections immediately. He wasn't 'government' which must have, but should never have led to the delay in his receiving the results. In the normal run of things, the South African and international corporation employees were super cared for medically and in every other way well ahead of government employees.

My role was not hands-on, but to implement and police the care plan. The far end of the isolation ward was isolated reducing my bed availability to five. Those caring were isolated along with the patient and the first cut off cubicle became an exchange depot for food, washing, and other equipment. Staff had been scrutinised for any skin abrasions and provided with a written schedule of 'Caring for patients with Rabies.' The only occasional admittance was to the doctor. The chosen care staff were started on anti-rabies injections before they took up residence.

One of the Afrikaner nurse aides told me that I should go into the room three times a day in full protective gear with a basin of water and flick a few drops at him. When he snarled at me, I'd know how far gone he was. Almost everyone I saw during his stay had a horror story to tell about rabies. It wasn't like any of that at all – it was just very sad. On arrival, he was clearly very sick and almost comatose. The window for nursing comfort was very short and he died within a few days.

Maybe he was lucky by being very sick with aching limbs and a high temperature and being treated for tick bite fever before the diagnosis, thus not realising he was dying. He was though. The only rabies patient during my tenure. Even a lick from an unknown dog and the whole anti-rabies treatment came on stream. People tended to be hypervigilant. A woman in outpatients was insisting on injections because she'd been scratched by a cat. Unable to tolerate the hysteria brought on by a tiny reddened but not blooded wrist, Dymphna asked her, 'was it a known cat?' Domestic animals were routinely vaccinated. There were always a goodly number of people on daily rabies jabs without consequence.

...

I was gutted when Bindie, a little Asian girl died. She was admitted in a comatose condition with a temperature of 106 and a diagnosis of PUO (Pyrexia of unknown origin). She was immediately 'specialled' and we put all we had into making sure she recovered. We had three tricky days before we were back on track. She was really bonny and a favourite with us all. One of the ones you miss when they leave the ward. Two days after she skipped out clutching her dolly, red ribbons in her hair and patent dancing shoes, she was dead; killed in a car accident. A stupid unnecessary avoidable head-on collision.

There were far more serious road traffic accidents in Northern Rhodesia than warranted by either volume of traffic or the roads. In town there was tarmac on Cairo Road and the trading street behind. Out of town, north, south and east, the road became a strip road. All roads were straight. You could see for miles. No dog legs or hairpins. The road was two strips of tarmac whereon you set your wheels and put your foot down. When a cloud of dust signalled an oncoming vehicle, your nearside tyres left the tarmac and you were one on tarmac and one on dirt. Once passed you went back to the easier and less dusty ride on the strips. The accidents were almost all head-on collisions. This was not the uneducated African in his first car. These boy racers were grown-ups playing chicken and leaving the strip too late to avoid written-off vehicles, bodies wrecked and the dead. Bindie had been with her uncles who also died.

Smashed elbows were the most common injury we saw in outpatients. Air conditioning had not been invented for cars, in fact you could only experience it in the poshest shops, Government House and the High Court. Some houses would have slow moving fans circulating the ambient hot air. We drove with the window down, elbow on sill, fingers clasped on the roof. The sheer delight of the cool breeze was only second to the icy sharpness of methylated spirits in shoes. Rebuilding elbows was hit and miss and much more miss than hit.

Our surgeons were general surgeons and any really fancy stuff went south to Salisbury. Orthopaedics and general accident surgery were not 'specialist' and orthopaedic meant the entire body. Maureen, a primary school teacher friend used to get overheated when it was suggested that despite teaching the whole curriculum, she was less qualified than those who taught one subject in secondary school. A relative began having joint problems and began with a wrist surgeon and by the time she really got going she had one for every possible joint that could be replaced. It wasn't like that in Lusaka. We were however a specialist eye hospital by virtue of Malcolm who could perform fast, magic sight restoration. The Africans were the main beneficiaries as they had dreadful eye conditions which caused blindness but with Malcolm's skill sight could be restored. He also had a large private practice and paying patients from all over Africa would travel to have surgery.

Mary was the sister in charge of theatre and long-standing mistress to Malcolm. Malcolm's wife, who may not have been but looked around thirty years older than he was, had for a number of years been unwilling to divorce him. Colin, my husband had a close friend who was a vet. That vet's wife's best friend was the wife of the eye surgeon whom he left to be with Mary. That meant that sides were taken. Strangely enough, in these semi-formal days I only ever knew the vet's wife, a South African as Mrs Van der something. Malcolm was a really happy-go-lucky chap and they had a lovely daughter whom he adored and who Majorie was not very keen of. Two things – she loved her dad and was a tomboy. Whenever we visited the Van ders, Malcolm's wife was in attendance, wearing her disapproval, disgust and determination not to let him get away with leaving her for Mary, like a shroud. On return visits her friend was always making snide remarks and seeking insider gossip. I could not help at all. I didn't work in theatre and I never came across either of them. I lied. Malcolm and Mary had regular Braais and any other excuse for a party to which we were all invited. Malcolm was invited to lecture at Moorfields in London so he and Mary went off for a short UK break. Unsure how it happened, but shortly after their return we were invited on posh ivory card with red text to – their wedding as Malcolm made an honest woman of Mary.

…

Yusuf had been swinging on the tail gate of his uncle's lorry. He wasn't quick enough jumping clear when it reversed. He was as near dead when he came in as he was a couple of weeks later, but he didn't die. Mr Macpherson removed his spleen; a lobe of his liver and he was returned to the ward to wait and see what happened with all the lesser bits and his head injury. He got no worse, but everything was wrong; his breathing, his temperature, his movements, and his level of consciousness. Time moved on and two weeks had passed. His family were in despair, and visitors to the ward were asking, 'How's Yusuf?' and by look and gesture wondering how it was he was still with us. There were dozens of religions in Lusaka which had clerics, priests, pastors, ministers, vicars and every other sort as well as medicine men and witch doctors. Yusuf's lot had gone and I was just looking at him when Father Murphy came on to do a bit of blessing around those with his star on their chart. He asked how he was. He told me he'd say Mass for him that morning. Shortly after an Anglican passed by and I told him what Father Murphy had said and he said in the grandiose superior style of the competition, 'We, too, will pray for Yusuf.' At 11am Yusuf opened his big brown eyes and said 'bookah'(hungry). That was it – he romped on and what was left of his liver, his squashed insides and fractured pelvis and hips all sorted themselves out.

I got a call from a school saying they were bringing in a girl who'd pushed her arm through a pane of glass and was badly cut. They could not get hold of the parents. I prepared a bed and alerted theatre. She was very shocked and her arm was wrapped in a grotty tea towel. I didn't like the look of her, so I spoke to the duty surgeon and said I didn't think we could wait for the parents. He said he'd go straight to theatre. I didn't touch the grotty tea towel, just removed her bloody clothes and put a gown on her good arm. I continued to try to find the mother as we'd established Daddy was out in the bundu. In theatre they set up a transfusion and as he undid the tea towel she virtually bled out. Sometime later the mother arrived.

I reassure her all was under control, offering tea and started to take the details. I did not ask where she had been. We get to religion and she said, Jehovah's Witness. My heart sank and I could see me and the surgical team in court. I firmly wrote in red – NO BLOOD TRANSFUSION. I excused myself to see where the nanny was with the tea – no way could I use the phone. I pelted down the veranda corridor and as I turned the corner there was the anaesthetist and a theatre orderly pushing a trolley with a little patient and a bag of blood. I blurted out my tale and dashed back. They reversed back, squeezed the rest of the blood into her and saline was running through when she came back to the ward. I thought I saw a pink tinge, but nothing was said. A few months later the mother had a hysterectomy and her religion was given as Baptist.

An older girl admitted for a ruptured appendix was another Jehovah's Witness and banned from any blood transfusion. She'd had a massive bleed and was so weak as to be barely able to lift up her head. The family hardly left her side – possibly just in case we slipped in a pint. There had been words spoken with the medics, but all they would allow was intramuscular iron. Her recovery took months rather than half an hour.

Doctors were not a permanent presence in the hospital. Although they did clinics and surgeries, they could only be called out of hours if there was an emergency. Out of hours had no casualty so customers would arrive and attract the attention of one of the wards who would deal with their emergency. Firstly, you established whether the patient was Government or Private. Thereafter you dealt with them as appropriate.

Dymphna and I quickly became friends and when her cousin Joe, a vet, went on long leave, we moved into his house as caretakers. We had parked and were walking towards the entrance one evening when a Game Warden Land Rover skidded to a stop and a blood-soaked driver tumbled out. I dived for the man in stinking bloody rags while Dymphna made for the phone/trolley/help. As his blood was saturating my uniform, I heard her bellow 'Government or Private?'

We were a good team, but as I was on my first 'tour' I tended to get the messy jobs. The warden had been mauled by a lion. He'd decided it was quicker to get to hospital under his own steam than wait for an ambulance; a good decision. He'd lost a lot of blood, needed a lot of stitches and immediate transfusions. We were short of blood so that night two members of staff lay down beside him and they did a direct transfusion. When done this way there isn't an exact 'stop when you reach the fill line'; they tended to be rather generous and only stopped when the donor began to look more exsanguinated than the patient.

Lions teeth are particularly filthy and the foul smell on the tattered bits of clothing sticking to his bits, meant instant recognition of the cause of his injuries. His wounds became infected making him very ill. When he left hospital, he said we should visit his game reserve and he'd show us the parts others never got to see.

24 Going Places

During the tumult of my arrival, one of the families I met were a government vet Chris and his wife Irene and their two children, Kenneth and Lydia. They were stationed at Chisamba about thirty-nine miles from Lusaka. Coming on-duty one night I found Chris and Irene obviously distressed sitting in the veranda corridor. Kenneth had choked on and inhaled a peanut and was unable to breathe. He was on his way back from theatre having had a bronchoscopy to remove the fulminating object and an emergency tracheotomy. He was heading to isolation and an oxygen tent. He had developed pneumonia and for a few days he was very unwell. Chris and Irene put his recovery down to me. It was helpful he knew me and on that first night I'd turned up the oxygen and spent time in the tent with him so he wasn't scared; but it's just what you do. He became attached – I was there every night when his parents went back to Chisamba. He declared his intention of marrying me before he left.

Chris and Irene insisted I spend my next time off with them but I was not over keen because after nights it was a full five days off. I was still rather wary of places where I was not in control and large platters of food could be set before me. I would, though, be able to spend my last two nights with them once I had met my other commitments. Sod's law and such like, my next night duty stint was extended due to a very sick child. A teenage Asian girl with tuberculous meningitis needing one-to-one care took precedence. What should have been the end of my time-off became the start of it.

When sleeping in the heat, during the day and without air conditioning, it was our habit in the morning to survey the drug cupboard and select a couple of sleeping pills. The previous day I'd not spent much time in bed. I'd been out for coffee in the morning, got to bed about one and knowing I was up at 3.30pm to go out to tea with someone, I'd have skipped the sleeping pill – just so you know we weren't total idiots. We lived it up. With no time for a kip, I set off as soon as the stores opened to shop for a wedding present for Dymphna and Ted, gifts for my hosts, then set off for Chisamba. Getting to your destination is easy and there's no need for a map. Everywhere is just off whichever of the main roads you leave Lusaka by. Correctly attired for a bush trip, I wore trousers tucked into socks, sturdy shoes and a long-sleeved shirt, made by me, with buttoned cuffs. Out of the store and onto Cairo Road it was straight ahead till a sign indicated Chisamba. Now on a dirt road it is dusty and bumpy, and you keep going until a sign says you have arrived. Lots of dirt roads lead off, but unless there is a sign, just keep going. Leaving the one you are on without a clear direction could take you into trouble.

I made good time and arrived in time for coffee, and for Kenneth and Lydia to introduce me to their toys before lunch. After lunch we all retired to bed giving me an expected good three hours which was the most I ever managed in daytime. I swallowed the pills, lay down and fell into the dead sleep as happens in the heat of the day assisted by a hypnotic. Very shortly Kenneth and Lydia tumbled in to join me; goodbye sleep.

Come four o'clock, Chris came home and we sat out in the garden and had tea. Later, I put the children to bed while Irene made supper. I got changed – we always changed for supper. For this occasion, it wasn't one of my home-made frocks but not significant enough an occasion for the blue frock. I was tired and I was ready for bed. Time passed and passed and there was no sign of supper. Keeping up the chat was an effort. Drink flowed, but I didn't dare have a drink, in case it reacted with the sleeping pills. Eventually there was a bit of movement. Chris left the room and returned with three men. Each was uniformly dressed. Grey pants, white shirt, cravat and a moustache. He led them in much as farmers show stock. Moved them round. Had I been a bit more alert, I might have suggested he turn them round and do another pass. One of the men was Colin the non-drinking, saving-up policeman I met at the time of the flag incident and Alan Middleton-Stewart; both police inspectors and their boss Chief Inspector – can't remember his name. Drinks were offered and as previously Colin declined. Apparently, they were Chris and Irene's next-door, and in fact, only neighbours. The moustaches were a competition. I don't know who won, but I know it would have been competitive. Eventually we dined and a lovely meal it was. Very much later I got to bed.

Because what would have been my last night off, was now my first, I wasn't due back for another five days, so I had absolutely no excuse not to stay. It was a very nice break. I did appreciate though just how much my visit meant for Irene as she was the only white woman in Chisamba. There were missionaries nearby, but not the kind of casual drop-in-for-coffee kind of neighbours as they were wholly committed to their work. Had Irene wanted to work, there was nothing available. She would in time school Kenneth and Lydia at home, but at seven they would become weekly boarders in Lusaka. She didn't have to as they were posted to Kitwe and they would be day pupils, and sadly, we lost touch.

Their home was government accommodation and like every other was equipped to the standard appropriate to the post holder, albeit within the limits of the local infrastructure and available utilities. There were three bedrooms with single beds provided as well as bedside lockers, a dressing table, hanging cupboard and a stand chair. Those wishing to sleep together had to shove the beds together and then the mattresses to mimic a double. The open-plan lounge, which was used for meals, had a two-seater settee and four chairs of the hardwood variety with the adjustable seating position which operated just like collapsible deck chairs on a ratchet. Two not very robust square cushions were provided for each seating in a green brown printed fabric. The covers were removed for washing. Random small drinks tables were personal possessions as were pictures on the whitewashed walls. The dining alcove hosted a table, six chairs and a sideboard. There was no electricity and two hissing oil lamps provided a dim light across both rooms. In the kitchen was a wood stove and a personal little Calor gas two-burner camping stove, which was the source of our excellent meals. Ironing was done with irons heated with burning charcoal. Washing left the house and was dealt with by their boy near his house. Africans are indisputably the most wonderful launderers in the world. With cold water in tubs and the help of stones, the results were worthy of the Persil advert and the immaculate starched and ironed uniforms of government staff a testament to their professionalism.

There was a kind of scullery next to the back door, where there was a bit of a shower and wash basin. The toilet was outside in a little hut. Irene's was a well thought out little facility. A torch on a shelf by the door showed you the way. Once inside the torch sat on a small ledge built for it and you could see to latch the door. A trick in Africa was to wait till someone got seated then re-do the latch and there they were, marooned till let out. In Irene's loo there was no chance someone would suddenly undo the bucket removal door when you were in mid flow because it was padlocked. Irene was fanatical over ensuring no human waste got near her vegetables.

Irene's life made me super aware of just how lucky I was. We had all mod cons, companionship, and a social life. We could read in bed. We could go out visiting. We had narrow gauge wire screens on our windows, but no need to sleep under a mosquito net. Irene had a telephone and a battery radio with limited stations. When Chris left in the early morning and until he came home – sometimes he had to be away overnight – she was on her own with the children. She could not contact him, and unless he was somewhere with a landline, he couldn't give her a call either. For emergences there was only the police radio. A wind-up gramophone and a few records were shared across the patch for rare social events.

Next afternoon we were having tea in the garden when Chris was called to the phone. He came back and said 'that was Scotland Yard'; they want me to look at one of the horses. Want to come?' Kids jumped up and down and scampered off with Irene and me behind. We were invited to play volleyball. They really enjoyed having us and invited us for tea and a re-match next day. Following the re-match, we had an invite to dinner the next night.

The police living quarters were very dark and they also lacked indoor sanitation. The children were in bed and being watched by the boy. The table was set as was the meal. It was curry. I had not until I went to Africa ever experienced curry. I knew of curry because my mother told me curry was a wartime way to disguise left-over beef that had gone off. I was getting the hang of it. We had curry regularly in the mess. There was always a wide selection of bits to boost or mellow the main dish. Diced tomato with onion, sliced banana, skinned orange segments, dried coconut, yoghurt, cucumber, chutney and naan bread. There were absolutely no refinements at Scotland Yard. The meal was curry and rice. I exaggerate; there was a jar of chutney. I took a mouthful and my mouth caught fire. There were no demulcents and it was stringy mutton, fatty and chewy. In the mess, the sweet after curry was always something like blancmange; there was no pudding at all at Scotland Yard.

Large quantities of beer were taken by all except Colin. I was advised against the water. It was explained the excess heat was because in the course of the preparation each of them had had a taste and decided it needed yet another spoonful of brimstone. After dinner we played cards and I needed to go to the toilet. Colin kindly escorted me with a torch outside. Their PK – Picaninny Kyah or child house wasn't quite up to Irene's standard. It had a wooden plank with a cut out to sit on and identified by sound, a bucket below, but no little back door because there was a howling gale. Worse, Colin had to lean on the door because they had no internal fitting and he kept the torch. Better though than one place where I asked where there was a PK and the boy, I asked waved his arm indicating – the whole of Africa. The next night we returned the favour, but the meal was duiker, not mutton, and not curried. The duiker had been shot by one of the African constables and was delicious.

What I didn't know, when a couple of years later a constable in Woodlands brought me some, was that you don't just cook it – it takes three days of marinating and nicking and stuffing before you can actually cook it. In Woodlands I had a wood stove to cook on – I called it the Black Devil. Sometimes it took all day to boil a kettle but on others it could cremate a pan of intended stew in three minutes. I just wished he'd gifted me mince. I've always been good with mince.

At Chisamba, we got pudding as well – mango mousse. That was 'the last supper.' During the day Colin had asked if I would like to go out on patrol with him. I did and he let me drive his Land Rover. He commended my driving – he did that only until after we were married. Once we were married, it was always a mystery to him how I had ever got a licence. It was an interesting outing as we visited several compounds. I'd been on compounds before, but for outpatient clinics. We never had occasion to really visit as the rondavel (a traditional circular African dwelling with a conical thatched roof) allocated to us was outside the perimeter. Crowds of all ages would be sat around when we arrived, but it was amazing how quickly we could get through a clinic. Less than twenty-five per cent were there for us, most just come along for the outing and travelled quite long distances for no shops, no entertainment; just a long walk. Going in on 'official business' was different. You could see what everyday life was like. The women would be busy, washing or sweeping or grinding meal or seeing to cooking pots. The men were just sat around, maybe smoking or chewing but nothing energetic.

I saw a grader – a bit like a snow plough in action. Main roads which are not strip roads are red sandy dirt which ridges and apart from sending up showers of dust is very uneven. The role of the grader is to try and even things out and prevent the knuckle ride due to ridges and fast driving. It doesn't help for long and causes even more dust. On the morning I left I was seen off by all and Colin asked if he could come down to Lusaka and take me out. I said yes. I later heard from Irene that he and Alan Middleton-Stewart had tossed up as to which would ask me out. Such was the shortage of women.

He came down the next week and we went to the bioscope and saw Hobson's Choice. I knew all about him by then due to the morning patrol. His parents, his sister, his ambition to have a farm. The reason he didn't drink – some very heavy drinkers meant the bar bill was substantial and if you were a moderate drinker like he was then it was unfair. He wasn't even any good as a moderate drinker either. Half a pint of Castle and he was legless. I could drink him under the table. He was saving for his farm and sent money to England every month; every penny was a prisoner. He was charming and such a gentleman. Boyish and earnest. We had lots in common. Sheep and cattle. Country life. Very hard working, too. He bought cars at auction, did them up and sold them at a profit. African constables were always in the market for cars, but not that good at mechanics. No way was the Colin I met, the guy I came to know whose DIY extended only to a hammer and a six-inch nail. His mechanical talent was much the same – spanner and a bash. He grew marvellous vegetables, though, and his beds were a joy to behold.

I didn't just latch on to Colin on the rebound. I was careful, very careful and he was the first man I ever had more than one date with. Had I even contemplated meeting anyone else I'd have hung on to the cake. Anything was an excuse for a party, but also many formal celebrations. I discovered Founder's Week was a bit like Thanksgiving in the USA.

25 Caretaking

Opportunity knocked when Dymphna invited me to co-caretake the house of her cousin, Joe who was going on long leave. He was Chief Veterinary Officer (CVO) for Northern Rhodesia and no longer lived in a tied house. Joe, his wife and children lived in a very desirable residence in the best area of Lusaka. Single-storey in a large well-maintained garden with a two-car porte-cochere. The piece de resistance was a swimming pool. The pool was not your everyday rectangle, but an edifice. The overall shape was that of a grand piano on kind of two tiers. The lower shape was plenty big enough to swim round, though perhaps more often a kind of cooling-off-with-a-cold-drink place. The upper tier was paddling depth with a fountain and was ideal for children.

The kindly gesture wasn't altruism, but a necessary provision made by home owners going on leave and at risk of their property being stripped in their absence. We were invited to dinner and appraised of the duties, tasks and responsibilities of our occupancy. We would not be responsible for their personal and expensive belongings, which would be locked away, reducing the accommodation available to two bedrooms and the rest of the house. The head boy and garden boy had been retained and we were provided with lists of their duties. We were not responsible for paying the garden boy or a pool boy anything, but were to pay 'scoff money' to the head boy who would cook and clean for us. There were other what-to-do lists. What to do when the electricity failed had pride of place.

Power failure was a frequent occurrence in Lusaka. At the hospital we had a temperamental standby generator, which more often than not, was having an off day when required to stand up for itself. I mentioned we had a Drinker in the isolation ward. Drinker was the guy who invented the Iron Lung. Very simply, the patient was placed up to his neck in a coffin and a rubber collar fitted round neck and below chin completed an air-tight seal. With only head out and a rear-view mirror, which was pretty pathetic for viewing anything, breathing was enabled by artificial respiration requiring electricity to feed the pump. When everything failed, survival depended on manual operation. Patients did survive being treated in Iron Lungs, a testimony to good nursing care. Only once was the Drinker needed in my time and for a short period. The patient with polio was transferred to the African Hospital's positive pressure respirator just as soon as we could lay hands on it. He was weaned off that and although he had some residual paralysis, recovered.

Joe's house didn't have a stand-by, but the circuits were temperamental and didn't automatically fire up when the power came back on. Another quirk in Lusaka was that when the power failed so too did the telephone system. You could not then ring to either report the failure or ask when it would be restored. So, we'd make frequent trips to trip the switch, just to check. Pool care was not our responsibility, but we had to know about changing filters and the filling up of chambers with various stuff. The bills for electricity and water had to be paid monthly. We were paid by cheque, but, in the shops and everywhere else you paid cash. At the end of each month you joined the queue of people paying in their salary and drawing out cash for their expenses. You took the wad of cash and went round town paying your bills. What was left over was what you hoped would see you through the month. If you misjudged, it was back to the bank where it was rare to find a queue. Always though a smattering of African males checking out the 'donas' (white women) for a chance to select the one who would be his on Fleedom (Independence – a cheque book, a white woman and a car).

Even in Lusaka, despite our much more responsible grown-up roles, we were subject to the same sort of guardianship of our physical and moral safety. A request for our temporary move had to be submitted then provisos, caveats and mutual agreements put in place. Our shifts had to be synchronised so we were never home alone. As ever, there were negotiations to be done. Because I had the biggest room, I paid for my room and Dymphna moved all her not-needed stuff into it. So, just a bit like the African scoff money, she drew rations for two.

The pool was a magnet and brought lots of company. During the day, we would offer cups of tea or coffee. Tea and coffee came with 'basic rations' so the only cost was the electricity and water. We did not have bottled water and in town the water was classed as fit to drink. Out of town we had water tablets which in theory, you could add to any mud and render it drinkable. The tablets coloured the liquid, but I can't say whether the taste was down to the tablet or the untreated water. I could have done a controlled test and now I would do, but I had other priorities then. Tea was not a preferred beverage due to strange taste so we mainly drank coffee. Our pot was black inside and out due to lingering on the stove. It was a tall metal jug with a narrow waist, and I have no idea how it worked because I never needed to know. If it ran dry then it was instant coffee.

Though our quarters were a bit Spartan, since most occasional furniture was locked away, we had space. We also had a record player, but no records. Between us, we had two LPs which we bought jointly out of our kitty. Johnny Mathis and Vic Damone. To provide this all-round sound, we had only to open up the patio doors and turn up the volume on the record player. People began to bring their own LPs, but never left them with us. They didn't think for a moment that we'd destroy them, just that records like many things, had legs in Lusaka. Johnny and Vic were played to death, but survived and returned to the UK in Dymphna's heavy luggage in 1976. We had lots of Braaivleis with music by the pool.

While we were being kindness personified, the Mess was burgled and being the only room without an occupant, my room was ransacked. The most serious loss was the sewing machine, which Dymphna borrowed to sew our frocks. The owner had said there was no rush to return it. Just come to dinner sometime and bring it with you. This went down as the dearest dinner she never had. Our luck was about to turn, as the police caught the thief.

My clothes and everything else were gone, but I wasn't getting upset over them because, the ones I wore I had with me. They left the trunks and bags which was good in a way, but would you not think how much easier transport would have been had they packed them? It took me a while to understand why my clothes on arrival were not fit for purpose. The person advising my mother had spent years in Africa. She still lived in Africa on a mission station where she and her husband were teachers, not missionaries. Missionaries and those around them didn't dress like ex-pats. A couple of lucky garments were saved, the blue dress and my camel coat.

In Lusaka, it wasn't a bit like when somebody says, 'You must come for a meal, I'll be in touch' and they don't. I'd learned that when an invitation is extended that is what it is, an invitation. If they say come and stay, they mean it. Back in the UK a relative once questioned why I always had people staying. We lived in a nice place for a break and it was a free holiday and I'd become used to the ex-pat way of community family. Only once did it get a bit much. My parents came on holiday and stayed for three years. Our invitation to visit the lion-mauled game warden was followed up.

While still at Joe's, we fixed it for the time off after night duty when we could add the extra public holidays for the Queen's Birthday and Cecil Rhodes. We planned on doing the game park first then travelling on to Livingstone, where we'd stay in the Victoria Falls Hotel. Visitors to the game reserve usually broke their journey by stopping overnight at a rest house. We should have planned to do that. We should have left as soon as we came off in the morning, but with things to do, it was lunch time before we left. Our boy had prepared us a 'peek-neek' – wicker basket picnic.

We did not set off in Hesperus, my twice round the clock Morris Minor, but in the pale blue VW with grey seats (PBVWGS). Dymphna's nearly new motor car. We were well on our way and into barren bush on a long straight road when red lights started flashing on the dashboard. We stopped. We didn't speak. We were in the middle of the bush in the middle of absolutely nowhere. We had one panga between two. There were no mobile phones. We hadn't seen a car for miles. What more could happen to us. We couldn't start walking. Where to and how far away were we. We had no map – you didn't need a map; you take the road till you arrive. Wild animals could get us. We could only wait and hope a vehicle will come along. I suppose in a way fortune had already shone because we were not surrounded by a mob of natives ready to strip the car. We were so far into the bush; nobody lived nearby.

After what seemed an age, we saw dust coming up behind a car, which whipped past at speed. We just had time to say, 'Hope you get a puncture,' when it skidded to a halt and reversed back. Nothing he could do, but he'd get the next garage to send help. It was quite a long time in the hot sun, but we had our picnic and were happy to see the grumpy mechanic who was a master of the deep sigh and grim prognostications. The sump had dropped out, we'd no oil, cap off, head scratch, bit of thinking then he pulled a branch off a scrubby bush. Hacking at it with a pen knife, he stuffs it up our sump and fills us up with an awful lot of oil. He followed us to the garage, but he was ninety-nine per cent sure he didn't have a part. Oh dear, fat lot of use the depleted wicker picnic set would be for a three-day wait. He may have been gloomy, but he was resourceful and another VW in for service was deprived of its sump and after another oil fill we were free to go. He suggested a stop off at the rest house, but we didn't waste time. We put our foot down and knew we'd be there before closing time. And we were.

The sight of yellow lights in the distance was welcome and at the perimeter gates a guard approached. A mistake occurred. Presenting our passes, Dymphna switched on the car lights. 'Thank you, madam, but you can't go in.' Even though the camp was within spitting distance and only the yellow insect repelling lamps were lit, you may not drive in a game reserve at night. If only she hadn't switched on the headlights. He suggested we could either go back to the rest house – a long drive or stay here. Here was Africa. However, he gestured towards the aircraft hangar that was the Tsetse Fly Shed and said, 'You stay here, madam?'

When guests left the camp, they would drive into the shed, the doors would be closed and the underside and wheels of the car would be sprayed with insecticide. You then drove out the other side, and got a stamp on your pass to confirm this had been done. We accepted his offer, drove in and asked if he had any hot water? We'd been hysterical when we'd we found our boy had packed a greaseproof 'poke' of tea leaves – he knew neither of us drank tea! He would have expected it to be there when he unpacked the basket and with anything else left over – his for the taking. We handed over the bag of tea. Quite a while later he returned bearing a missionary-size iron cooking pot of tea – lots left for those in the compound and no need to return the dry leaves left over! You just know how it works.

Another car joined us when we'd settled for the night, with a couple inside. PBVWGS didn't allow stretching out, but it wasn't that which bothered us. The wife could nag and she did – all night long she berated the poor sod for not leaving when she said they should and everything else she could drag up that he had let her down over since the day they met – and since that was a very long time ago, she had much ammunition! We didn't know them, and though our paths did cross in the dining room, I don't know whether they stayed married or not. Definitely six of one and half a dozen of the other based on the reciprocal verbal combat.

Dawn came; we were let out, admitted and drove up the hill to the gated complex where the chalets were. All mod cons and good food in a communal area. A bath and breakfast set us up and the next two days were a definite experience of a lifetime. The guy who had bled all over me was true to his word and we were the envy of the rest of the guests, who had to be satisfied with African rangers and set tours. It isn't like a zoo. It wasn't an elephant behind bars waving its trunk at you or a lion pacing up and down. They were at home and we were tolerated tourists. The only animal we failed to see was an elephant, but we saw elephant spoor (tracks) and I have a picture somewhere among my souvenirs. To see whole herds having a bit of gallop or impala drinking at a water hole and having animals I'd never seen before explained. It was peaceful and the beauty and serenity of Africa I can bring to mind today. Even a group of lions feasting on a zebra who hadn't got away seemed more interesting than scary. The order and method of the dismemberment and mastication was part of life. Tourists would be unwise to step out of line. It wasn't noisy though at night and especially when we were bedded in the shed, the sound of a lion roaring, the screeching of birds of prey and the raucous laughter of the hyena broke the silence. A bit like on the ward, one wakes up and disturbs everyone else.

We looked round the camp itself as did the less privileged visitors and were encouraged to photograph the staff at home. It was a small compound built round a yard just like the laager explorers would build when they camped for the night. What was presented for our entertainment was energetic dramatic fiction. Men in long un-pressed, holey trousers, ragged coloured shirts and trilbies, were dancing round a tub, using long sticks to pound corn into mealie meal. Not something they ever did in real life. Another woman's job on show was an energetic barefoot dance in a basin to aid the washing of clothes. There were quite a few children playing with sticks and mud; the women were all away water gathering.

Breakfasting prior to driving to Victoria Falls for our next two nights, a radio message was received and relayed to all asking me to report to reception. Never were we unavailable, the courts contacted the hospital and the hospital told them where to find me and I had to present myself in court the following morning to give evidence in the prosecution of our burglar. As far as I knew they were proceeding with enquiries. So, no trip to Livingstone, we had to hot foot it back to Lusaka. No telephones and radio contact only, their knowing where we were at any time meant we were always on call. The trial was interesting – particularly the witness to whom the accused tried to fence the sewing machine. The cross examination. What happened? 'I am asleep and I hear 'knock, knock' then what happened 'I hear knock, knock' then what happened this went on a few more times and eventually he said, 'Then I wake up.'

We got back the sewing machine and my little travel iron. There was more good news. Witness fees. I was paid for my time and mileage and because I was away from home, they paid mileage to and from the game park, then my onward mileage to Victoria Falls, two nights' accommodation and subsistence at a set rate – a lot more than we would ever have spent subsisting. It paid for our entire break and the PBVWGS repair.

It was while we were looking after Joe's house that Dymphna met Ted. Headmaster of the best local primary school, which was not only academically ahead of the game, but had a swimming pool, changing rooms and a spectator stand. Ted had custody of his seven-year-old son. The child was amazing and a testament to a chap bringing up a boy on his own, she said. In time I became his occasional sitter and he was never any trouble. In public, however, I failed to see any of these wonderful attributes as he was perpetually whining and clinging to his father. Despite his making it clear there was no room for anyone in his life apart from his dad, he turned out fine. They lived on a plot out at Chelston, where Ted had had his house built, had chickens, kept a pig and an Alsatian guard dog. Ted was seriously security minded and carried a revolver in a shoulder holster. Courting was somewhat limited due to the boy and theirs was rather more sedate and of the afternoon tea kind unless one of us took care of the lad. It was quite some time before Ted was relaxed enough to allow us to care for his son so quite some time had passed before I or any of the others met Ted. My first meeting was when Dymphna had malaria, again. I called to the Female Ward on my way off-duty and my first sight was a large man on Dymphna's bed and a revolver by his side. Introduced, Ted was our social inclusion to the education circuit.

As a parting gift for our lovely stay, we decided at great expense, to empty, clean and refill the swimming pool. When Dymphna called to return the keys, she was gutted to find Joe, paint brush in hand, giving the now-empty pool a fresh coat of sky blue. I have no words which could convey the fury, deep sorrow and utter devastation Dymphna felt over this utter, criminal waste of money.

26 Out in the Community

I got out and about in the community because I wanted to learn more about it. None of the outreach in Lusaka was comparable with the UK. When I experienced some later in Bechuanaland, the contrast was even greater. Bush stations ran their own clinics, but we covered about a fifteen-mile radius of Lusaka. Mother and baby clinics were run from Maternity and held in the suburbs. Since they were wholly attended by mothers and babies delivered in the hospital, I felt no great urge to see how they ran. We were regularly updated on what went on, any juicy gossip and the silly questions asked by first-time mothers. Without exception, our midwives were of the common sense routine, 'let them cry and make sure they know who is in charge' school. If the crying bothers you, move the pram.

Midwives do tend to be pragmatic about their work; straightforward from start to finish. Is this the reason that young men take fright when they learn that their next hit is a midwife? One lady had been visiting the clinic weekly with her fretful infant who never slept. Week after week advice had been given. The worried mother reported that this week the infant had slept for three hours and then she was so anxious, she had to wake him up in case he was dead. The immediate response was, 'If he was dead you were too late!' Apparently, the mother and midwife shared the joke. Overall, the baby clinics were good customers of the Children's Ward.

Most of the mothers were strangers in a foreign land. There were no mothers or sisters nearby and often neighbours were foreign as well. The climate was a challenge to the newly-born as well as a learner mum. Most of our babies could have been discharged with the diagnosis of Anxious Mother. Breastfeeding seemed to fail easily. There was no National Dried Milk, but a wide variety of brands of replacement, all with wonderful marketing and generous with samples. After a few weeks of chopping and changing and things going from bad to worse, the baby would be admitted as a failure to thrive or maybe just GP desperation consigning them to us to sort out. Unhappy mums, with fretful babies who wouldn't feed, cried a lot, didn't sleep, hung on to wind with drawn up knees and tummies like drums, were as much in need of care as the child. With few exceptions, there was nothing to blame except lack of maternal knowledge, loneliness, fear and anxiety, leading to windy posseting and crotchety little sprouts confused with different tastes, rate of flow and the assumption of mum's insecurity. Care plans in the 1950s all began exactly the same way. Reassure the patient.

The real issue of the fretful child and frantic mother required whole system thinking. Nurses have been whole system thinking since Florence Nightingale's day, but smart people dream up new names, often at great cost, for stuff we've done forever and think they've invented something new and better. It is always tempting to accept the praise when a screaming tot relaxes, and mum wants to know how you did it. I've always been very good at this except for the super challenges thrown at me by my own screaming infants when I kind of lost my touch. The desired outcome was for a confident mother to leave with a transformed baby in full knowledge that it was this very special baby who had been out of kilter and nothing to do with any ineptitude on her part. We spent a long time getting a full history of everything from the pregnancy through to delivery, social and economic, hour by hour sleeping, feeding, brand and teat type, physical conditions and clothing and having reassured the mother we sent her home for a kip. Though we didn't have spread sheets, we had a start and finish chart. We introduced mum to the wonders of gripe water and asked only that she adopt our laid-back not-bothered way of relaxing to allow her inner calm to transmit to the child and learn the full range of our top tips for bringing up wind.

Other baby clinics were in the African townships and the coloured quarter. Northern Rhodesia did not have apartheid as in South Africa. It was a well-advertised multi-racial country, but not really because it all depended on ability to pay and acceptance. We knew the true meaning of apartheid was parallel development. Preparing for Independence, health, education, policing and administration services for all, were all run from one office. Statutory services and mandatory compliance applied to all. The children's clinics were primarily geared to ensuring children were vaccinated and immunised. You were a lucky little African if you reached the age of five. The mortality rates were horrendous. Babies rolled into fires, got bitten, dropped, drowned in buckets, caught communicable diseases, had vitamin deficiencies or just left behind. The loss of a child was heart-rending and gave rise to high-pitched wailing at the moment, but bereavement was not sustained. Everything just carried on as usual. The main provider of African education had been the mission schools, but the education department managed from Salisbury was making inroads to the bush. However, to be accepted into a government school required a certificate of vaccination.

There were two kinds of African clinics; the urban ones were in compounds in the suburbs, English was spoken and, the children went to school and the roads in and through were kept graded. The huts were round and thatched and cooking was over a fire. Water came from a standpipe and little boys and girls tended to wee on the spot. The compound clinic attracted mothers and small children and was not the great occasion it was in the bush.

Beyond the town, the clinics were an occasion and people travelled long distances on foot or occasionally by bicycle to participate. There was a crowd when you arrived and there was still a crowd afterwards. As far as possible grown-ups were referred on to the days when the provision was for general outpatient services. Sometimes urgency demanded immediate referral to hospital and the whole family would pick up their kutundu and travel to hospital with the patient. Families advised to wait would just settle themselves and do just that for however many days it was till the next clinic. Africans don't do urgent. Once they came to a clinic, there was no hesitation in accepting vaccination and immunisation as the power of injections was well known and sought after. Unfortunately, there was a growing trend for artificial feeding which was being encouraged by limited but free supplies of branded powdered milk. People today are still boycotting Nestle SA for marketing the product initially by disposing of supplies, which were nearly out of date, free of charge.

We are still catching up and not learning in the UK today. Preliminary research in Burnley in 1998, found children were lacking in their five-a-day so free fruit was made available. For the period of the project the intake rose from one to three. When no longer provided, they fell below the start figure of one. When a small charge was introduced, mothers would decline to pay, with the excuse that they had a snack before they came. My head keeps filling up with the way in which we in the UK are falling into the same trap Kenneth Kaunda did in the late 50s and 60s. He thought that by upskilling the workforce and getting rid of the Europeans that the indigent population would upskill themselves to work in what could have been a great economy. It didn't work. The natural way of life and the subsidised lifestyle of the urban citizen was not conducive to striving and working towards a better and more affluent life without subsidy.

Another outside clinic was in the coloured quarters on the Great North Road and close to the town. The houses were less native in that they were red rendered and the roof corrugated iron. It was a much poorer-seeming place than the African townships; the mood was low the whole place lacked life. There were more dogs and too many men just sitting on their doorstep smoking. It really confirmed the writings of Chirapula Stephenson, pre-World War II, who pointed out to the Prime Minister of England his disappointment that his natural sons had little drive and were lacking in moral fibre. I know a bit about John Edward Chirapula Stephenson and maybe some of what I know is not in the public domain, but it is fascinating.

What I know about Chirapula comes from visiting his home. On one of my privileged trips round the beat, I was taken there. He'd been dead over two years and to get to his house we came off a dirt road and into the bundu for a bit then into a deserted quadrangle. It was quiet and there was no human presence and the buildings around the square were all three storeys high. One was clearly the mansion house. Wide and double fronted, there had been glass in now dead window spaces and the entire complex had been rendered and painted but had faded to a tired yellow. The other houses were of narrow Victorian terrace-style and their window apertures were slits. One in each side of the square was the home of one of his wives while the others were of lesser width and internal standard, likely home to his children, concubines, servants and storage.

This was the home of an Englishman who came to Africa to seek his fortune and became a telegraph clerk till Cecil Rhodes asked him to head up another expedition to claim more land for Queen Victoria. Until he died, he was still in contact with the higher echelons of the British Government and clearly despite his lifestyle was listened to and not disparaged. He went native after a while and his three wives were all of noble tribal birth. The wives in no way restricted his activities and though history mentions nine children, I prefer to subscribe to what I saw and heard which was that Chirapula had three wives and twenty-three natural children and was considered a god by the natives. When he died native bearers carried him in a wicker coffin open at the head. As they walked, grain was sprinkled on him to feed him in the afterlife. When the lengthy procession reached the 'highway,' the coffin was taken over by an official burial detail from the High Commission. His grave, only a short way off the road is marked by a large headstone giving his name, John Edward Chirapula Stephenson. There is a Masonic symbol and a verse which includes the words 'in a grave where a Mason has laid him.'

His home had been stripped. Apart from being multi-storey it was just like any other ex-pat house till we got to the top floor – round and round a narrow circular stairway and we were in his office. Apparently, MI5 or 6 or whatever had bulldozed in as soon as he died and removed all sensitive material. The place had been ransacked, but there was an abundance of personal and to me very sensitive material littering the room and available to read. I think what forensics had done was remove correspondence embellished with crowns and portcullis and typed or written on vellum. What there was, was riveting, interesting, fascinating, open and honest. Chirapula had a carbon copy of letters he had sent, and he had politicians, writers, minsters and aristocracy among his pen friends. There were two museum piece typewriters which must have been for the use of his clerical 'boys' and still operational. His correspondence was pen and ink. Some letters were to people he knew, asking them to offer employment to his natural children. Offa John was one he referred to as lacking in ambition and not having a proper job so seeking assistance from the head of Rhodesian Railways in Bulawayo to find him a clerical post. I could have read all day but we were on a working journey. How could he, the father of twenty-three, suggest his natural children lacked moral fibre. I left without taking a single sheet of paper with me.

Back to the coloured quarter and the lack of opportunity for their advancement. Indian, African and European; none were enthusiastic and few accepting of mixed race. The mixed marriage fared quite well with acceptance within whatever social circle their work put them. The next generation were the problem and a poor fit as they were neither one thing or another and so migrated to a ghetto. There were limited employment opportunities because the coloured would not stoop to the kind of jobs taken by the working African. The upwardly mobile African despised his own kind and was even more disparaging of mixed race. We didn't get the same crowds at clinic, mother and child and maybe another at foot, but no relatives and no buzz. They conducted the business they attended for and left. The Africans weren't noisy – well yes, they were, but the noise was always indicative of the mood. At the clinics it was an all-day opportunity to meet up and chat, but the noise level was never disruptive and there was no aggravation. Sweets were a great way to gain co-operation from little Africans. The children once persuaded into our orbit were shy and much less boisterous than their European counterparts who'd be hanging onto your leg five minutes after you'd picked up his little brother. There was always an exudation of noise from a native mob from which you could anticipate the mood and outcome.

The only group without a separate clinic was Indian. Several Asians lived over the shops they owned, and the more affluent lived in the suburbs. There was only one Asian living over the store with a toilet and that became an aspiration for all storekeepers when I was there, and also to move away from the shop to live. My first run-in after arriving was with the local shopkeeper patronised by our boys in the mess.

Our boys were paid monthly, and each week received their scoff money. During the month they bought on tick and paid up plus interest when they were paid. Ticky had financial problems and the drama was playing out in his day to day life. You could always tell when they were put out for any reason from a splinter to a puncture to a bit of a headache. They droop; they flounce; they sigh, and their normal pace becomes general malaise. Ticky was our drama queen, but this was a sad tale. The shopkeeper was telling him he owed too much money. I listened to his tale of woe; he showed me his repayment book and it was clear he was being diddled. The shopkeeper had a unique system where at the bottom of each page the amount carried forward was always plus the amount owed, month one, plus compound interest, plus the balance on the day. So, since the book began, he'd been accruing interest on a sum of money he had already paid. I took the matter up with Grace, who was most helpful, agreed with me, said it was really bad. But these things happened, and she said I needed to go with Ticky and sort it out. I had to go with him to the compound to the store. Luckily, I could use a driver and meet Ticky on site. The store in a shack stank, outside were festering sacks of wriggling maggots and the little whitebait fish and other sticky looking bits as well as metal buckets and mugs hanging round. Inside it was smelly, oppressive and dark so you couldn't actually see the goodies on sale. There was a little counter where I slapped down the offending book and said, 'there seems to be a mistake here.' The horrible smells, plus Ticky shaking and sweating beside me meant I had to breathe through my mouth. It was unbelievably easy. They admitted it was a complete mistake and when we left, Ticky was solvent for the first time since he'd started working at the hospital.

The Afrikaner opinion was that all the Indians in Africa were Sweeper Class. The very lowest caste in the Indian hierarchy. This was cast in stone because they first came to South Africa to build the railways. It wasn't true in Lusaka, where there were Indian doctors, lawyers, teachers and gradually some of the larger Indian Corporations were making inroads. Savita Patel was one of the sisters on the Children's

Ward. Trained in England, she had returned to the family home in Lusaka, not to work, but to have her marriage arranged. Initially this was not known to us. She wore uniform and was picked up and dropped off by hospital transport. Things began to emerge as we got to know each other. Savita had to wear Indian dress at home. She missed her lovely European clothes and she never got out. They were thinking of marrying her into a family in Tanganyika because she'd turned down the first chap. Her brother was on her back because they were required to marry in age order, and she was next and he was already suited and wanted to get on with things. Then Savita went off sick.

We didn't know what was wrong, but her father had informed Rose. Rose's suggested visit by GMO was considered unnecessary. A few days passed without contact and still no doctor was required. Then a driver brought in me a crumpled bit of paper 'from the Dona.' Inside was scrawled 'they are poisoning me.' Straight down to Rose. She read the note and Grace was called in and plans made. I would go and visit unannounced because I was her direct line manager. I would take Sister Landsberg with me as an Afrikaner. She was better versed in their ways, was calm and unthreatening and today was the day. We would go under our own steam. Hesperus was up to the task and we parked outside their store.

Definitely a more salubrious establishment than the one in the compound only though because it was a much larger store with a cellar below and three floors above. We made our way in and with the chirpiness of chums visiting a sick friend, said hello to a lady we took to be her mum. She looked nervous and referred to a man who was already making his way towards us. She introduced Savita's brother and fled. There was just a flicker of uncertainty as we stood there trying not to look as though we found the smell offensive when her father came through a bead curtain and made us welcome. Thrilled he was, and all over us like a rash he couldn't do enough for us, except allow us to see Savita unsupervised. We were ushered through the curtain into a stone-floored store with more sacks, drums of oil and piles of plaited mats and bolts of cheap cotton. At the back was a narrow steep staircase which we climbed., On each landing, we travelled the width of the building to the next flight where we could clearly see the squatting hole every time. This was not the one Indian store in Lusaka with a domestic toilet. In these homes it was not necessary to make your way outside when you needed to go. Dead easy, a hole in the corner replicated directly above/below. I don't know, I didn't look to see if there was toilet roll, I just knew that was what it was. It was one of Savita's gripes about how stuck in the past were her family and the risks you took should you choose to do what you needed to do and someone else joined in from above.

We are now on the top floor where there are four closed doors and her father leads us to one which he opens without knocking and ushers us in. Not a pretty girl's bedroom, just bare walls and a very wishy-washy Savita completely taken by surprise. Her hair wasn't shining, nor was it in its usual swept-up dressed-up style, but lanky and greasy and we made nicer shrouds at Sick Kids than the plain cotton gown she wore. Mother by now hovering, was dispatched to make tea and we sat down either side of the bed and tried to chat nonchalantly. The tea arrived in pint size mugs made as they make tea. Leaves, water and condensed milk are heated together. I don't like tea. I'm getting better at tastes and smells, but it is downhill all the way. Father is replaced by two uncles for a short period then returns with Mother, who lays down a tray of assorted Indian delicacies. One of them was thin white wax with flecks of dead insects which he actually put a price to as he'd imported it for its flavour and rarity. He'd been robbed; it was awful and the next one was worse as it had little red bits in and when they hit your mouth ignited. The uncles said little just a watching presence, but father kept up a spiel. We were reaching the end of our second cup of tea and considering our departure when Mother came back with long glasses of coconut milk. Not keen and so much fluid was making our need to depart urgent. Squatting hole – no way. I asked if the GMO had been to see Savita and he said she was almost better and would be back to work soon. I just casually dropped a few hints about telling matron how she was, and that the Medical Director sent his best wishes.

Savita herself telephoned Rose next day to say how much better she was and would soon be back and she was. Soon after, she agreed to marry a doctor in Kenya, whom she had been allowed to meet and reckoned was OK and a better offer than those she had refused. She had by now another sister champing at the bit, so the pressure was on. She married the doctor and had twins, but it didn't last. We lost touch when they left Africa after which they separated.

27 The Way Things Worked

Health was managed from Salisbury, whence came bureaucracy by which we were all required to abide. Very little impacted on our daily lives, but those which did were applied to the letter. Often only when the occasion demanded, like the occasion of the annual visit of the Chief Nursing Officer. The visit was short. She had the whole of Rhodesia and Nyasaland to cover so they were whistle-stop tours. The preparation took time and planning because we had to ensure that our customisation was un-customised and set out as set out in the policies and standing orders.

Though there was much to do, one thing was certain and that was the route she took and the time spent at each pit stop. Before the day, each ward and department had to ensure that what they had belonged to them was where it belonged, and in the right stock quantity. First on the list was to look around and see what you had that belonged to the African Hospital and get it back there and reclaim anything they had of yours. I was the only ward with any regular give and take in that direction. It was very much a one-way system as they never seemed to need anything of mine, but I seemed to be forever on the mooch. I'd an occasional adult bed loan, but by and large everything else was the wrong size for any of the other wards. The wards were a bit trickier, because you could never rely on equal numbers of male and female. Beds were trundled between the two and one bed looks very much like another, unless you have the eagle eye of the CNO and could notice the paint blob which read MW instead of FW. Linen was a nightmare because bed sheets, pillow cases, draw sheets and blankets are all white lookalike. Why get upset as long as you get back the number you sent? But, on this day you cared. We appreciated Rose and Grace and would try hard not to cause them to be censured. All this could be pre-planned and in place in advance – this was no CQC Unannounced Inspection.

Prior to the day it was essential that some training updates were implemented to ensure that all the nannies and boys were word perfect on a long list of supposedly frequently asked questions. I never noticed her approach any of mine because they seemed to scarper before she set foot in the place. She never asked. The ward aides were also primed and committed to being correctly dressed and know the protocol should they be addressed. One thing I never had to do was insist they looked busy. We rarely had quiet times and with nannies and boys having cleared off – no chance. Our major issue was the clothes that we wore.

Not one qualified nurse on the payroll wore the uniform specified for her position. Some of the Afrikaners came on-duty bare-legged, but we UK ex-pats never did. I've no idea why we were so strait-laced, silly and impractical in all that heat and wore stockings and suspender belts, but we did. Certainly not for fear of censure because Rose was totally on the common sense approach. The white frock was not an issue, no revolt there. Shoes were supposed to be brown flat lace-ups and I know that there were only three pairs in the whole place. Caps were Sister Dora perched on the back of your head or if you were I/C and taking the government extra payment for the privilege, you wore a veil – a silly floppy thing for children to grab and pull and rubbish to keep in place. Again, if in charge, you were entitled to wear a coloured belt with hospital buckle.

For us all to be correctly dressed was as tricky as an Olympic relay. So, while the CNO was walking the corridors, there was frantic activity round the back doors as caps, belts and shoes were swopped, so we were correctly dressed as we welcomed her on to our ward. I never felt quite myself, out of breath, with this mass of muslin which seriously needed more than two Kirby grips and the shoes that were at least a size too big. Once, she'd only just left when I was called to the phone. It was Grace asking if she could urgently have her shoes back as she was invited to Rose's flat to have tea with the CNO.

Another bit of protocol was 'inventory.' Teaspoons were inventoried every day. It was serious stuff but THE inventory that counted even the beds was horrendous because like our uniforms, we swopped stuff that had to be in the right pile in the right ward when the entourage came around. We weren't like the Africans who took stuff and sold it. Rose and Grace were well aware we had a lending library system, they were part of the activity. We were totally justified in dealing in this way, because most of us were not only employed by the government but housed as well. Housing included basic fixtures and fittings and some things which were never used at all. Our homes too were inventoried and we had to drag out the government property we couldn't live with just to reassure them. At the hospital, everything had to be back and, in a pile, when they came to count accompanied by a senior store person from out of town. It wasn't the things that might be on another ward that was tricky, that could be sorted by a bit of back door sorting. The off-site loans were a nightmare. Finding you were three blankets short, trying to remember if you've lost them or lent them to someone then getting them back in time. Another dropping it off at the back-door scenario.

We were big in hospitality and when friends from bush stations came to town, we put them up. That always involved a bit of sheet, pillow and blanket borrowing. On the Children's Ward we had lightweight strong cotton webbing harness embroidered CW to ensure children didn't fall out of or into things. They laundered well and we had a frequent call on stock since we were the only source of supply in the country and long-term loans to staff, inevitable. Up to about the age of two, Central Hospital-generated young were parked in their prams, in the shade wearing a nappy and a CW harness. I was two short and when I recalled them, the borrower duly pulled up to add them to the pile. She was really panicking about what she would do with this child until she could get them back. Put him on the floor! We did not advertise our nefarious trade beyond our own circle. One of our number at the local baby clinic was asked what CW stood for. Christopher William, she came back with – just like that. This could have spread like the roll fiasco at Sick Kids and we could have lost our benefits. Not long enough after the war for us not to know what loose talk did. The average African believed that Independence or as they called it 'Fleedom' was a white woman, a cheque book and a car. Entrepreneurs did a good trade 'selling' white women. How much the poor sod that bought me paid, I don't know. He told Bwana Colin; he'd bought the Dona for 'fleedom.' We were meticulous in our recording because the locals were just so skilled at acquiring items for sale. Teaspoons were more than inventoried daily. If you had any sense you kept a running total in your head at all time and particularly when you asked for a tea tray for relatives. Is it possible than an occasional visitor pocketed a teaspoon? According to Joseph and our nannies, they were all kleptomaniacs and collectors, desperate to add a few more teaspoons stamped Government Property.

It wasn't all them. Once, when one of our number was being dined at the Ridgeway and overtaken in strong drink, a silver-plated condiment set jumped into her evening bag. Note: she was on this occasion wearing 'the blue dress,' my only real success from the aborted trousseau and in high demand. Returning the refreshed blue dress, she suggested I could return them next time I went to the Ridgeway. Hello, I'm returning these; my friend accidentally popped them in her handbag. On your bike! After our bad experience with the journalists, who thought we were call girls, more care had been exercised in permitting our social skills to be on offer. They were a bit of a lucky dip these nights, never on our own, and not a bit as organised as police or armed forces. Some weren't a lot of fun. One night I got one who was teetotal, must have been from a sect. He had an enormous Adam's apple, a beak and a strong belief in his own rectitude, which turned into an embarrassing inability to get over himself. Not a bundle of laughs, but I knew that early in my life that never was there ever a free lunch.

Another of these accompanied jaunts took us to Kariba Dam. The dam was not fully operational with only one sluice gate open, but such power in the width and force of the water thundering down to the rocks below. There was no cafe or tourist kiosk, but there was a small round chapel that was a replica of one in Rome and quite the loveliest I had ever seen. Dedicated to St Barbara, the patron saint of engineers, it was built by the Italians in memory of the engineers and builders who had died creating Lake Kariba and building of the dam. Although it was open all around, it had a wonderful ambience of cool tranquillity. Standing on the wall and seeing the lake and knowing how much effort had gone into transforming the landscape and re-homing the wildlife and marvelling at the sheer wonder of the water, I will never forget. Sadly, in later years the capacity was overtaken by development and Zambia and Zimbabwe suffered power cuts.

Preparation for Independence was taking place in all departments, but in particular in the BOMA – High Commission – town hall. The wives of senior government officers were being paired with the wife and family of the African, who would in time replace her husband. None of the wives I met found this an easy task. Muriel had lots of tales to tell, now she was affianced to James, who although not top notch, was on his way and in the know. She knew that once they were married, she would be a bit like a vicar's wife, she was part and parcel of James's job. She revelled in the weird and wonderful matters arising. Once an African had reached a level as to be allocated a P3 or even P4, the wives would be introduced. They, too, would be provided with the basic furniture and fittings just as we were, but to complete the commissioning, they needed to shop on Cairo Road. That is where the wives came in. They would invite the new post holder and his wife for tea, later to dinner, thus introducing them to life at a high level in the BOMA.

These events weren't easy. We ex-pats would not want any new friends to think our children were badly behaved, our houses messy, our stuff tatty or our catering substandard. Everybody tried and mostly the new friend was, while overwhelmed initially, left determined she could keep up with the Joneses and not only that, but surpass the wives of any of her husband's colleagues. The food they would eat at home would not change much, but rather be of higher quality and all kinds of relish affordable. Entertaining and furnishing items were a big playing field. Choosing cutlery in Greaterman's was fraught for one lady. You can buy a canteen of cutlery, lovely box, Viner's EPNS and get fish eaters and serving spoons included. If you want more than a six-place setting, you can make it up by purchasing place settings of each. This was not an option because fish knives and forks were not included in the everyday place setting. Suggesting that maybe fish knives and forks were not absolutely essential was useless – she needed twenty places and that meant four canteens. A very similar situation arose with dinner services and the need to have complete sets. Let loose in the bedding department wasn't any better and, in a country, where you could wash and dry in a few hours, the one-on-one off and one-in-the-wash meant nothing.

Plagues of flying ants were a diversion. Crunching on cockroaches in the dark at the Western wasn't worth mentioning when compared to being assaulted by a fast moving, humming black mass of massive white flying ants which didn't crunch underfoot, but squelched. They arrived uninvited on the open, but covered, way between the main hospital and the Children's Ward. The sound must percolate because no sooner did I make for cover than a crowd of Africans arrived manically shovelling the fluttering ants into basins, bowls and buckets. The water in the receptacles weighs down the wings and the bodies are ready to cook a dish on a par with truffles. I've never tried either but accept the ardour they were harvested as a sign of value.

While on insects it's the right time to explain just why laundry was vital to our survival. It wasn't just that we ex-pats couldn't get whites white by slapping them on stones in cold water with a bar of soap. Nor was it that we were incapable of ironing with a mini cast iron stove with a fire burning inside it. It wasn't about the fact that spray starch had not been invented either. It was a health and safety issue. The clothes we wore could kill us. Africa is the natural habitat of hundreds of insects, beetles, spiders and flies, which if the penetrate the skin or even just defecate on it, can cause you to be very ill or even die. The only way to counter this risk is to ensure every crease, seam or buttonhole has been seared with a hot iron before any item of clothing makes skin contact.

A visit to a tobacco farm in Southern Rhodesia let me see another way of life. Betty Keith had delivered babies the length and breadth of Africa. Days off and she'd dash to somewhere else where she was a welcome visitor. She took me to stay with an Afrikaans family near Salisbury. Separate from the main house was kind of open terrace of bedrooms with a toilet/wash facility at either end. Guests and the older children slept here. Being special guests, Betty and I were housed in the main house which was single-storey five bedrooms, mod cons and very large veranda lounge and dining rooms. In this patriarchal establishment we all ate together and once all were seated with parents either end, mother pinged a bell and food was brought in, something she repeated between each course. Soup was placed before the father, who then bowed his head. We did so too, and grace was said. He then served the soup. The conversation was inclusive and informal and enjoyable and after each course, the bell was pinged, plates were collected up by two of the daughters and the servants brought in great tureens of vegetables and platter with roasted something which was carved by the father.

On the Sunday evening after dinner, the children left for school. All five were weekly boarders in Salisbury. The oldest boy drove them in and dropped them off at their various boarding houses. Once done, he drove himself back out to the suburbs and parked the car at the home of an uncle. Uncle then drove him into town and dropped him off at school. Though the boy was old enough to have a licence, he was not allowed to have a car at school. Come Friday, the process would be reversed.

Because it was my first visit, I was taken to see the tobacco auctions. This took place in warehouses, where piles of sacks labelled with the source and with one of the batch open to test. People went around with clipboards and did a lot of pinching and smelling. There was a buzz of conversation and warning shouts when piles were shifted and lifted; but see one and you've seen them all. What was interesting though was the 'No Smoking' signs.

The most interesting part of my stay was when I went out in the Land Rover on a tour. The miles of growing tobacco weren't riveting, but it was fascinating to learn about the process and the difficulties posed by insects, animals and the weather threats to a crop. The living arrangements for the workers and their families were inspiring. It was a large plantation and there was more than one compound, but the facilities and services provided to each were the same. They shared services all free-at-point of delivery. There was a school, which provided primary education; and if a child showed promise and passed an entry examination, it could go on to further education as a boarder. There was a foreman in each compound, who was not only responsible for his own workforce but also for ensuring the environs were kept neat and tidy, vegetable gardens planted, and order maintained. The workforce and families had access to a weekly clinic on site and emergency care when necessary. There was no church, but missions abounded and the view held that they could go as and when and where they chose. There was a store. Tommy shops have a really bad name for charging what they like, but their store was different. The idea was to prevent the Africans being conned by the Indian traders. The owner was committed to ensuring his workforce were as self-sustaining as possible by encouraging vegetable and fruit growing and keeping a small herd of cows for milk and scraggy hens for eggs.

The saddest and most awful outcome was that when Southern Rhodesia became Zimbabwe, the land and the house were seized and the family evicted.

28 Kapiri Mposhi

Time passed and Colin and I spent time together, his ambitions coincided with mine. A farm and a lot of children. We have to save. If we got married, we could live in police accommodation free. I wouldn't have to pay for board and lodging. I earned more than he did and he already had his salary paid in the UK so he would be able to send a further £40 a month out. Then not only his allowance of £40 a month be transferred home, but I could as well – how much more quickly we would have the money we needed for the farm we hoped to buy. The situation was tricky as he, being single, was in a bush posting which would be difficult for me getting to work. However, as a married man, he could get posted to the Copperbelt towns like Kitwe, Ndola or Mufulira and I could just transfer, or he might even get a Lusaka posting.

After our engagement in 1961, and before our wedding Colin was posted to Kapiri Mposhi. I stayed there once – just the once. North of the Copper Belt and a long drive up the Great North Road, it was much more primitive than his previous outpost, Chisamba. Pastoral care of the workforce being paramount, safety, circumspection and chastity was policed. No risk – no way. Travelling alone so far in my elderly motor car was not an option, I would travel with Betty Keith. Betty on that day would be on her way to Mufulira, where she had yet another birthed family looking forward to seeing her.

If I suggested our being 'I am sir, your obedient servant' of HM Govt. of Rhodesia and Nyasaland and living in a convent, I'd say these were a reflection of how it was.

Chaperoned on the journey, delivered by Betty and just to make sure there would be no possibility of carnal relations, she was formally introduced to Mrs Erasmus. Mrs Erasmus whom she believed would be my hostess. Well I did as well.

This was the real bush; you could count the white people on one hand. Women were a rare breed, just Mrs Erasmus and me for two nights. There was a railway yard, police station and the Erasmus' garage, shop and bar. I was never permitted to enter the bar. Mrs Erasmus was a towering Afrikaner whose first name I never learned. Colin called her Mrs Erasmus and he more or less lived with them! They came to our wedding as Mr and Mrs Erasmus. They had two grown-up sons who said little – well, nothing. Apart from at the table I never saw them, and they certainly had nothing to say there. Colin had some great times with the lads, he said, but whether it was all grunts and guns I do not know. When a new railway bloke called McDonald paid his first visit to the bar, Mr Erasmus introduced him to the only other guy in the bar. He'd only said 'Campbell' and the newcomer said 'Campbells! – a smile on their lips and black murder in their hearts' – turned on his heel and walked out. The Massacre of Glencoe was 1692!

In preparation for Kapiri it was important I was safe around guns. I learned to 'lean in' and 'be ready for the recoil.' One of his fellow inspectors stood to the side of the tree with the target attached. First two shots and I hit the target – not a bull's eye, but the little piece of paper. I'm brilliant for a woman, not only was I fit to drive a constabulary Land Rover, but 'she can shoot.' I was re-loaded, and our friend stepped up to the tree. I was so unnerved by his proximity to the tree, I shot wide with no idea where it landed. I was now considered sufficiently competent to bear arms.

I thought I was staying with the Erasmuses and came bearing appropriate gifts for my hostess and her family. I wasn't staying with them at all. I was sleeping in the police station and Colin was sleeping on the Erasmuses' stoep with the lads, Piet and Hennie! Really safe – all I had to do was fire a warning shot and they'd be straight over. Dymphna and Ted had been married that day in Lusaka. Betty and I set off after the reception. No evening celebrations in Zambia – get married in the morning, have a bit of a reception and clear off before it gets dark. Driving in the dark is not done and guests have a long way to go home. We arrived as instructed at the garage, introductions were made. Because of approaching dusk, Betty declined the offer of tea and went on her way.

I was not even to cross the threshold of the Erasmus establishment. That's when I realised, I was not having B&B. Colin picked up my gear and we set off on foot for the police station. To welcome us he was smartly turned out in his every-day uniform. He had a clean one every day. Khaki shorts and bush jacket, starched so well you could set them down and they stood to attention. Very neat about the neck and with knee socks and shiny shoes the entire ensemble was a tribute to his boy. He had the elaborate cross over shiny brown leather; I think Sam Browne is the name for it and, of course, his holster. Then there were the crowns, pips and shiny silver buttons. He still had hair then, but on-duty he had a cap. That was only one of his uniforms. There was a more casual than this, his day dress. There was evening dress and No 1s. No 1 had variations as well as maybe just not official ones like the one he got married in. Anyway, he smartly escorted me to the police station.

Squalor I knew about. Nurses homes can be a bit that way and I've been on the district and seen how people live, but Kapiri Mposhi police station was such as I'd never experienced. The police station and police house combined was a hut. Steps up and you were in an entry hall with a sink with one tap in a metal frame, Calor gas ring, desk then straight ahead a small room. The small room, small window, two standard government-issue easy chairs, deal table and two chairs. A government easy chair is wooden with two thin cushions and lights are max 40-watt, just the one central; shades not supplied.

Leading off the 'lounge' was the bedroom. Low wooden single bed with a rifle handcuffed to it. A door and small window faced us. On our honeymoon we stayed in 'The Tatty Hotel' and that was five-star compared to Kapiri police house. How glad he was to see me, and the sheets were clean – we had better blankets at the African Hospital – there was cold water from a tap in the entrance and a gas ring – such luxury. Anyway, this was where I was to sleep and he would be just across Africa sleeping with Hennie and Piet on the Erasmuses' stoep. Clearly the Erasmuses had only limited accommodation and all but Mr and Mrs slept outside. Oh yes, I had a loo – outside, plank and bucket, torch provided. Colin was the only European and had a number of African constables and his boy. I never discovered where the boy did his washing and starching because my intended was immaculate. And yes, the sheets were starched as well. The constables lived in a compound apart from the station, quite a bit away, but in line with my toilet.

We ate with the Erasmus family, I can't remember what, except it was served at the table from an enormous pot and there were literally buckets of vegetables and we ate off serving platters.

Mr Erasmus 'boomed' as he and Colin exchanged man talk then I was escorted back in the pitch dark across rough ground to my room. Mrs Erasmus and I exchanged smiles and occasional pleasantries, but this was a patriarchal establishment. Piet and Hennie said nowt save an occasional grunt and the buckets were shifted or Mr Erasmus shovelled another couple of ladles on to their platters from the cauldron.

Pitch dark and over stony ground, Colin couldn't stay long, or Mr and Mrs Erasmus might think we were up to no good. He just ensured I knew where the PK was, gave me his revolver for under my pillow and left to slum it with the boys. It was fine as I could read. but what I hadn't counted on was what to do when I needed to go. Torch, pistol, toilet roll might have been OK if I could have opened the door and walked out, but as at the front, the floor was a long way above ground and there were no steps. A Tesco poly bag would have been a solution. What if I left the door open and a snake got in? What if I left the gun and a burglar got in? What if I jumped down and the gun went off? Despite all this I managed.

I was wakened in the morning by a banging on the door and Colin in true Taggart fashion announced – 'there's been a murder.' He'd never had one before. So, he and a posse of constables took off into the bush in two Land Rovers. I was a bit wary of going outside because obviously the news had spread and there was a growing crowd outside. They weren't baying or anything but male and restless. He came back a bit later with a constable to update me, have breakfast and borrow my camera. A girl had been killed and her eyes gouged out. The Africans believed that the eyes of the corpse retain a picture of their assassin, a bit like CCTV so by removing them, they cannot be identified. This time I was required to accompany him since he wasn't sure how the camera worked. That's true but understated; I couldn't stay there on my own with a gathering, and no way of knowing how and if it would kick off.

We set off on a track but soon took to the bundu, where traces of his earlier route were obvious and much denser that I'd ever experienced before. There were hordes of bystanders but the driver just drove through them and they moved. No crime scene tape or attempt at securing the crime scene. The place was heaving. We did what had to be done and returned to wait for the constables, who were apparently hot on the trail of the murderer. About four o'clock they returned in high spirits, hot and sweating with a sweaty, stinky prisoner. They fixed his handcuffs to the sink leg and he just sat there on the floor exhausted and terrified while they set about getting drinks for themselves. The crowd outside began chanting. The prisoner was ignored. I didn't like that, so I filled the only receptacle left, a pop bottle, with water and gave it to him. There was a lot of 'over-and-outing' on the radio. We were to head straight off for Ndola with the prisoner because as the rising clamour outside indicated there was a potential riot situation. I could not be left behind, so with prisoner and two constables in the back I set off with Colin for Ndola.

We were making good time when the fan belt went. Usual, middle of nowhere I was forced to remove my stockings, to affect a repair. We were considerably slowed down till we came to an Army post.

As usual to keep cool as we drove, I had my elbow on the open window and my fingers curled on the roof. We stopped and with not even a 'Who goes there?' a bayonet just missed me. As well as the African sentries, in the hut, shed, guard house were four Army officers playing cards. We had the usual formal exchange of introductions, banter and tea and I was abandoned there to wait. It seems it was inappropriate to turn up at a proper police station with a prisoner and a fiancé in an official vehicle. Till he eventually returned, I played cards with the soldiers, but lost nothing since I had no money with me. It was the middle of the night when we got back to Kapiri and things were quiet. It was a different sort of break.

The murder was of a local virgin. The murderer was the tribe stud. African girls were 'tried out' before they were given in marriage and it was the job of this man to carry out this role with the girls in the village reaching marriage age – anything after about thirteen. I suspect a lot of the unrest was about it being the fault of the girl, who spurned his advances. In the eyes of the elders, he had done no more than his job.

I had been taking photographs at Dymphna and Ted's wedding, but in true crime scene fashion, once the camera had been used for evidential purpose, the film was impounded as evidence. NRP were fast responders and their clear-up rate really good, but getting my snaps back didn't happen. Colin thought I should be over the moon at getting a free film, but I wanted the wedding pictures I'd taken. The trial was complex owing to the combination of tribal customs and he went to prison. Justice was very difficult in ways of ensuring equality.

I had cared for a male patient, a European in the Isolation ward, who had recently been released from prison. His crime was an almost accidental infringement, but he was sent down.

Hard labour was for all prisoners and the food was abysmal. His knees were scabby and infected, but he wasn't actually infectious, just suffering from malnutrition and infected bites. One of the labouring jobs he was given was to paint the white stones which lined the pathways in the prison compound with a child's paintbrush.

Damaged knees I saw another time were on a deceased bishop, on whom Dymphna and I were performing the last offices. She drew my attention to the damage done through a life of prayer. The callouses were enormous and deforming.

Kafue is lovely. The river is wide and Africa stretches out all around. The land is dry with scruffy bits of scrub, but there's always a bit of colour – bright colour – weeds with vibrant shades. The bridge that was the border between Northern Rhodesia and Southern Rhodesia is at Kafue. It has no architectural merit, just a Meccano kind of erection. You would not sit out and picnic because it is bush, but the wide river and the steel bridge is a place to stand and stare. In a warm land a trip down to Kafue was a treat. The Zambesi was wide and fast flowing and the banks were green. Apart from Lake Kariba, the river at Kafue was the only stretch of water I saw. The first place I wanted to go when I returned to the UK was to see the sea. There may even be a McDonald's there now. Animals of all sorts are to be seen by the road and crossing it. Crocodiles, zebra, hippo and wildebeest are most common. Men fished and hunted, but it was dangerous.

It was my good fortune to be part of the first Sirolli Enterprise Facilitation ™ in Europe in the late 90s. The Sirolli Institute, established in 1985, is a social enterprise that teaches entrepreneurs, corporations, governments and community leaders how to *capture the passion* of their communities, using the intelligence of local people. Convinced that the future of every community lies in capturing the energy, intelligence and passion of its people, Enterprise Facilitation was developed by Dr Ernesto Sirolli as a social technology application to train anyone ready to add tools for sustainable economic development. It is a brilliant initiative, based on his knowledge that development can only be indigenous and on what is already present in every community. It began in Australia then spread to New Zealand and the wider world and eventually Ernesto came to talk to us in East Lancashire and we recognised his message was something we were trying to achieve, but hadn't the underpinning knowledge to ensure its sustainability, continuity and reach. His inspiration came from events at Kafue.

USA leaders thinking to improve the native lot sent a bunch of experts with student volunteers to show them how to grow food easily and cheaply. 'These people are lazy they lie around in the sun and don't grow anything because the land is dry.' The banks of the Zambezi were ideal for their purpose and they chose to plant tomatoes and were very successful. The natives showed only perfunctory interest in the scheme. However, these 'pioneers' knew what was good for them and persevered with committed altruistic volunteers with missionary zeal. One night the hippos had a bit of a wander and destroyed the lot. The Africans just shrugged and carried on doing what bush Africans do. In the UK women have a 'sniff' that speaks volumes. The Africans do a shrug.

Kafue was the beautiful place, where a terrible thing happened. The son of Mary Lansberg, one of the sisters at the hospital, was taken by a crocodile. It was the most awful thing and there was a pall of shock and dread that spread beyond the hospital. The Lansbergs were a South African family and he'd gone with his dad and uncle on an expedition as a treat. A grown-up outing, he was thrilled to be allowed to go on. His mother wasn't happy about the trip and he was well warned before he left, as were the adults. There was no sign, no hint of danger, just a sudden swift, silent slither on to the bank and snap he was dragged into the deep fast-flowing river. The men in the party dived all day but failed to find him. His father found him next day. Crocodiles do not kill and eat. Crocodiles kill, conceal, store and save for later when the flesh is rotting. Mary never got over it and I don't expect his dad did either, but I never knew him. Though very tall and statuesque, she just withered until in no time at all she was small, drip white and thin. 'Shilpit' is the Scottish word that describes.

29 Married in Africa

We are now approaching our wedding day, September 30th, 1961. I've just checked in my little brown book stamped – Northern Rhodesia – Notebook – Government use only! It is important the date is checked because of gestation times, as will be revealed later in this narrative. We had a fairy-tale wedding for less than £50, all inclusive. My Dad was disbelieving when I told him what it would be costing him. He'd already paid for one abortive attempt at getting me off his hands and I was reluctant to accept, but he insisted. It was a bit Blue Peter in that I just happened to have a little box with a veil and tiara in stock. Dymphna was married first, so she provided the nearly new wedding dress. Irene and Bill's little girl Irene just happened to have been a bridesmaid for her auntie and hadn't outgrown her frock. Somebody knew somebody who knew somebody who iced wedding cakes. Edgar Gatt, the anaesthetist, was a keen photographer, so he provided two films with forty-eight pictures of the day. The reception was in the garden of the mess. Food was funded by a one-off and a bit of a government subsidy prepared by the 'boys.' It was a lovely day. We needed nothing else. Flying wasn't common and a three-week journey just wasn't something people did, so weddings were like ours; home-made. No parents or in-laws in waiting. Rose and Grace were professional wedding planners. In their capacity as Matron and

Assistant Matron, they extended their parental oversight of our morals until we were no longer their responsibility.

It would be unfair to portray Rose and Grace as Mother Superior types because they were anything but. Neither was married, but for both it was non-contributory to their lifestyle. Rose was Irish and devout, but off-duty and after mass, off came the mantilla until next time. She had a chap and though he was brought out on occasion when available or necessary, this was not a formally recognised liaison. He had a recognised problem with alcohol and like others was periodically admitted to dry out. The situation neither matured nor disintegrated during my time and was reputed to have been like that for many years before. Rose was efficient and ran both Central and African Hospitals with a certainty that nothing anyone was involved with in her ambit escaped her, on or off-duty. Such was her control that when Alistair, my first born, was less than two weeks old she required me to look after Muriel and James's six-week-old baby, Patrick. Muriel and James married a week before we did and delivered four weeks before we did. My fertility was questioned. The shame Colin felt was a reflection on his manhood and a constant irritation and recriminatory matter for some time. When Rose rang to tell me, I would be having Muriel's baby for some shifts, I thought to mention the 'breast feeding.' Wrong. Muriel had kicked breast feeding into touch that very day. Of course, having young Patrick would not interfere with my having Donald – Dymphna's first born, during the day. Grace was not the social animal Rose was. She had a badly-behaved dog and a cat. She was quiet, efficient and very kind, on and off-duty. Grace became a friend and was the first person we invited to dinner after the honeymoon.

I was given away by Tom Little. Very tall and very bald, he was a pharmacist in town. I'd met him and his wife at the Presbyterian Church the first Sunday I arrived. We all had to attend somewhere and if we had no transport a driver took us and collected us. Once we were independent, we could choose to go or not. It was only the RCs who stuck with it and more often than not we'd go there before going wherever we planned to go afterwards. Father Murphy could say mass fast; we could be in and out in twenty minutes. An important part of the wedding was the passport. I had to have a new one to travel and there was a system for that. Apply for a new passport in your married name by filling in a lot of forms including one that was filled in by the minister who would do the job. The new passport was then sent to him and he retained it and presented it after the signing of the register.

Colin's best man was Alan Middleton-Stewart a fellow inspector. He later became a radio presenter in the UK and a prominent member of the old boy's reunion mob of the Northern Rhodesia police. The groom and best man wore No 1 uniform, long navy-blue trousers with dangerously sharp creases, shiny belt and shoes and a lanyard which finished up in the top left pocket of the tunic via a little opening on the side. On the end of this lanyard was a little whistle! Just like the whistles we had in the Girl Guides when we reached the heady heights of patrol leader. That's what should have been in his pocket, but it wasn't. Apparently, he and Alan were on their way to the church when it was discovered Colin was incorrectly dressed. He had in his excitement or apprehension forgotten his whistle. There was no time to go back so they had stopped off at Alan's and got his spare lanyard. Not being of the tight and teetotal brigade, Alan's spare lanyard didn't have a little silver whistle, but a bottle opener on the end.

I'm afraid I have only scanty memories of the wedding itself. I remember nobody seemed to know the hymns, so I felt the need to add volume to *Love Divine*. The minister made a performance out of the presentation of the passport by reading my new married name out loud. I remember I had the key to my suitcase pinned to my bra so nobody could stuff it full of confetti. I remember Elaine double fixing my veil because it was a bit windy. I remember Dymphna being very pregnant in her best maternity dress which she had made herself. A dress which I later wore. It wasn't my very best frock. My very best was a navy one with little white spots and a floaty bow, which served me well, even onto the twins. There were about fifty guests and the garden looked lovely. Tom Little made a speech and read a letter my Dad had sent him. Then Colin did his 'my wife and myself' to hoots and raucous laughter from very coarse policemen! We didn't stay long as we had a way to go before dark. Naturally we went in Hesperus as we were not a two-car family. Duly stuffed with confetti and rattling cans and lipstick writing, we left on the first leg of our honeymoon. On our way to start our married life together, to carry on saving for our farm which would prosper so Colin could be an antique collecting gentleman farmer.

We left the reception and stopped around the corner to cut off the clattering cans, rip off the placards and wipe off the suggestive texts. Cutting and ripping didn't take long but cleaning the windscreen with hankie and spit took a bit longer. We set off again for Monze, where we were to spend 'our first night.' It's only about twenty miles away, but far enough because of having to travel in daylight. For the benefit of any reader, it is quite possible to drive at night in Africa, just not sensible. The roads are mostly strip roads and straight. You can drive for hundreds of miles in the middle of the road. In daytime the monotony can be relieved by seeing wild animals or meeting another vehicle head on. At night there is the hypnotic monotony of tarmac strips in your headlights and falling asleep. The possibility of a puncture and being an early breakfast for some animal is annoying because safety dictates you stay in your vehicle until daylight. Then of course there are the head-on collision statistics. The most frequent night hazard in town or bush is African plus bicycle. Africans do not have lights on their bikes. The locals do not use Pickford's for removals, though Pickford's is big business in Africa. Always give cyclists a wide berth, but often that is not enough. The African townships are not visible from the road and seldom is there any foot traffic; unless you happen to run full pelt into a zebra or some other creature who knows nothing of the Green Cross Code. When that happens, suddenly, out of nowhere hordes of Africans, men, women and children pour into the road fully equipped and in good voice swoop on the roadkill. Your only sensible course of action is to close the window, lock your doors and put your foot down. You can observe via your rear mirror a carcass stripped bare in seconds.

We congratulated ourselves on getting away with only surface confetti and my key was still attached to my bra when we had an emergency stop! Colin needing his razor etc. had not packed his toilet bag and it was still in Alan's car. Back we went. The guests still enjoying my Dad's hospitality, found this very entertaining, the shortest honeymoon on record. On the subject of funding, the total cost was standing at £56 until the hire glasses and sale or return booze was returned and the refund took us back down to under £50. This time we managed to reach Monze, where there was a motel.

I thought a motel was a place where you parked outside your chalet which would have all mod cons and privacy. Wrong. It was a shack with rooms, a bar/canteen and outside ablutions. The food was plentiful as befits a truck stop. Our fellow guests all male, tickled to bits with the arrival of a couple and newlywed into the bargain. That put a damper on our nocturnal expectations and for the second time Colin had to accompany me to the lavatory. It's one thing being in a bucket-n-chuck-it when it's your own or you know the neighbours, but a load of rough men was inhibiting.

A 'not quite nice' part of life to a formerly well brought up free church Presbyterian of teetotal parentage, was the reluctance of any European male to look for a 'gents.' Any party, any event, if you ventured outside there was a line of men, backs to the light, competing to pee highest, furthest and longest. Anyway, their ribald send-off with suggestions, when we left the table, was totally inhibiting. We just quietly went to bed and left early next morning. This may well be the reason we lost a month in the reproduction stakes.

We were going to Molepolole in Bechuanaland, 648 miles away, to visit the Merriweathers as the furthest point south on our trip. A wonderful cosmopolitan trip to those who may have had a week in Blackpool, but it was the ex-pat equivalent of a few days at Fleetwood. We could not afford posh, since I met Colin and knew he was the person I would spend the rest of my life with, I'd occasionally put petrol in Hesperus and we'd been to the bioscope. Everything else was a bunch of flowers in return for somebody else's hospitality. As for Colin, he'd been there longer than I had and only ever spent his salary on essentials not provided as part of his package. So, the first night at the motel at Monze, then five stars in Salisbury was extravagance. I've looked up Kapiri since I began to write this and today it has supermarkets and hotels and an airport style railway station.

Meikles Hotel, five-star luxury, as described then and now was decayed, colonial and unchanged since Cecil Rhodes. Plush velvet and chintz, large settees and elegant potted plants scattered the entrance. Dozens of white gloves and Boys' Brigade uniformed boys were on hand to take our luggage. Proudly signed in as Mr and Mrs, we were shown upstairs to our room. Our room was not en-suite, but there was a bathroom nearby with large claw-foot bath and a proper Thomas Crapper toilet. Within our rooms the curtains and bedspread were heavy folk-woven tapestry in wine and red. There were even blankets on the bed and a proper double bed it was. There was no hospitality tray, but an extensive room service menu which we resisted as we were booked for dinner. An orchestra played in the dining room.

We missed out on so much by penny pinching. I should have had some inkling. but Colin was endowed with a courtly gentility loved by old ladies and the wind never blew on me, I was diverted from temptation by the promise of pedigree Charolaise and 'name your price' prize bulls. You see, by this time, Antonina, one of the nursing assistants, had told my fortune, people paid for her services but all I had to do was have Chubby cover my ward while I watched hers and I had my palm read. I would have twins and caramel coloured cows. She was a little out in the longevity as I was supposed to peg out in middle life. This gave Colin an opportunity to educate me in single-suckle special breeds. His mother sent him the

Farmers Guardian every week. We had few mementoes to bring back to the UK because souvenirs were an unnecessary expense. In the end it made it easier on the distribution of the assets. One luxury night in Salisbury and we were on our way, next stop Gaborone.

Gaborone, the capital of Bechuanaland, a desert land teeming with wildlife and the world's second poorest nation, had much in common with the Wild West in having just the one street. Only the hitching posts were missing. The street was cluttered with bicycles, pickups and a sprinkling of sturdy cars. Vauxhall Vanguards were popular. We were booked in at the Tatti Hotel, the Ritz of Gaborone. The entrance was directly off the front street, a street which didn't even have a tarmac strip. There was no pavement. The hotel entrance directly off the road was green saloon type swing doors. I suppose you could say it was airy because in the whole complex only the bedrooms had doors and they were only half doors with a fitted metal mesh screen for the top part. The Tatti Hotel was not the place to go if you were looking for honeymoon privacy.

The reception was short and wide and between two sets of more green swing doors, a desk where passports were scrutinised, and we checked in. The whole area was hazy with a thick fug of African odour, tobacco and beer. The first swing led into the bar which was shoulder-to-shoulder drinkers and a lot of mixed language noise. The other led into the dining room, which was again smoky and busy, but neither room had a window. From the dining room two doors lay straight ahead leading to kitchen and sleeping quarters.

The sleeping accommodation was straight ahead and out of the back door – another green saloon door. Outside you had a choice even on the left, odd on the right. Seaside bathing huts, attached, ten each side, you walked past a half-screen door with an adjacent window with a lace curtain, then the next screen door. The rooms were identical and open to view. A chest with a Gordon's gin bottle, with a tumbler perched on it, sat between twin beds. Some beds had bodies resting on them, others were just rumpled. We were half-way up on the left.

Warm water for drinking was provided in matching green bottles and a request for more brought another perhaps a little bit less aired. You were not intended to drink water; strong drink was the beverage of choice in Bechuanaland and half of the residents were in the bar practising. The smell from the multi-racial bar was overwhelming. Not so in the dining room as the Africans, while keen on Castle beer were less keen on the food. It was not haute cuisine. There was no menu. Boil in the bag fish in white sauce, not Bird's Eye because there was a lot of it and string beans. Could have been an Afrikaner speciality of the house.

A building across the end of the bedrooms housed friendly toilet and washing facilities. The toilet cubicles had bog roll provided and a three-foot partition between each allowed a little privacy. As usual, I never encountered a male user. The baths were user-friendly, the partitions, a mere gesture. Conversation and 'pass me the soap' happened to me. There was potential for voyeurism night and day in the bedrooms. The nets or rather the net, was on a wire, sagged and hung either to the right or the left, but not all the way. The corridor between the rooms was lit night and day for two reasons. The orange bulb kept insects away at night and lit our way to bed. After the tiny bit of corridor, there was a bit of a ravine before the sides rose again for walkway at the other side. I don't think this was a storm drain because they never get much rain in the desert and some years none at all. They needed a bit of width to accommodate the toilet block and make the whole building square.

Next morning, we set off for Molepolole a United Free Church of Scotland mission station. Alfred Merriweather was the doctor son of our minister in Edinburgh and a friend of my dad's. I'd known him since I was small and being a nurse had an interest in his work. There was a hospital and lots of outpatient places in the bush. It was Alfred my dad contacted when I had my bit of a problem when I first arrived.

Alfred and Mary, his wife, had a little girl Joy and their bungalow was lovely with all mod cons. What it didn't have though were through walls. In the sleeping part of the house there were just low tongue and groove partitions which didn't encourage whatever it is parents do that their children believe never took place.

Bechuanaland was a new experience in every way. The Kalahari Desert is nothing like the bush in Rhodesia. It is dry and sandy with little vegetation. How far did the natives have to travel to find the sharpened staves that built the corrals to keep their skinny cattle safe from predators? Out of Molepolole there weren't even tracks to follow. Until 1966, when it became Botswana, this was a British Protectorate. The UK government tried to hang on to it for the wealth they wanted to keep. King Seretse Khama was prevented from returning until 1956 with his English wife. A barrister, he became interested in politics and had a vision for his country which has resulted in Botswana having the highest standard of living in Africa. A country where education and health care are free. It is based second only to Kenya as a tourist destination. It was nothing like that when we went there on our honeymoon.

Alfred and Mary weren't stuffy as missionaries go and we had a good time. They had lots of friends and in later years I caught up with some of them again who'd been in Abercorn and Lusaka. Alfred was physician to Seretse Khama, chief of the local tribe and his family and socialised with them. Alfred and Seretse were a surprising pair of friends as Alfred was lifelong teetotal and the drink eventually contributed to Seretse's early death. There was a lot of adverse publicity when Seretse, son of the chief of the Bamangwata tribe, met and married Ruth Williams, a white shorthand-typist, when he was at Oxford. They were jointly interested in public health and education and Alfred ran some pilot projects funded by the World Health Organisation. Alfred had been in Molepolole since he was demobbed directly there after the war. He was fluent in the local language and trusted by the tribes so his transition to becoming Speaker in Seretse's first parliament was a good appointment. I believe their friendship had much to do with Botswana emerging as a stable and wealthy nation.

The Livingstone Hospital in Molepolole was similar to the African Hospital in Lusaka. The relatives came too. The only real difference was that education and religion combined with health, and no one was immune. Alfred was the only doctor, but he had so many letters after his name you could have said the only one he lacked, was PDS – Pure Damn Swank. Every furlough time he completed yet another degree. Starting with tropical diseases, he carried on to MRCP, FRCS and MD then, just to top it, of theology. As the Reverend Doctor, he covered a broad spectrum.

Like anywhere in Africa, there was an ex-pat community, but it was slightly different, due to Seretse's father having made friends with the UF church people and the British Government and invited them to his country. In 1961, there was a growing European workforce doing what they were doing in Lusaka with a different slant. It was assimilating modernisation organically and history shows just how well it worked.

I know what I did while we were there, but not just sure how Colin filled in his time. I know he got involved in fixing the water tower and made friends with the police station, but I went out and about in a truck to clinics with Alfred. In the cab were me, a nurse, and Alfred driving. It had a very long wheelbase and before we left it was loaded up with carboys of medicine, and cases of dressings and some files and folders, a dispenser boy and another boy who was clerical and crowd control. We set off early and did not travel fast as we were on a road, but a very dusty sandy one and how we ever got there without getting lost I don't know. There did not seem to be any landmarks. Every few miles we'd come on groups of people waiting and no sign of human habitation in sight. Maybe they saw the dust storm. I don't know how we kept going because every time we stopped, we seemed to be in deep sand and the revs needed to get started got heavier. We kept picking up more and more people who were making their way to the clinic. By the time we got there, it was a bit like the buses in India with people hanging out. We never turned anyone away and the surprising thing was that with all the bumps nobody fell off and under the wheels. No suspension in the cab so what it was like lurching and clinging on in the back God only knows.

We eventually came to a village. Though the houses looked similar to those in Lusaka, everything else was different. There was spare land amid the houses with a wooden stockade, where very lean cattle were kept overnight. Boys went out with them each day to forage. In Africa, Botswana has the most elephants, and we'd seen lots of wildlife on our way, but that didn't seem to stop the nomadic people wandering about waiting for the lorry. In another area, oxen, were walking round and round dragging a wooden pole which was drawing water. There were no bikes, nor were there any broken-down vehicles. Women with babies on their backs and scraggy dogs mingling with children kept clear of groups of elders – gentlemen all – who sat in groups outside of the huts sucking pipes and deep in conversation.

There was a goodly mob waiting outside a little shed. Most of the people were clutching bottles of all shapes and sizes. Later, I realised you brought your own container for your moutie (medicine). Inside the shed was the dispensary, a hallway and the doctor's office. The usual offices were bucket and chuck it and a basin on a stand in the surgery and dispensary. The passengers had by this time jumped off and were mingling with the crowd. We had a drink then got stuck in.

Outpatients were like no other. Crowd control was a little Hitler and we got just one at a time, but 'one out one in' was remorseless – hand over prescription and next patient is already describing his ailment after Alfred had done his 'Good morning. What seems to be your problem today?' in fluent whatever. In true African fashion the explanation is long winded, but while they are getting it off their chest, Alfred has turned their head away from him, so he is not breathing in TB and is listening to their chest. If the situation required it, they lay down on the portable couch for him to see to that. More linguistic exchanges, a bit of rapid writing on a prescription and the next patient was on his way in. Nobody ever left without either an injection or a bottle of medicine.

The dispensary does not carry much because we were not yet at broad-spectrum antibiotics. They did, however, carry penicillin, sulphonamides and quinine. The carboys contained the liquid that will fill the 'bring your own' containers. Simply, we had on offer, kaolin and morph for diarrhoea, mist pot cit for urinary infections, cough mixture and a tonic. It was hot and smelly and the queue seemed endless, but we did stop for a very brief drink and carried on until crowd control shut the door and he and dispenser began to pack up, nurse finished her weighing and dressings. Alfred and I were led by the caretaker to the 'home visits.' The insides of the huts were dark with mud floors kept swept clean and the room tidy. They had few possessions, just pots and pans and they were wearing their limited wardrobes so there was no need for cupboards and drawers.

We saw some very old people, who were not really old at all – just worn out and crippled with musculo-skeletal problems which had followed on from rickets, TB or osteomyelitis. We saw a young woman in advanced pregnancy dying of TB. Will she or won't she deliver before she dies? We decided we would take her back to the hospital as well as two other people seen in clinic, who needed nursing care. These and their relatives were preparing to travel with us. The hospital did have an ambulance, but if we could fit them in, we would take them. There was an arbitrary hierarchical selection carried out by dispenser and crowd control as to who else might be lucky enough to get a lift. We left and were back mid-afternoon for a shower and light snack before hospital rounds.

Next stop Livingstone and the Victoria Falls. After the dry sandy Botswana, Livingstone was a wonderful experience. The greenery, the forest and the roar of the water was you walked through its cathedral-like arches and the growing sound of the falls is almost a mystical experience. The spray was so cool, the rain forest soft and cold underfoot and the rainbows enchanting. Sitting outside in the evening with a cool drink and the roar of the water, was grand. This was the first time I'd been to Livingstone. The previous time we were meant to go, we were called back to Lusaka for the court case about my burglary. The hotel was of a much more modern style than Meikles and the food streets ahead of the Tatti Hotel, but my last hotel stay for about ten years.

30 Married life

The honeymoon was over and it was back to work and living in our new home. Colin had a new posting to Woodlands, a suburb of Lusaka. Our accommodation however was the single flat above the police station because there were no P2s available. A P2 had two bedrooms. Our flat had one. Like all government accommodation it had been designed by a male architect who had never washed up; didn't understand the need for the facility either side of the kitchen sink for before and after dishes. The layout was impossible, impracticable and required an advanced degree in logistics.

We had our own entrance. No letterbox. An external staircase led up from the cell block to our door. The door opened directly into our lounge dining room with windows at either end. There was a red stone floor, table, sideboard and four chairs at one end and our two easy chairs at the other. We had little to add in the furniture line, but we had lovely glasses and crystal sundae dishes. In the facing wall were two doors. The left door led to our bedroom furnished as standard with twin beds and not much else. There was no room for anymore and two in the bedroom at the same time was an invasion of personal space.

The right-hand door raised issues. The architect had started with a square space and two windows to the left and two windows to the right. The left provides a window each to bedroom and diner end and right a lounge window and the problem. The room is the same shape and size as the bedroom and with window mid-wall has to service kitchen and bathroom. The kitchen came first, and the bathroom was clearly an afterthought and led off it. Was thought ever given to ventilation? Were there building regulations? It was probably the smallest toilet and shower ever. Colin's boy, Luke, who was vital for the laundry, was in attendance during the day, which led to complications if I was on nights. Wandering out to the loo half asleep, bare feet and nightie was tricky. However, Luke went walkabout and instead we got a girl called Emma.

Emma too could wash and starch like a professional and reputedly cook, but not for me. I fed my man myself. I had my recipe books and in the flat a little gas cooker. Our first dinner guest was Grace. I went to town with the menu. I bought a chicken. I had some crystal sundae dishes Betty Keith had bought us and we had grapefruit to start. Not just plonked in the dish. but plonked in frosted dishes. It seems daft now, but I smeared juice round the rims then dipped them in sugar and put them in the fridge. When I took them out, they had sparkly rims and half a grapefruit in its skin but with the refinement of my having carved out the segments in advance.

I placed the chicken on the table in front of the master of the house who threw a wobbler at being faced with this alien task. Grace more or less said, 'Give it to me, you wally' and proceeded to carve. My shame, the knife hit a foreign body, and she drew out neck, liver and gizzards and said, 'We don't normally leave these inside.' But it was cooked, and I knew then that 'wash the chicken' meant inside and out. Not my finest hour, but I'd made a trifle and that was and ever more has been my specialty. A P2 became available and we moved around the corner.

The P2 had two bedrooms, twin beds, lounge with dining area, bathroom and kitchen. You just moved your clothes and any odds that put your stamp on a place. Colin had a unique system for moving. He tipped all his goods and chattels into his riot shield then upended them into the back of the Land Rover. You entered our plot across a bridge over the storm drain and we had a stoep (veranda) with the standard yellow bulb – to deter flying insects – and a couple of canvas chairs. In the back garden we had fruit trees, well, mangoes and bananas. Naturally, we ate the entire crop because it was free, and I was a bit OTT on mangoes when I was pregnant. At the bottom of the garden was Emma's living quarters.

We paid Emma £6 a month and £2 a week scoff money. She had free accommodation and somehow always managed to cook enough to have some left over. I virtually gave up on the good wife bit when we moved to Woodlands because of the facilities. We had a wood stove which I called the black devil. It was temperamental and I never got the hang of it. It could take six hours to boil the kettle but turn a casserole into cinders in three minutes. Augmenting this, we had a single Calor gas ring. Our next-door neighbours were really set up properly and she had a proper cooker. We used to eat there regularly. They came to us, but only for drinks and snacks. Please don't think we were so mean as not to offer a return meal; they had one school-age child, the husband worked days and wife stayed at home with staff. They were a P3 and in mitigation; we both worked shifts and were subject to the vagaries of the black devil. I use her braised onion recipe today.

Not much changed apart from the living arrangements and car ownership. Colin didn't have a car in Lusaka, though when younger and a trial to his mother, he had an open top MG he called Annie. First thing we had to have was a vehicle more suited to our status than Hesperus and off he went to an auction. As a side-line it was lucrative. I never saw it and certainly it did nothing to raise our standard of living. He bought up wrecks, I drove them to work, he fettled them then sold them on to an eager queue of constables and it all began again. Life was full of surprises. I'd come off-duty in the morning driving a Ford Escort then look out in the afternoon to see what I'd be driving later. One two-week night duty I had three cars. I was sometimes envy of the boys at the hospital but just as easily the laughing stock.

One day I looked out and there it was a gleaming black monster – Sunbeam Talbot, I think. Our paths seldom crossed so I'd get ready, pick up the keys, always left in the same place and go to work. This car was a true unknown in that it had a column gear change. I worked out the forward gears and got there. Parked in my slot beside the ward – nose to wall, storm drain left, wall on right. Only when I got in to get out in the morning did I realise I had no idea where reverse was. Not an inch to make a mistake; the head ambulance boy swaggered over and got it out for me.

In Lusaka, we seldom went out with ambulances, we were in short supply and to take us out would put patients at risk. The drivers were not paramedics and the kindly women usually went with them. One Sunday lunch time I was just coming off when I got an Isolation admission. A female with chicken pox! Just an unbelievable bit of drama! Silly woman, what a fuss, I blame the GMO he was a bit like a GP we had in Lancashire once, needed a second opinion for dandruff. In Scotland you could only use the siren if you had a police escort. Not in Lusaka. If they spotted a car it was foot up and a sharp blast on the siren. I couldn't believe it – chicken pox!

I've got a little ahead of myself. I've jumped from being competent to manage my wards, fairly self-sufficient, fit to drive and giving birth as if there was no intermediate stage. Muriel and James who married on the same day as we did, beat us by four weeks in the baby stakes. We caught up but were only allowed to continue working until week twenty, when you had to resign your post until your baby was twelve hours old. Then, just like the Africans, get up and get on with it. During weeks twenty to forty, I provided a baby minding service for those nurses already delivered and required to be available to work.

I'd never heard of 'baby brain,' but apparently Colin had and realised he was now in charge of an idiot. I was discouraged from driving. That meant he took the car to work where previously he'd used an NRP Land Rover or a constable picked him up. So, when he's on-duty – I am marooned. Getting to hold on to the car was a struggle because nothing – nothing at all was important enough for me to use petrol in my car when I was not earning, and we were deprived of my salary. That is when my Edinburgh middle-class snobbery was thrown up. Regularly thrown up. I'm sorry, but I just didn't get it. From the day we married, I kept this bloke; I saved and could maintain his lifestyle until it was time for us to go on home leave. I had become a parasite and my profligacy meant we would be held back in buying our first farm. It blew up in his face – or rather the wall – because I'd thrown away good money on a home perm!!! A home perm because it was cheaper than a proper salon job. Not just perm lotion but I expected to keep the car and drive somewhere to have the perm! Well the perm lotion flew out of my hand, he ducked, bottle hit wall and broke. I burst into tears and he had to buy me another bottle.

Once I finished work there were other new rules. I may have places to go and people to see, but once permission was given, I was forbidden to go anywhere near the African townships. Popping over to see Dymphna was a doddle – through the township behind us, cross the road and through the township that led to Ted's plot – no distance. No. No. No. You drive all the way into town and then all the way out of town and miles up the East road. I got fed up and went how I used to go before the draconian rules and just as I was getting near the proper road, what should cross the intersection but an NRP Land Rover. And people talk now about the way police deal with the public. My children will be familiar with this scene. It involves a sort of body inflation, steaming ears and shouting; cap flung off head and stamped on. I'm still too far in front of myself, I haven't mentioned the in-laws.

I could understand my parents being somewhat anxious about me getting married again and took all possible steps to assuage their worries. This included Colin writing to ask for my hand in marriage which was the start of my mother thinking the sun shone out of his whatsit. I had to explain myself to his parents. I'm sure for both parties there was a feeling of impending doom. I was Scottish and Colin was English.

Meanwhile, back in Lusaka, we now dutifully wrote home every week with my doing a keep you going in the middle to maintain the 'reassurance.' The thing was we did a bit, and the other added a bit, so they heard from us both. Prudence required we filled the whole of the airmail letter and that meant up the sides as well. 'Don't leave me much space.' At one stage during Alistair's gestation there was a mail strike and letters arrived out of sequence. To his parents I confirmed when we would be travelling back to the UK 'plus infant' of course. Shock horror – the times I've heard this story. His mother used to open the letters and leave them on the mantelpiece for when his dad came home. She said nothing until he read it and then they both went into meltdown thinking I'd been pregnant before we got married. Oh, the shame. Anyway come a few days and the mail caught up and they got the announcement, fingers were counted, and sighs heaved.

It was a normal evening, warm, muggy, but what about a little treat? The garage had taken ownership of a chest freezer and was selling Fanta. There was a choice of orange or lemon. With great purse string loosening, we walked there and chose one each to savour as we sat out on the stoep. I felt a few twinges walking back, but only mentioned once I'd got my Fanta in a glass. This was a sharp learning curve – keep it to yourself. A very casual comment and the only thing I can liken the panic to is that which occurs in submarine war films and that horrible hooter goes off and someone yells 'Dive, dive, dive.' I was only mentioning it, but he was frantic and needed to rush off and fill up with petrol. It was Friday and the weekly ration had been trickled into the tank. The hospital was only five miles away. He got back and left the engine running. I managed to delay matters until 10 p.m., but the pressure and agitation was too much for him and we screamed off to the hospital. I've got out my government use only book and see that Alistair James Mitchell (AJ) weighing 7 lb 4 oz. was born

FTFD (full term, forceps delivery) at 12.40p.m on 25th August, 1962.

Because of the timing, there were no florist flowers and the announcement of the birth couldn't be cabled until Sunday opening, but I'd written the words for either sex so all he had to do was chose the correct sex and name, insert the weight and hand over the counter with the two addresses. When Colin came to visit, I proudly proffered Alistair and he backed off and said – 'Oh no I might drop him.' As soon as I was out, I was back on-duty and looking after Dymphna's first born, Donald and my decrepit pram had two occupants. Donald used to go at the hood end where the pillow prop made a little pen then Alistair in the flat bit. Two infants in nappies and CW harness. It was the fashion then for babies to lie on their tummies. When Alistair was ten days old, I strolled up to the baby clinic with them. Donald standing up straining against his harness and swaying side to side waving his arms in the air and making happy sounds with Alistair snuggled below – probably 'at risk.' When we got to the clinic, I picked up Alistair, tucked Donald under my arm and in I went. I dropped Alistair on the table and got on with divesting Donald of his harness and nappy for the big weigh in. Not something I kept up with mine, as long as I liked the look of them, I gave the scales a miss. Alistair raised his head, held it and turned it over before doing a little frog movement with his legs and doing it all over again. A very observant mother did the – 'are they twins' – do they look like twins chat, then asked how old Alistair was and I said with pride – ten days. 'My baby is three months old and he can't do that!'

I became an 'ad hoc' from the week after I was discharged. There was no barrier to my working. Most shifts I would drop off Alistair somewhere and when I was finished pick him up and the child of his minder who would then take up where I left off. Sometimes we swapped in the hospital car park. Rose knew not only what stage our babies were at regarding breast or bottle, she also knew the working hours of our husbands. One day she got me to do an 11p.m until 5a.m on the basis that she knew Colin was on lates, and would be there to see to Alistair. That was a sad story – on that shift we had a patient with a head injury. At a tennis party a man leaping over the net to shake his partner's hand tripped and fell on his head. He required specialist one-to-one, but it was no good and he died four days later.

Meanwhile, back at Woodlands, Emma, our girl, had been getting plump and I realised she too was pregnant and shortly after Alistair was born, she gave birth to a girl – all black. That meant when Donald wasn't in the pram with him, Emma's baby Kathryn was. Emma was back at work promptly and she and Kathryn lived in her little house at the bottom of the back garden, but of course she had nothing for the poor child. I drew the line at a Children's Ward CW harness, but from Alistair's vast layette was able to clothe her. The bottom drawer of Colin's tallboy provided her with a cot. Emma had loads of milk and Kathryn grew plumper than Alistair.

The time seemed to fly once Alistair was born and we were preparing for our new life. We had long leave so would be paid for that time and then would decide whether or not to return. We were to fly home, but we did not have to worry too much about baggage weight because we were ex-pats. We couldn't be too lavish but we managed as many cigarettes and of course three months' supply of SMA for Alistair. I got it all free from the rep and no way would I consider spending our leave money on the most expensive baby food on the market when I could bring it home for free. Then I had all Alistair's woollies – I knitted an awful lot including pram suits complete with leggings and helmets in blue and lemon not knowing sex in advance. I was a keen knitter. On night duty, I always had orders for pullovers for husbands. No, I did not get paid – selling was never something I could do with ease.

Leaving was sad. We had no families – the people we lived among and worked with were our families. We relied on each other. There was a permanence yet a fleeting one. We were all going to be going places where we would not be going together. The airport was open, and we met planes and saw people off at the plane itself. I never saw most of these people again. We had mega hand luggage – tins of SMA could not go in the hold. Cigarettes we could have 900 each as ex-pats. Opened packets didn't count so every bag, pocket, and nappy bag had a pack of 49. Despite Colin's dislike of the filthy habit, he too was padded out with Life cigarettes. He was a St Bruno tobacco user since he had a pipe which he mostly chewed. More matches than tobacco. Alistair of course needed lots of changes of clothes and we needed to have woollies for landing in the UK. Not that we travelled casually – proper afternoon attire we wore. We were going first to Edinburgh and were booked through.

There were no direct flights. The first time we came down was Entebbe, but we were not allowed to disembark so it was a hot wait. We had a sky cot for Alistair, which was a bit like a hammock, but it wasn't much use. It may have been had the chap in front not kept getting up and down and bouncing it with his head. The fact that he was very drunk did not help. I cannot remember the airline food. London was fog-bound so we had to land in Nice. We got off the plane there. The most amazing thing was the icy air when you breathed. It was a complete shock and an experience I have never experienced since. We hung around in Nice for a while then piled back on for the last leg to London. On arrival there, Alistair's dirty washing bag was bulging – no disposable nappies and lots of posseting had really made inroads into my pre-planning. In the toilets at Heathrow I got him all dressed up in a blue and cream romper suit and his yellow knitted pram suit to meet his grandparents. We had a bit of spat with the baggage people who wanted to charge us over £100 for our excess weight. We sorted that one by explaining our human rights as ex-pats and HM Government employees; something that they had not encountered before, but they swallowed it and next stop Turnhouse Airport (Edinburgh).

Arriving at Turnhouse wasn't a lot different than Lusaka because the airport was relatively unmanned, free and easy. When I got off, I didn't have to follow the line to arrivals, I just walked over to the low fence where Mum and Dad and Margaret were madly waving and handed over my grumpy little yellow bundle. By the time I joined them, he was a bit damp due to the emotion dripping all over him. We had eleven pieces of hand luggage! I think we may have got down to nine by Turnhouse because our UK clothes were now worn and not in suit bags. We had a really naff pale blue plastic carry cot, which in Lusaka, was packed to the last inch with the mattress hovering over Alistair's outfits. By the time we got to Edinburgh they were stiffening up with sick in my old hospital laundry bag. I'd swilled the nappies at Heathrow so there was a damp bag as well. Not a big worry for us because every time we were challenged all we had to do was explain the ex-pat rules. We hadn't paid either, all funded by HM government, Rhodesia & Nyasaland. Since we didn't use our return tickets we'll never know if there was an excess baggage claim in our PO Box. Same place as my overdue tax return?

In case there is anyone reading this, who may feel like dobbing me in, don't bother. I left more than I owed and never got it back. I entered Northern Rhodesia with £105, without a visa and left without a tax clearance certificate. I put that down to the fact that any African scrutinising our leaving schedule wouldn't dream of a woman earning enough to pay tax. Colin was in the clear because he never had much money in the country and after marrying me had no need of money. He had his 'wad' from cars and vegetables to cover anything he had been forced to pay for when I became the parasite; I continued to be for many years to come. In a voluntary capacity, in communities I have lived in, my training has been useful. What I learned from my nursing years has stayed with me all of my life.